PAGEANT-MASTER OF THE REPUBLIC

I. SELF PORTRAIT

Painting by David

Courtesy of Le Musée du Louvre

PAGEANT-MASTER OF THE REPUBLIC

Jacques-Louis David and the French Revolution

★ ★ ★

DAVID LLOYD DOWD

Select Bibliographies Reprint Series

BOOKS FOR LIBRARIES PRESS
FREEPORT, NEW YORK

Reprinted 1969 by arrangement with
University of Nebraska Press

LIBRARY OF CONGRESS CATALOG CARD NUMBER:
72-75507

PRINTED IN THE UNITED STATES OF AMERICA

To the Memory of
My Mother

CONTENTS

ILLUSTRATIONS

Preface

The bicentennial of Jacques-Louis David this year provides an appropriate occasion for a revaluation of the great artist. The absence of any work in English and the lack of a scholarly and comprehensive synthesis in any language on David would seem to make even a partial contribution desirable at this time. The present study constitutes a modest attempt to analyze and reinterpret one aspect of David's long and varied career, namely, his role as propagandist of the French Revolution, on the basis of historical research. David's artistic contribution and the development and signifiance of his style are subordinated to the main theme. The Jacobin artist's political career, while indicated in passing, is reserved for detailed treatment in a monograph now in preparation. Also incidentally involved is the fascinating problem of the influence of the creative arts upon the political events of a given period—particularly a period of revolutionary crisis.

This study is concerned primarily with the character and effect of the propaganda activities of David. It is intended as an unpretentious contribution to a neglected aspect of the history of the French Revolution rather than as an addition to the already extensive critical and aesthetic literature on David's art. It attempts to show the development of the idea of the use of art as a method of social control prior to 1789 and how it became a social weapon in the hands of the political leaders during the period 1789–1794. The various artistic techniques and media employed as propaganda by the revolutionists are described and analyzed. Finally an attempt has been made to determine how effective the arts were in molding public opinion and political events thereby during the Revolution. Though music, drama, the dance, and other arts have received some consideration, the emphasis has been placed upon the plastic arts, including painting, sculpture, and architecture, and above all upon the festivals, which combined and coordinated all of these.

The materials upon which this study is primarily based are contemporary sources: archival documents, official papers, memoirs, journals, and diaries, public and private correspondence, *nouvelles à la main,* almanacs, pamphlets and the like. These have been employed either in original editions or reprinted by modern scholars in documentary collections, books, and learned journals. More than one hundred contemporary newspapers and periodicals have been analyzed for the reactions of the observers of the time. These contemporary materials have been supplemented by specialized monographs and articles and standard histories of the period. Perhaps most important of all have been original works of art from the hand of David himself and his followers. Of particular significance are the numerous sketchbooks and drawings which were studied and to which a section of the discussion of the evidence is devoted.

I take this opportunity to express my gratitude and appreciation to the many individuals and institutions that facilitated the research for this study. Professor Franklin C. Palm under whose direction this work was begun, has been an unfailing source of support and encouragement. During a period when research in France was impossible, the Amy Bowles Johnson Traveling Fellowship, granted through the University of California, provided funds for study in the major libraries of the United States. Kindly assistance was given me by the library staffs of the Universities of California (Berkeley), Stanford, Nebraska, Iowa, Chicago, Northwestern, Illinois, Michigan, Western Reserve, Cornell, Princeton, Columbia, Brown, Yale, and Harvard. The art reference libraries of the Metropolitan Museum, the Frick Collection, the Chicago Art Institute, the Fogg Museum of Art of Harvard, and the Princeton Art Museum, and the architecture and town planning libraries of Columbia and Harvard extended me many privileges. The staffs of the Public Libraries of New York, Boston, and Cleveland and the Library of Congress as well as the Newberry Library, the John Carter Brown Library, the Boston Athenaeum, and the New England Deposit Library were extremely cooperative. The libraries of the Universities of Rochester, Illinois, Toronto, Wisconsin, Minnesota, New York and of the Brooklyn Museum and the Peabody Institute provided important materials through the Interlibrary Loan Service. Moreover, I am deeply indebted to various scholars who went out of their way to aid me with suggestions, assistance and encouragement. Among these special mention must be made of Professor Jakob Rosenberg of Harvard University, Dr. W. R. Valentiner, and M. Georges Wildenstein, who introduced me to the first-hand study of David's original drawings and paintings. Professors Edgar N. Johnson, University of Nebraska, Robert R. Palmer, Princeton University, Richard M. Brace, Northwestern University, and Eugen Neuhaus and Raymond J. Sontag, University of California read the manuscript at various stages and contributed helpful suggestions. In a very real sense the Committee on Publications of University Studies of the University of Nebraska and the University of Nebraska Press have made the publication of this study possible. To them also goes my sincere gratitude for encouragement and interest. Finally, all thanks go to my wife who has helped in innumerable ways of which translating from the Russian and checking bibliographical data were among her simpler tasks. For any errors in fact or interpretation, I assume full responsibility.

DAVID LLOYD DOWD.

Lincoln, Nebraska
May, 1948

LIST OF ABBREVIATIONS

A. A. F.: *Archives de l'art français. Recueil de documents inédits,* published by P. de Chennevières, A. de C. de Montaiglon and others (Paris, 1851–1863), 8 vols. in 2 ser.

A. H. R. F.: *Annales historiques de la révolution française,* published by Société des Etudes Robespierristes (Paris, 1924–), 20 vols. to date.

A. P.: *Archives parlementaires de 1787 à 1860; Recueil complete des débats législatifs . . . 1 sér. 1787–1799* ed. J. Mandal, E. Laivient and others (Paris, 1867–1913), 82 vols.

A. R.: *Annales révolutionnaires,* published by Société des Etudes Robespierristes (Paris, 1908–1924), 32 vols.

C. G. A.: *Procès-verbaux, de la Commune générale des arts,* ed. H. Lapauze (Paris, 1903).

C. I. P.: *Procès-verbaux du Comité d'instruction publique de la convention nationale,* ed. J. Guillaume (Paris, 1891–1907), 6 vols.

C. I. P. Leg.: *Procès-verbaux au Comité d'instruction publique de l'Assemblée législative,* ed. J. Guillaume (Paris, 1889), 2 vols.

Col. Baud.: *Collection générale des décrets rendus . . . [mai, 1789-nivôse an VIII],* ed. F. J. Baudouin (Paris, 1789–1799), 79 vols.

Col. Vinck.: *Un siècle d'histoire de France par l'estampes 1770–1871; Collection de Vinck; inventaire analytique,* by F. L. Bruel and others, t. I–III (Paris, 1909–1921), 3 vols.

Cor. Ang.: *Correspondance de M. d'Angiviller avec Pierre [et Vièn],* ed. M. Furcy-Raynaud (Paris, 1906–1907), 2 vols.

Cor. dir.: *Correspondance des Directeurs de l'Académie de France à Rome avec les Surintendants de bâtiments, 1666–1804,* ed. A. de C. de Montaiglon and others (Paris, 1887–1908), 17 vols.

Cor. lit.: F. M. Grimm and others, *Correspondance littéraire, philosophique et critique,* ed. M. Tourneux (Paris, 1877–1882), 16 vols.

Cor. sec.: *Correspondance secrète, politique et littéraire . . .* by F. Metra and others (London, 1787–1790), 18 vols.

C. S. P.: *Recueil des actes du Comité de salut publique,* ed. F. A. Aulard (Paris, 1889–1933), 27 vols.

G. B. A.: *Gazette des beaux-arts,* ed. G. Wildenstein and others (Paris, 1859–).

Inv. dess.: *Inventaire général des dessins du Louvre et . . . Versailles, Ecole française,* ed. J. Guiffrey and others, t. I–XI (Paris, 1907–1938), 11 vols.

J. D. D.: *Journal des débats et des décrets,* (Versailles and Paris, August 30, 1789–May 17, 1797), 42 vols.

Mem. sec.: *Memoires secrètes pour servir à l'histoire de la république des lettres en France* by L. P. de Bachaumont and others (London, 1784–1787), 36 vols.

N. A. A. F.:*Nouvelles archives de l'art français. Recueil de documents inédits,* published by Société de l'Histoire de l'art français (Paris, 1872–1938), 53 vols., 4 ser.

Notice: *Notice sur la vie et les ouvrages de M. J.-L. David,* (Paris, 1824).

Peint. Louvre: *La Peinture au Muséum du Louvre,* ed. J. Guiffrey (Paris, 1929), 2 vols.

P. V. Acad.: *Procès-verbaux de l'Académie royale de peinture et de sculpture, 1648–1793,* ed. A. de C. de Montaiglon (Paris, 1875–1909), 11 vols.

P. V. Conv.: *Procès-verbal de la Convention nationale imprimé par son ordre,* (Paris, 1792–1795), 72 vols.

P. V. Leg.: *Procès-verbal de l'Assemblée nationale [législative] imprimé par son ordre,* (Paris, 1791–1792), 16 vols.

P. V. Nat.: *Procès-verbal de l'Assemblée nationale [Constituante] imprimé par son ordre,* (Paris, 1789–1791), 75 vols.

R. F.: *La Révolution française,* ed. F. A. Aulard and others (Paris, 1881–1939), 87 vols. + 18 nos.

S. H. A. F.: Société de l'Histoire de l'Art Français.

Tableaux historiques: *Collection complète des tableaux historiques de la révolution française,* (Paris, 1802), 3 vols.

CHAPTER I

Neoclassicism and the Revolution

One day, early in the French Revolution, a peasant stood fascinated before a picture hanging in the Louvre:[1] Jacques-Louis David's *Oath of the Horatii.*[2] The vast and somber canvas represented with archaeological exactness three young Roman warriors. With hands raised in the Roman salute they were taking an oath on the swords which their father held aloft, to win or die in the struggle against the enemy. The style of the painting was austerely neoclassical. It revealed the inspiration of antique sculpture and a penetrating study of the living model. The picture itself was clearly intended to be less a work of art than a lesson in civic virtue and heroism. If this simple peasant could not read the chapters of Livy or the play of Corneille[3] which had inspired the painting, he could clearly perceive the patriotic and revolutionary message of David's severe and simple work of art. "It made one think."[4] In these heroic Romans he saw himself on Federation Day[5] taking his oath to be faithful to the nation. He felt, like them, a fanatical zeal to defend the Fatherland.[6] The reception accorded by the bourgeoisie to this pictorial exaltation of patriotism and civic virtue was if possible, even more enthusiastic. Their classi-

[1] During the Salon of 1791: *Lettre bougrement patriotique du véritable Père Duchêne,* no. 212 [n.d.], pp. 3–4.

[2] Today in the Louvre: Catalogue no. 189 (10′ 10″ high by 14′ wide) J. Guiffrey, ed., *La Peinture au Muséum du Louvre* (Paris: L'Illustration, 1929), v. I, pt. 1, pp. 5–7, pl. V (hereafter cited as *Peint. Louvre*); R. Cantinelli, *Jacques-Louis David* (Paris: Van Oest, 1939), p. 103, no. 45, pl. XVI; F. Engerand, ed. *Inventaire des tableaux commandés et achetés par la Direction des Bâtiments du roi* (Paris: Leroux, 1901), pp. 137–139. Cf. E. Wind, "The Sources of David's *Horaces,*" Warburg and Courtauld Institutes, *Journal,* IV (1940–41), 124–38. Opposite p. 2.

[3] Titus Livius, *Ab urbe condita,* trans. by B. O. Foster (London: Heinemann, 1919), Bk. I, Chap. XXIII-XXVI. P. Corneille, "Horaces" in *Oeuvres,* ed. Marty-Laveaux (Paris: Hachette, 1862), III, 282–358.

[4] A. Péron, *Examen du tableau du Serment des Horaces . . .* (Paris: Ducessois, 1839), p. 27.

[5] *See* pp. 45–46, 54–55.

[6] *Lettre bougrement patriotique du véritable Père Duchêne,* no. 212 [n.d], p. 4.

cal education [7] made them especially susceptible to propaganda which was given a Graeco-Roman setting.

It was David's characteristic combination of classicism and naturalism which made his paintings appeal to all classes. Classicism, which had been to date the habitual and almost inevitable vehicle for historical subjects, by its very form reinforced the simplicity, strength, and heroism of the message. Naturalism emphasized that these statuesque figures were men of flesh and blood like the observer himself; thus it helped the beholder to associate himself with their patriotic action. It imparted a persuasive vitality to what would otherwise have been a somewhat academic and theatrically posed tableau. Here was no esoteric abstraction comprehensible only to the chosen few, but rather a realistic and vivid scene in which the arrangement of significant objects clearly emphasized the moral content, and in which the formal clarity of classicism had its counterpart in a clarity of concept which appealed to the "common man."

The rationalism of his art was one of its significant characteristics and David has not ineptly been called "the philosopher painter." [8] This feature, together with moral virtue and emotional power, enabled the master of the neoclassic school to appeal to the reason, the conscience and the emotions of his audience.

That "most veritable of veritable Père Duchênes," Lemaire, who recounted the episode of the peasant, went on to say that David's paintings "had inflamed more souls for liberty than the best books." [9] In his opinion the work of David had prepared the people for the Revolution just as much as the writings of Voltaire and Rousseau.[10] The picture which captured the imagination of the illiterate peasant and expressed the new ideology of the bourgeois revolutionaries had been painted seven years before. Its exhibition in 1785 marked the triumph of neoclassicism over the rococo style of the old regime four years prior to the Revolution of 1789. Accordingly, David's contemporaries regarded him as the founder of neoclassicism and as a forerun-

[7] H. T. Parker, *The Cult of Antiquity and the French Revolutionaries* (Chicago: Chicago University Press, 1937), pp. 8–36.

[8] A. Th[omé de Gamond], *Vie de David* (Brussels: Tarlier, 1826), p. 229.

[9] *Lettre bougrement patriotique du véritable Père Duchêne,* no. 212 [n.d.], p. 4.

[10] *Loc. cit.*

II. THE OATH OF THE HORATII

Painting by David

Courtesy of Le Musée du Louvre

ner of the Revolution.[11] Historically speaking, however, David was not the creator of the new school but rather represents its culmination; 1785 marks the fruition rather than the inception of the style. For even if the *Oath of the Horatii,* was the "manifesto" [12] of the new school, the origins of the movement can be traced back as early as 1747,[13] the year before David was born.

During the first half of the eighteenth century the charming and decadent rococo style, an expression of the luxury-loving aristocracy and court, dominated the artistic scene. About 1750, there began a reaction against the erotic and petty mannerisms of the French School in favor of a revival of the "grand style" of monumental art going back to the classical tradition of Poussin and Greek and Roman antiquity. Four forces operated against the rococo French taste in favor of the neoclassic style: court influence exerted through official channels, the philosophy of the enlightenment, the rise of art criticism, and the international aesthetic and archaeological interest emanating from Rome.[14]

The various Superintendents of the King's Buildings exercised their powers to encourage the painting of history and the return to the antique. Count Angiviller (1773-1791) followed the policies of Madame de Pompadour's uncle and brother, Lenormant de Tournehem (1745-1751) and the Marquis de Marigny (1751-1773). These men encouraged the "grand style" by granting royal commissions and special privileges, such as pensions, positions, studios and patents of nobility to painters of history. They also strengthened the material and moral power of the Royal Academy of Painting and Sculpture through the revival of the aristocratic spirit, the destruction of the rival community of Saint Luke, the medieval artists' guild, and the insurance of the academic monopoly of instruction and public exhibition. Convinced of the "moral, political and social value of art" as a means "to

[11] To give only two examples: F. A. Aulard, ed., *La Société des Jacobins* (Paris: Jouaust, 1889), I, 333; E. Charavay, ed., *Assemblée électorale de Paris* (Paris: Jouaust, 1894), II, 260.

[12] L. Hautecoeur, *Rome et la renaissance de l'antiquité* (Paris: Fontemoing, 1912), p. 158.

[13] According to J. Locquin, *La peinture d'histoire en France* (Paris: Laurens, 1912). Other scholars propose dates between 1749 and 1755.

[14] The fundamental works are J. Locquin, *op. cit.;* A. Fontaine, *Les doctrines d'art en France . . . de Poussin à Diderot* (Paris: Renouard, 1909) and L. Hautecoeur, *op. cit.*

revive the virtues and *patriotic* sentiments,"[15] they considered the painting of history as "an emanation of the throne"[16]—a buttress for the preservation of the monarchy.

At the same time the central authority was joined in its crusade against rococo art by the *philosophes* who likewise believed in the regenerative effects of the fine arts but for quite a different purpose—reform. Lafont de Saint-Yenne inaugurated modern art criticism and called for the restoration of the painting of history and a return to antique models.[17] Diderot, that "explosive encyclopedist,"[18] in his famous "Salons,"[19] upheld the political, social, and moral utility of the arts, fulminated against the bad taste of Boucher, recommended study of classical sculpture and lauded the anecdotal and sentimental canvases of Greuze. The Enlightenment appealed to "classic reason" to destroy feudalism and obscurantism, and moralizing and classical canvases were expected to reform mankind. "Philosophy was the fire in which art was forged as a sword of the Revolution."[20]

The classic revival which produced the propaganda art of the Revolution was born amidst the ancient monuments in Rome. The eclectic Academic school was classical only in theory. It was the cosmopolitan art colony at Rome which created true neoclassicism. The vogue of classical antiquity was stimulated by a continuation of the excavations at Herculaneum and Pompeii and the revelation of Paestum. The contemporary romantic interest in ruins was nurtured by the paintings of Hubert Robert, (1733-1808), (Robert des Ruines), and the magnificent engravings of Piranesi,[21] and nourished by the publication of lavishly illustrated volumes on archaeology such as those of Count Caylus, Stuart and Revett, and Hancarville.[22]

[15] Letter of Angiviller to Pierre, March 14, 1776: Engerand, *op. cit.*, p. xxix.

[16] The *Journal de Paris,* no. 89 (March 30, 1777), p. 2.

[17] *Réflexions sur quelques causes de l'état présent de la peinture en France* (Paris, 1747), pp. 2–4.

[18] G. V. Plekhanov, *Sochineniia,* ed. Riazanov (Moscow: Gosudarstvennoe izdatel'stvo, 1924), XIV, 109.

[19] *Oeuvres complètes,* ed. Assézat (Paris: Garnier, 1875–77), X-XII.

[20] M. W. Brown, *The Painting of the French Revolution* (New York: Critics Group, 1938), p. 17.

[21] *Della magnificenza ed architettura de' Romani* (Rome, 1761), and numerous other works.

[22] *Recueil d'antiquités* (Paris, 1752-67), 7 v.; *Antiquities of Athens* (London, 1761), 4 v.; *Antiquités étrusques, grecques et romaines tirées du cabinet de M. Hamilton* (Naples, 1766–67), 4 v.

Popularization of classicism was due in large measure to the collaboration of two Germans working at Rome: Johann Jakob Winckelmann, the archaeologist, and Raphael Mengs, the painter. The latter applied Winckelmann's ideal of "the noble simplicity and serene grandeur of the ancients" by the imitation of ideal nature as found in classic art, and at the same time emphasized the moral virtues they both believed inherent therein. Under their aegis a school of painters developed at Rome (1765-1775) which included the Swiss Angelica Kaufmann and Solomon Gessner and the Englishmen Gavin Hamilton and Benjamin West. Their influence was exerted on French artists through the artists' colony at Rome and the French Academy there, and at Paris through zealous admirers among the *philosophes* such as Diderot, [23] and through published engravings of their works.[24]

In France, Count Caylus acted as liaison between the artists and the archaeologists. He had a great influence on the former and popularized the findings of the latter.[25] Joseph Vien, influenced by Caylus, encouraged by Diderot, and inspired by the ideas of Winckelmann and the examples of the School of Mengs, was the recognized leader of the pseudo-classical movement in France before David. Nevertheless Vien's classicism was far from the "noble and sublime" style of David; it sought simplicity rather than the expression of any profound moral philosophy and was steeped in the sentimentalism and sensuousness of the eighteenth century.[26] Nor can the polished and artificial archaeological reconstructions of Mengs and his followers, which gratified the tastes of a few dilettantes, be compared to the highly popular and intensely moving canvases of the painter of the *Horatii.*

Before neoclassic art could become the "sword of the Revolution," it was necessary that a forceful and virile artist should, while perfecting the form of the new style, fuse into it the morality and philosophy of the bourgeoisie and a vital and powerful realism comprehensible

[23] *Correspondance littéraire, philosophique et critique,* ed. Tourneux (Paris: Garnier, 1878), III, 234–7 (hereafter cited as *Cor. lit.*).

[24] J. Locquin, "Le retour à l'antique . . . avant David," *Renaissance,* V (August, 1922), 481.

[25] S. Rocheblave, *Essai sur le Comte de Caylus; l'homme, l'artiste, l'antiquaire* (Paris: Hachette, 1889).

[26] As Vien himself expressed it: "J'ai entr'ouvert la porte, David l'a poussée." A. Lenoir, "David, souvenirs historiques," *Journal de l'Institut Historique,* III (August, 1835), 4.

to the masses. It was the forceful mind, virile talent and revolutionary spirit of Jacques-Louis David which transformed neoclassicism from a fashion into a style and from a fad into a propaganda weapon of the new order. He completed the work of his predecessors by carrying the imitation of antique art to its fullest expression in modern times. He endowed his statuesque antique figures with a concrete and powerful naturalism—a vital core of flesh and blood. He imbued his canvases with the "heroic morality" and the political and social reformist philosophy of the rising middle classes and tried to make his pictures "so many open books." [27] Thus he brought neoclassicism to its technical perfection, established its artistic hegemony for two generations, gave it "a new structure and vision," [28] and endowed it with a new ideological content. In so doing he reformed and dominated the art of his own day, fathered the painting of the nineteenth century and became a propagandist of the French Revolution. These achievements constitute his personal contributions to art and history.

While his artistic forerunners were returning to antiquity for their models during the third quarter of the eighteenth century, David was growing up in Paris.[29] From birth to exile he spent most of his life within sight of the Pont Neuf—that is to say in the heart of the French capital. He was born in an old house on the Quai de la Mégisserie

[27] A. Cantaloube, "Les dessins de Louis David," *G.B.A.*, [ser. 1], VII (September 1, 1860), 284.

[28] K. Berger, "Courbet in his Century," *G.B.A.*, ser. 6, XXIV (July, 1943), 34.

[29] For the early life of David *see* P. J. B. Chaussard, "Notice historique et inédite sur Louis David," in his *Le Pausanius français* (Paris: Buisson, 1806), pp. 145–174; *Notice sur la vie et les ouvrages de M. J.-L. David* (Paris: Dondey-Dupré, 1824), pp. 7 ff. (hereafter cited as *Notice*); Thomé, *op. cit.*, pp. 3–48; [A. Rabbe], "Notice sur J. L. David," *Biographie universelle et portative des contemporaines* (Paris: au bureau de la biographie, 1830), II, 1216-17; P. A. Coupin, "Notice nécrologique sur J. L. David," *Revue encyclopédique*, XXXIV, no. 100 (April, 1827), 34–36; "J. L. David," *Biographie nouvelle des contemporaines* (Paris: Ledentu, 1827), V, 231–33; E.F.A. Miel, "David," *Encyclopédie des gens du monde* (Paris: Treuttel, 1836), VII, 572 ff. A. Lenoir, *loc. cit.*, p. 1 f.; [J. N. Paillot de Montibert and V. Parisot], "David," *Biographie universelle*, ed. Michaud (Paris: Dupont, 1837), XLII, 124–6; Miette de Villars, *Mémoires de David* (Paris: chez tous les libraires, 1850), pp. 49 f; E. J. Delécluze, *Louis David, son école et son temps, souvenirs* (Paris: Didier, 1855), pp. 106–32; A. Jal, "David," *Dictionnaire critique de biographie et d'histoire* (Paris: Plon, 1867), p. 475; J.L.J. David, *op. cit.*, pp. 2–8; All the biographies since have been based on these works but in most cases upon Delécluze and Jules David.

on August 30, 1748 [30] and was baptized that same day in the ancient church of Saint-Germain-l'Auxerrois, the parish church of the artists who inhabited the neighboring Louvre. His father, an enterprising merchant who purchased the office of Excise Tax Clerk, was killed in a duel when Jacques-Louis was only nine. His architect uncles Jacques Buron and Jacques Desmaisons saw to it that he received the usual classical education at the Collège de Quatre Nations. Here he covered his books with sketches and in other ways indicated a great talent for drawing. His mother opposed his desire for an artistic career and his uncles wanted him to be an architect. David persevered however, and finally overcame parental opposition. At an early age he manifested the "indomitable will" and "passion for glory" which stamped his character.

The young artist's training was entrusted to his aged relative, François Boucher,[31] the leading artist of the day. In turn this rococo painter recommended the youth to his friend Vien, the mediocre but conscientious partisan of the classical reaction. David made rapid progress during the next few years and finally decided to compete for the *Prix de Rome,* a highly coveted art scholarship which provided three years of study at the French Academy at Rome. According to tradition it was only the interference of his master whom he had not consulted which deprived him of first place in 1771.[32] The next year he was again denied the prize by what he considered the "injustice" of the Academic judges so he tried to starve himself to death. However, his next failure only stiffened his determination to win.

David produced much at this time. Besides several fine portraits, the first of which was that of his aunt, Mme. Buron,[33] he was commissioned to complete Fragonard's decorations for the salon of Mlle. Guimard, the famous opera dancer. These murals, for her Palace

[30] The date is variously given by his biographers ranging from 1747 to 1750. His baptismal act (*Nouvelles archives de l'art français,* ser. 1, III [1874–75], 374–5 [hereafter cited *N.A.A.F.*]) definitely fixes it as given and also proves that Sedaine was not his godfather, as claimed by Chaussard, *loc. cit.,* p. 145; Coupin, *loc. cit.,* p. 35; and Delécluze, *op. cit.,* p. 109.

[31] The tradition that he was a relative of David has usually been denied by recent writers.

[32] *Notice,* pp. 9–10; Thomé, p. 9; Paillot, *loc. cit.,* p. 124; Miette de Villars, *op. cit.,* p. 54; Delécluze, pp. 109–10. His entry, *The Combat of Minerva against Mars and Venus* is in the Louvre.

[33] Painted in 1769. Now at Wildenstein & Co., New York. Opposite p. 8.

of Terpsichore were, like the rest of his paintings to date, in the rococo manner.[34]

The young artist had a great regard for Boucher [35] and his art. One scholar maintains that David would have been only an "understudy for Fragonard" if he had followed his youthful preference.[36] Nevertheless the realism of his portraits and an occasional vigorous figure in otherwise rococo allegories indicate that his powerful personal style was already developing.[37] This fact lends support to the tradition that Diderot praised his work and encouraged him at this time.[38]

Then, suddenly, David was brought face to face with the classical revival. On August 27, 1774, he was finally awarded the long coveted *Prix de Rome*.[39] Warned by an academician against the "corrupting influence" of the classic goddess he was about to confront, David declared "Antiquity will not seduce me, it lacks warmth, and does not move." [40] The aspiring young artist was soon to discover that he had vastly underrated the potent charms of that cold and bloodless beauty. For neoclassicism which reflected the philosophical, moral and aesthetic aspirations of the age so well, was all powerful at Rome. The influence of Wincklemann was still exerted through the "School of Mengs" and David was soon to join the ranks of the artists, scholars and scientists who had fallen under the spell of the Eternal City.

Vien had just been named Director of the French School at Rome

[34] Chaussard, pp. 145–7; Lenoir, p. 2; Coupin, pp. 35–6; Paillot, p. 125; Miette de Villars, pp. 61–3. Unfortunately the house in the Chaussée d'Antin, designed by Ledoux, has disappeared. It can be judged from the engraved plates in Ledoux, *Architecture,* ed. Ramée (Paris: Lenoir, 1847), II, pl. 175–7 and the description in M. F. Pidanzat de Mairobert, *L'Espion anglais* (London: Adamson, 1785), X, 324–6.

[35] *Notice,* p. 14; Chaussard, p. 147; Lenoir, p. 3.

[36] Saunier, "La'Mort de Sénèque' par Louis David," *G.B.A.,* ser. 3, XXXIII (March, 1905), 233–6 and "'Jupiter et Antiope,' oeuvre de jeunesse de Louis David," *G.B.A.,* ser. 4, VI (September, 1911), 254–60.

[37] *E.g.* The figure of Mars in his *Combat of Minerva.*

[38] C. A. Sainte-Beuve, "Diderot," lundi, 20 Janvier 1851; *Causeries de lundi* (3. ed., Paris: Garnier, 1885), III, 309–10.

[39] *Archives de l'art français,* ser. 1, IX (1857–58), 302 (hereafter cited *A.A.F.).* David's *Brevet de pensionnaire,* dated August 31, 1775: A. de C. de Montaiglon and others, eds., *Correspondance des directeurs de l'Académie de France à Rome avec les surintendants des bâtiments, 1666–1804* (Paris: Charavay, 1904), XIII, 124. (hereafter cited as *Cor. dir.*)

[40] The Academician was Cochin: Miette de Villars, p. 65; David, p. 9.

III. PORTRAIT OF MADAME BURON

Painting by David *Courtesy of Wildenstein & Co., Inc.*

by fat old Count Angiviller,[41] and David accompanied his teacher to his new post at the Palazzo Mancini.[42] On October 21, 1775, they set out for Rome. Their journey took them through Turin, Parma and Bologna, where the sight of the Italian masterpieces began to undermine David's confidence in the French School. Once they reached their destination, the ruined splendors of ancient Rome made a profound impression upon the young artist. His master advised him to begin his new studies by sketching from the old masters and especially from antique sculpture.[43]

David, with ever-growing interest, investigated the art galleries, the classical collections and the ancient monuments at Rome. Abandoning the brush for the pencil, he spent his days sketching and his nights copying. The twelve notebooks which he filled with drawings at this time were to be a constant source of inspiration to him all his life.[44]

A careful study of these sketchbooks,[45] the most reliable and original source for David's ideas at this period, reveals both his varied interests and his increasing proficiency in his art. Graeco-Roman statues, bas-reliefs, sarcophagi, cameos, trophies and other objects from the Villa Medici, the Capitol, the Palazzo Farnese and other collections; tracings from the engraved plates of Greek vase paintings in Sir William Hamilton's collections;[46] red chalk *contre-preuves* of ancient utensils and accessories: all these indicated his mounting passion for classicism.

Nevertheless, David did not neglect the picturesque beauties of his surroundings and many of the sketchbook studies reveal the young

[41] August 28, 1775: *Cor. dir.*, XII, 115–17, 128–29, 138–39.

[42] J. C. V. Mannlich (*Lebenserinnerungen*, ed. Strollreither [2. ed., Berlin: Mittler, 1913], pp. 91–137, 152–80) a former pupil of Boucher gives a vivid account of the life of a foreign art student there at this period. For an exact description of the School *see* J. J. Lalande, *Voyage d'un français en Italie* (Paris, 1769), III, 591 ff. Since 1803 it has been located in the Villa Medici.

[43] *Notice*, pp. 14–15; Thomé, p. 17; Coupin, p. 36; Paillot, p. 27; Delécluze, pp. 111, 113; David, pp. 9–11; Miette de Villars, pp. 65–67.

[44] These "douze grands livres de crocquis" figured as no. 66 at the David sale of 1826 after the artist's death: Pérignon, ed., *Catalogue des tableaux* [*etc*] *de M. Louis David . . . dont la vente publique . . . aura lieu . . . 19 avril 1826 . . .* (Brussels: Stapleaux, 1826), pp. 16–17. Today they are divided among the Louvre, the Ecole des Beaux-Arts, Fogg Museum of Art, and various private collections.

[45] For a discussion of the sketchbooks used for this study *see* p. 195. Opposite p. 10.

[46] *See* p. 4, note 22.

artist's realism and love of nature. Some remarkable landscapes—views in Rome and scenes of the Campagna with ancient ruins, medieval castles and quaint villages—are conceived in an idyllic and, at times, impressionistic spirit. On other leaves appear life-like human and animal figures sketched from nature—a Roman street beggar, a peasant sleeping in the sun, a donkey, a goat, a horse. Some of these reappear ultimately in his famous paintings.[47] Still other pages present, in a few quick lines, the first ideas for some of his later works: the artist's inspiration of the moment is here recorded in a "kind of compositional shorthand." [48] Finally, the sketchbooks contain small pencil and wash copies of Italian paintings. Insofar as they can be identified, they confirm the tradition that David studied the work of the Bolognese eclectics, the Caracci, Guido Reni and Domenichino and the revolutionary art of Caravaggio as well as his idols Raphael, Michelangelo and Poussin.[49] His greatest admiration was for Raphael, who, in David's own words, "elevates me to the antique." [50] Though the pages of his albums lack the perfection and expression of his mature drawings, these student notebooks reveal as no other source can, the youthful artist's technical proficiency, feeling for composition and monumental simplicity, and mastery of plastic form. Besides demonstrating David's artistic genius and versatility, these folios also corroborate the stories of his conscientious thoroughness and tireless energy in the pursuit of his ideal. It is said that he would carry off plaster casts of Trajan's column to his room, and spend the entire night studying them.[51]

Though French scholars minimize the influence of Winckelmann's writings and Mengs' paintings upon David, it is certain that Vien, who had the highest regard for these two distinguished Germans, must have recommended them to his special protégé.[52] As a matter of

[47] For example the Italian in a cloak (no. 3366 Guiffrey, ed., *Inventaire général des dessins du Louvre et . . . Versailles, Ecole française* [Paris: Librairie centrale d'art et d'architecture, 1909], IV, 104, ill., p. 105 [hereafter cited *Inv. dess.*]) reappears as Plato in *The Death of Socrates.*

[48] E. Scheyer, "French drawings of the Great Revolution . . ," *Art Quarterly,* IV (Summer, 1941), 188.

[49] Chaussard, p. 148; *Notice,* p. 15; Thomé, p. 18; Miette de Villars, pp. 65–67; David, pp. 10–11.

[50] David, p. 10.

[51] Miette de Villars, p. 6.

[52] Vien was a personal friend of Mengs and painted an "Apotheosis of Winckelmann." Scheyer, *loc. cit.,* pp. 187–88.

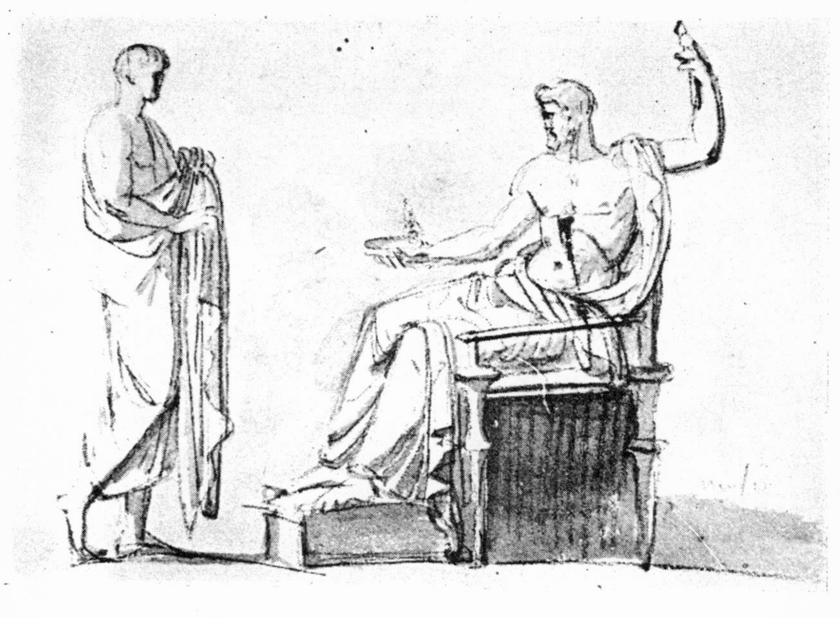

IV. ITALIAN SKETCH BOOK

Drawings by David
Above: Classical Figures

Courtesy of W. R. Valentiner
Below: View of Italian Town

fact, Miette de Villars includes Winckelmann among the books which David studied.[53] He also informs us that the artist pored over plates in Montfaucon,[54] Hamilton,[55] the *Antichità di Ercolano,*[56] Winckelmann [57] and other illustrated archaeological works of the period; and steeped himself in Homer, Virgil, Corneille, Molière and, above all, Plutarch. His copy of the *Parallel Lives* was well thumbed and annotated [58] and he could quote long passages from it from memory.[59] Another influence on David's art which has been established is the series of engravings after Gavin Hamilton and other classicists of the School of Mengs.[60] It is generally believed that conversations with friends rather than the direct influence of Mengs and the archaeologists and aestheticians brought David under the sway of the classical ideal. He appears to have engaged in long discussions regarding the theories of the German classicists, Lessing, Sulzer, Heyne and Winckelmann with his fellow students Giraud and Peyron, and with the studious young antiquarian Quatremère de Quincy.[61] Nevertheless it seems likely that this "pedantic Romaniser" had less influence on David's style than the sculptor Lemaire who urged him to emphasize the outline in his drawing.[62]

More than theoretical discussions were required to win completely the intense young artist to the new dispensation. The classical collections at Rome, the illustrated archaeological publications and the

[53] *Mémoires de David,* p. 37. If the young artist did not digest the monumental *Geschichte der Kunst des Altertums* (Dresden, 1764; French translation, Paris, 1766) he must have been familiar with the *Gedanken über die Nachahmung der griechischen Werke in der Malerei und Bildhauerkunst* (Dresden, 1755; French translation, Paris, 1756) which contained the essence of Winckelmann's theories.

[54] *L'Antiquité expliquée et représentée en figures* with *Supplément* (Paris, 1719–24), 10 v.

[55] *See* p. 4, note 22.

[56] Ed. O. A. Bayardi and P. Carcani (Naples, 1757–92), 8 v.

[57] *Monumenti antichi inediti* (Rome, 1767), 2 v.

[58] Miette de Villars, p. 37.

[59] Lenoir p. 9. Contrary to Delécluze (pp. 107, 132), Couder maintains David was both studious and well read: "Protestation en faveur de l'école de David," *Revue universelle des arts,* VI (February, 1858), 421.

[60] Locquin, "Le retour à l'antique avant David," p. 481.

[61] Delécluze, pp. 129–32.

[62] Miette de Villars, p. 68. Cf. H. Fierens-Gavaert, "Jacques-Louis David," *Le Flambeau,* IX (January, 1926), 43. For a contrary view *see* R. Schneider, *Quartremère de Quincy et son intervention dans les arts* (Paris: Hachette, 1910), pp. 397–98.

monuments—particularly the bas-reliefs of Trajan's column [63]—prepared him for conversion, but he was not fully satisfied. Excited by the enthusiastic reports of the amazing discoveries at Herculaneum and Pompeii[64] he determined to see the excavations for himself. In July 1779, he went south to Naples with the sculptor Suzanne and young Quatremère.[65] Already prepared by his classical education, his passion for Plutarch and his art studies at Rome, the revelation of the archaeological remains of the buried cities is credited with producing a revolution in David's ideas. Like Paul after his encounter on the road to Damascus "his eyes were opened and he became another man." [66] It is possible that the severe attack of fever [67] which closely followed his visit to the ruins may have reinforced the psychological impression he had received. At any rate this vision of the concrete and vivid reality of the life and art of the classic past exerted a profound and lasting effect upon David's career. When he returned to Rome and looked at the monuments with new eyes, he is supposed to have said: "I have been cured of a cataract." [68] After the initial discouragement he set out to revolutionize the decadent art of his day by bringing it back to nature and to what he regarded as the eternal principles of classicism.

David discovered that his passionate expression of the new ideas, together with his intense independence and solitary, industrious habits did not endear him to his fellow students. His turbulent and quarrelsome comrades regarded him as morose and misanthropic.[69]

[63] J. J. Sue ("Rapport sur les tableaux de David," *L'Espirit des journaux*, VIII [August, 1793], 275) says the artist devoted his first year at Rome to studying these sculptures.

[64] These ancient Roman cities had been overwhelmed in the eruption of Vesuvius in A.D. 79 and preserved under layers of volcanic ash and tufa. Excavations at Herculaneum began in 1738 and continued to 1780, at which time activity shifted to Pompeii which had been discovered in 1748.

[65] Vien to Angiviller, July 21, 1779: *N.A.A.F.*, ser. 1, III (1874–75), 377; Angiviller to Vien, August 15: *Cor. dir.*, XIII, 454. The trip and its effect upon David was first mentioned by Coupin (p. 37) in 1827. The anonymous *Notice* (p. 15) and Thomé (p. 18) place his conversion soon after his arrival in Italy and attribute it to the monuments at Rome.

[66] Miel's account (p. 579) is quoted verbatim by Miette de Villars (p. 70) and repeated by David (p. 13). Cf. *Acts* 9: 3–18.

[67] Vien to Angiviller, August 24: *Cor. dir.*, XIII, 455.

[68] Miel, p. 579; Paillot, p. 126; Miette de Villars, p. 70.

[69] Coupin, p. 38; Paillot, p. 126.

Although they were jealous of his superior talent, they praised his work, and the Italian artists and the Academy shared their enthusiasm.[70] In fact, as a mark of special favor, he was accorded an extra year at the School at Rome. The extended correspondence between Vien, Angiviller, and Pierre, the First Painter of the King, on this matter showed the kind regard for and confidence in the ability of David of the first two and the hostility of the third.[71]

David used the extension to paint *Saint Roch Interceding for the Plague Victims*[72] for the Lazaret of Marseille. This work, which showed the influence of the school of Caravaggio, first revealed David's characteristic style: a neoclassical fusion of nature and the antique.[73] The Roman public and art world flocked to admire it, and old Pompeo Battoni, the patriarch of the Italian School, hailed it as "entirely worthy of Michelangelo."[74] With this praise ringing in his ears, David returned home at the end of almost five years at Rome bringing with him some unfinished works, a passion for Italian music, a boundless veneration for classical antiquity[75] and probably the inspiration for many of his later propaganda endeavors.

Back in Paris, David discovered that news of his success had preceded him and that he enjoyed a considerable reputation among artists of the city. Friends and relatives were ready to use their influence to aid him. They obtained for him a studio in the Hôtel de Ville where he completed a *Belisarius* and a great portrait of Count Potocki,[76] begun in Italy. These he submitted to the Academy August 24, 1781, "for advice and instruction." His work was so highly regarded that without further delay he was made an *agréé* of the Academy.[77]

[70] Sue, *loc. cit.*, p. 275; Coupin, pp. 37–38; Paillot, pp. 126; David, pp. 11–12. Reports of Commissioners of the Academy: *A.A.F.*, ser. 1, I (1852), 340–44; A. de C. de Montaiglon and others, eds., *Procès-verbaux de l'Académie royale de peinture et de sculpture, 1648–1793* (Paris: Baur [etc], 1875–92), VIII, 320, 376 and IX, 12, 13 (hereafter cited *P.V. Acad.*)

[71] *Cor. dir.*, XIII, 455–75, XIV, 10, 27; *N.A.A.F.*, ser. 1, III (1874–75), 379.

[72] Today in the Musée de la Santé, Marseille.

[73] Delécluze, pp. 114–15.

[74] *Notice*, pp. 17–18.

[75] *Notice*, p. 18; Thomé, p. 20. He left Rome on July 17, 1780.

[76] In the Museum of Lille and the Collection of Count Adam Branicki, Willanow Palace, near Warsaw, Poland, respectively.

[77] *P.V. Acad.*, IX, 76–77; L. P. de Bachaumont and others, *Mémoires secrètes pour servir à l'histoire de la république des lettres en France* (London: Adamson, 1784), XVIII, 10 (hereafter cited as *Mem. sec.*); *Journal de Paris*, no. 237 (August 25, 1781), p. 953.

The Salon of 1781, which opened the next day, included David's paintings [78] and proved to be a brilliant success for the young artist. Critics such as Diderot,[79] Grimm,[80] Métra,[81] and Moufle d'Angerville [82] praised his work highly, and their view that his talents presaged a new artistic renaissance seems to have been shared by many contemporaries.[83]

The high nobility made much of him and commissioned their portraits; Count Angiviller encouraged him; and according to Sedaine, the crowd carried the young artist in triumph on its shoulders.[84] Irritated by David's popularity and disquieted by the artistic revolution it reflected, some of the older members of the Academy were unable to conceal their hostility. It is said that Pierre, the Director, who had promised the painter of *Belisarius* that the government would buy his picture for 4000 livres, now offered him 50 louis. David kept his painting, later selling it to the Elector of Trier for a much larger sum than the one originally offered.[85]

David's fame spread throughout France and numerous young artists applied for instruction in his studio. The pupils of the first year included such important painters of the future as Girodet, Fabre, Debret, Wicar, and Drouais. This school of painting soon became a veritable art mecca for distinguished travelers from all parts of Europe, and a salon where the leading French social, political and

[78] *Explications des peintures, sculptures et gravures des messieurs de l'Académie royale . . .* (Paris: Herissant, 1781), nos. 311–18. Besides the *Belisarius* and the *Potocki,* there were a *Funeral of Patroclus* (sketch), three academic figures and several small studies. *Journal de Paris,* no. 241 (August 29, 1781), p. 973.

[79] "Salon de 1781," *Oeuvres Complètes,* XII, 63–64.

[80] *Cor. lit.,* XIII, 27.

[81] *Correspondance secrète, politique et littéraire* (London: Adamson, 1787–90), XII, 84 (hereafter cited as *Cor. sec.*)

[82] *Mem. sec.,* XVIII, 68–69, XIX, 286, 289.

[83] *Mercure de France,* (October 6, 1781), pp. 37–39; *Journal de Paris,* no. 273 (September 30), pp. 1100–01.

[84] Letter of David to his mother: David, pp. 19–20. *Notice,* p. 19; Thomé, p. 25; Miette de Villars, pp. 75–76.

[85] T. C. Bruun-Neergaard, *Sur la situation des beaux-arts en France* (Paris, 1801), pp. 83–85; Chaussard, p. 151; Paillot, p. 127. Cf. M. Furcy-Raynaud, "Notes sur les tableaux de Bélisaire par David," Société de l'Histoire de l'Art Français, (hereafter cited S.H.A.F.) *Bulletin,* (1915–17), pp. 115–20.

artistic figures gathered during the next three decades.[86] Before long his reputation became European, and soon he was recognized as the master of neoclassicism and the greatest painter of the day.

After David's success at the Salon of 1781, the King granted him lodgings in the Louvre:[87] a most ancient and sought-after privilege of artists, dating from the reign of Henry IV.[88] Thus David took up his residence for the next quarter century, along with other celebrated artists of the day, in the vast rabbit warren of winding corridors, narrow stairways, and innumerable rooms, which they constructed for themselves in the semi-ruinous halls of the old royal palace.[89] Here, in addition to his living quarters, David eventually acquired an immense private studio on the top floor overlooking the quai opposite the Collège de Quatre Nations, and two others for his students in the north east angle of the Louvre.[90]

It was with regard to the arrangement of his new quarters that the young artist approached M. Pécoul, Contractor of the King's Buildings. In the course of their negotiations, the Contractor persuaded David to accept the hand of his seventeen-year old daughter Marguerite Charlotte. The marriage, celebrated May 16, 1782, in the church of Saint-Germain-l'Auxerrois, brought the rising young artist a fortune which assured him financial independence, a charming, vivacious and devoted wife, and, in time, a family of four children.[91]

On August 23, 1783, the painter presented his "reception piece," *The Grief of Andromache over the body of Hector,* to the Royal Academy and was admitted to full membership in that august and

[86] Count Ségur, *Mémoires* (3. ed., Paris: Eymery, 1827), II, 34, Sir J. Carr, *The Stranger in France* (London: Johnson, 1803), p. 109.

[87] Chaussard, p. 151; *Notice,* p. 20; Thomé, p. 26.

[88] O. Mersen, "Les logements d'artistes au Louvre," *G.B.A.*, ser. 2, XXIII (March, 1881), 264–5. *A.A.F.*, ser. 1, I (1851–52), 194.

[89] *Loc. cit.*, pp. 203–4; [L. S. Mercier] *Tableau de Paris* (Amsterdam, 1788), XII, 285; Report on the lodgings of artists in the Old Louvre in 1773: *N.A.A.F.*, ser. 1, II (1873), 214–18; State of the lodgings . . . 1790: *loc. cit.*, p. 147.

[90] Administration of the Museum to the Minister of the Interior, May 3, 1800: L. de Lanzac de Laborie, *Paris sous Napoléon* (Paris: Plon-Nourrit, 1913), VIII, 398. The best description of his studios in the Louvre is the vivid and interesting account in Delécluze, pp. 15–24. *See also* Carr, *op. cit.*, pp. 109–10 and other contemporary accounts such as F. J. L. Meyer, *Fragmente aus Paris* (Hamburg: Bohn, 1798), II, 215 ff.

[91] Chaussard, p. 151; *Notice,* pp. 20–24; Thomé, pp. 20, 27–31; Miette de Villars, pp. 74, 79–80; David, pp. 17–18, 22–23; Jal. *loc. cit.*

venerable body.[92] The neoclassical beauty of his latest work, which of course appeared at the Salon that year,[93] was praised by the critics as warmly as its predecessors.[94] The realism with which he painted a figure of Christ crucified for the Marquise de Noailles, wife of the Minister of War, was well received by the public, but the ease with which the identity of his soldier model was recognized, led to a scandal and a law suit which David won.[95] Students overcrowded his studio and he was beginning to enjoy the prestige which the role of *chef d'école* was to bring him.

Prior to his election to the Academy, David had been working on a composition ordered by the government: *Horace defended by his father,*[96] inspired by Corneille's great tragedy.[97] The artist changed his mind, however, and the picture did not appear at the Salon of 1783. Nevertheless, he received a new commission for 1785. When he decided that "only at Rome could he paint Romans," his father-in-law generously provided the funds for a year in Italy.[98] Taking leave of the Academy on July 20, 1784,[99] David, accompanied by his wife and favorite pupil, Drouais, *Prix de Rome* winner that year, returned to the scene of his earlier studies.

For eleven months David shut himself up in his studio at Rome, only leaving it to commune with Raphael, antique marbles and the the-

[92] *P.V. Acad.,* IX, 164, The appointment was confirmed September 6: *ibid.,* p. 166.

[93] *Explication des peintures . . .* (Paris: Herissant, 1783), no. 162. He also exhibited fine portraits of his uncle Pierre Jacques Desmaisons (now in the Albright Gallery, Buffalo, N. Y.) and the doctor Alphons Le Roy (now in the Museum of Montpellier).

[94] *Cor. lit.,* XIII, 444–5; *Mem. sec.,* XXIV, 20; *Cor. sec.,* XV, 82; *Journal de Paris,* no. 266 (September 23, 1783) , pp. 1098–9; *Mercure de France,* no. 38 (September 20), p. 132.

[95] Chaussard, pp. 152–3; *Notice,* pp. 23–24; Thomé, pp. 31–33; Lenoir, p. 5; Miette de Villars, pp. 88–90.

[96] Engerand, *Inventaire,* p. 137. A drawing he made for this work is in the Louvre: *Inv. dess.,* no. 3196, IV, 76–77. Repr. in David, vol. II, and Cantinelli .

[97] Péron, *Examen des Horaces,* pp. 27ff.; "Horace," act V: *Oeuvres de P. Corneille,* III, 282–358. E. Wind, *loc, cit.,* argues that David's design was based on Charles Rollin's, *Histoire Romaine.* However, there appears to be no reason to suppose that David was not inspired directly by Livy: Livius, *op. cit.,* Bk. I, Chap. XXVI.

[98] *Notice,* pp. 25, 26; Thomé, p. 35; Coupin, p. 39; Péron, *Examen des Horaces,* pp. 17, 32; Delécluze, p. 117; Miette de Villars, pp. 91–92; David, p. 26.

[99] *Congé*: *N.A.A.F.,* ser. 1, VI (1878), 58–59; Angiviller to Pierre, July 21: *Correspondance de M. d'Angiviller avec Pierre* (Paris: S.H.A.F., 1907), II, 53 (hereafter cited *Cor. Ang.*)

ories of his friends, the German aestheticians and the archaeologists.[100] Finally the painting was finished—it was the *Oath of the Horatii*. When he opened his studio to the public, an eyewitness declared: "Every day it was like a procession: princes and princesses . . . , cardinals and prelates, monsignori and priests, bourgeoisie and workers, all came to see it." [101] Rome rang with the praises of his latest opus and even the Pope asked for a showing.[102]

At the Paris Salon the reception was equally flattering.[103] But powers within the Academy showed their spite at David's success by hanging his painting in an unfavorable position.[104] Angiviller was said to have reproached David on account of the size and composition of his picture.[105] Nevertheless, in response to popular murmurs, he ordered Pierre to hang it in a better place and continued to support the young innovator.[106] Despite the disagreeable notes sounded by the Academy, enthusiastic critics hailed the *Horatii* as a masterpiece [107] and its author as the "Corneille of painting."[108] Even Cochin, the hostile secretary of the Academy, was forced to admit "David was the real victor of the Salon." [109] Henceforth, the painter of the *Horatii* exerted such a great influence over the other artists that he was regarded as chief of the French School and the leader of the

[100] Lagrenée to Angiviller, December 1, 1784: *Cor. dir.*, XIV, 467; W. Tischbein, *Aus meinem Leben*, ed. Schiller (Brunswick, 1861), II, 44–6; *Memorie per le belle arti . . . dell'anno 1785* (Rome, 1785), I, cxxxv; Péron, p. 33.

[101] Tischbein, *ibid.*, p. 47.

[102] Letter of Drouais, August 14, 1785: Péron, pp. 34–5. David to Marquis de Bièvre, August 28: David, pp. 27–28. Sue, p. 277; *Notice*, p. 27; Thomé, pp. 38–39; Couder, "Protestation," p. 422; Miel, pp. 579–80; Delécluze, p. 118; Miette de Villars, pp. 93–4.

[103] *Notice*, p. 28; Thomé, p. 41.

[104] *Explication des peintures . . .* (Paris: Herissant, 1785), no. 103. *See* P. A. Martini's contemporary engraving, "Le Salon du Louvre," reproduced in A. Calabi, *La gravure italienne au XVIII siècle* (Paris: Van Oest, 1931), pl. LXIV.

[105] Chaussard, p. 155; *Notice*, pp. 29–30; Thomé, pp. 42, 44; Coupin, p. 40; Paillot, p. 128; Delécluze, pp. 118–19; Miette de Villars, p. 96.

[106] Angiviller to Pierre, September 23; same to Cochin, November 9: David, pp. 32–33. Cf. Paillot, p. 126.

[107] *Journal encyclopédique*, VIII, pt. 3 (December 15, 1785), pp. 512, 515, 526–7; *Journal de Paris*, no. 260 (September 17), p. 1072; *Mercure de France*, no. 40 (October 1), p. 33; *Mem. sec.*, XXX, 156–7, *Cor. sec.*, XVIII, 367.

[108] *Notice*, p. 31; Paillot, p. 137.

[109] Cantinelli, p. 23.

neoclassic art movement.[110] Though the return to antiquity had begun long since, the *Horatii* served as "the manifesto" of the new artistic order.[111]

In 1787, David failed to win the appointment as Director of the French Academy at Rome, which he coveted. Although Angiviller expressed his high regard for the artist, he felt he was as yet too young and too low in the academic hierarchy for the position. Nevertheless, he hinted quite strongly that he would support him "in six or twelve years" when the position would again be vacant.[112] David's enemies later alleged that his rancor against the Academy stemmed from this rebuff.[113]

At the Salon of 1787, David's *Death of Socrates*[114] created an immense sensation. The absence of its author's name from the list of painters honored by royal "works of encouragement" was attributed to the intrigues of Pierre and was decried as an "injustice."[115] The critics praised his *Socrates* highly and the detractions of his rivals were discounted.[116] Although its general popularity was not so great as that of the *Horatii*, it was praised by artists and connoisseurs as the supreme artistic achievement of the time.[117]

[110] Locquin, *Peinture d'histoire,* p. 287.

[111] Hautecoeur, p. 158. Moreover, the furniture, costumes and coiffures of the painting were widely copied and exerted a marked influence upon taste and style: Delécluze, pp. 134–36.

[112] Angiviller to Bièvre, June 22, 1787: S.H.A.F., *Bulletin,* (1907), pp. 32–33.

[113] Renou to President of National Assembly: *Procès-verbaux de la Commune générale des arts,* ed. Lapauze (Paris: Imprimerie Nationale, 1903), p. xxiii.

[114] *Explication des peintures . . .* (Paris: Imp. Bâtimens du Roi, 1787), no. 119. Now in the Metropolitan Museum of Art, New York. Opposite p. 18.

[115] *Mem. sec.,* XXXVI, 318. An injury which the artist had suffered prevented him from completing his commission, a *Coriolanus,* for the Salon of 1787.

[116] *Mem. sec.,* XXXVI, 318–20, 346–7; *Cor. lit.,* XV, 165–7; *Journal de Paris,* no. 266 (September 23, 1787), pp. 1152–3; *Mercure de France,* no. 9 (September 22, 1787), pp. 177–8. The interesting comments of the Polish amateur Potocki, printed in N.E. Restif de la Bretonne, *Nuits de Paris* (Paris, 1789), VII, 3150–52, 3326–48 are highly favorable to David.

[117] R. H. Wilenski (*French painting* [Boston: Hale, Cushman and Flint, 1931], p. 184 n) shows that David's biographers have erred in attributing a eulogy of the *Socrates* to Sir Joshua Reynolds, but Edgar Wind ("A Lost Article on David by Reynolds," Warburg and Courtauld Institutes, *Journal* VI [1943], 223–24) suggests that the article missing from Sir Joshua's writings was deliberately suppressed by his literary executor because of political bias.

V. THE DEATH OF SOCRATES

Painting by David

Courtesy of The Metropolitan Museum of Art

Before the next Academic Exposition (1789), Pierre tried to have David's name stricken from the lists, but Angiviller restrained the Director and insisted that David's work was essential.[118] Instead of painting the *Coriolanus* ordered by the King, David busied himself with *The Lictors bringing back to Brutus the Bodies of his Sons.*[119] Such a representation of the virtuous republican defender of Roman liberty sacrificing his sons for the fatherland, had a triple appeal to the public: it was inspired by the classical spirit, so alien to the medievalism they were destroying; it glorified the simple moral virtues of a republican hero; and it faithfully displayed the picturesque externals of antiquity which enjoyed the popular fancy. Then, even before it was exhibited, an ill-considered act of the government stimulated the curiosity of the crowd still more and made David a popular figure.

Before the opening of the Salon on August 25, the Revolution had of course begun. The peaceful movement which had established the National Assembly had been followed in July by the outbreak of armed violence, the fall of the Bastille, and the beginning of the emigration. The court was determined that the Salon should not become an avenue for revolutionary propaganda and therefore all paintings were carefully censored before being hung. Portraits of certain well-known figures were banned such as David's magnificent portrait of Lavoisier, the great chemist who happened to be one of the hated Farmers-General.[120] When the newspapers reported that the government had prohibited the exhibition of David's *Brutus,* public opinion was outraged.[121] In fact, popular feeling was so aroused that the "subversive" picture had to take its appointed place at the Exhibition where it was protected by art students wearing the uniform of the newly created National Guard.[122]

Popular attention was naturally concentrated upon the political symbolism of *Brutus* rather than upon the artistic qualities of David's painting. The image of the virtuous Roman consul sacrificing his

[118] David, pp. 53–54.

[119] *Ibid.,* p. 54; Engerand, *Inventaire,* p. 138.

[120] Cuvillier to Pierre, August 19, 1789:*Cor. Ang.,* II, 263–64.

[121] Angiviller had to bear the onus for this prohibition. ***L'Observateur,*** **no. 3** [August 11, 1789], pp. 9–10; no. 4 [n.d.], sup. p. 22.

[122] *Explication des peintures . . .* (Paris: Imp. Bâtimens du Roi, 1789), no. 88. J. G. Wille, *Mémoires et Journal* (Paris: Renouard, 1857), II, 214; Cuvillier to Vien, August 7: *Cor. Ang.,* II, 263. Opposite p. 20.

treacherous family for the sake of liberty and the fatherland was regarded by some Frenchmen as a "coup d'état," for the patriotic Brutus was compared to their own feeble king who lacked the "virtue" to punish the conspirators in his family.[123] The triumph of *Brutus* was of a political nature: the painting was regarded as more than a glorification of patriotic virtue; Brutus was proposed as a model for the French people. Public fervor proclaimed the author of this "revolutionary document" as a "precursor of liberty." The austere republican sentiments of Brutus were ascribed to his portrayer, and David became the idol of the day.

David's position as leader of the French school of painting was now even more firmly established than before. The Exhibition proved that this supremacy was unassailable. His disciples and emulators shared the favor of the public; two of his pupils won first and second prize at the Salon that year. Moreover, David exercised an almost unbelievable ascendancy over his devoted pupils and inspired in them a fanatical admiration. Thus at the outbreak of the Revolution, David was the most powerful as well as the most famous artist in all France. The rapture with which the populace greeted his *Brutus* indicated that his services would be of considerable value in manipulating public opinion during the rapidly approaching struggle for control of the State. The exhibition of *Brutus* was regarded as a signal of revolt and David was regarded as a precursor of the Revolution.

The immense effect of this painting upon his contemporaries and the close association of David with the Revolution, brings up the problem of a possible relationship between an artistic style and an historical movement; namely, whether or not there is any intrinsic connection between neoclassicism and the French Revolution. More specifically, is there anything in the style which David employed which was particularly suitable for the expression of the revolutionary program?

When formulated in this way, the question would seem to call for an affirmative answer. Certainly the new artistic style represented a revolt against the characteristic style of the eighteenth century, the aristocratic rococo art which indulged in the frivolities of courtly pastimes. While the Greek and Roman subject matter preferred by

[123] E.L.A.H. and J.A.H. de Goncourt, *Histoire de la société française pendant la révolution* (n. ed., Paris: Charpentier,1904), p. 44.

VI. LICTORS BRINGING BACK TO BRUTUS THE BODIES OF HIS SONS

Repetition by David

Courtesy of Wadsworth Atheneum, Hartford, Conn.

the School of David was not new, still the particular incidents depicted often illustrated a revolutionary theme. For example, blind Belisarius was the victim of the ingratitude of kings, and Brutus was the heroic defender of republican freedom. Moreover, this subject matter was treated in quite a different manner than before, as a comparison of Poussin and David will illustrate. Most important was the new moral content. David imbued his canvases with the philosophy of the Enlightenment, thus providing a new ideological content for art. In his hands neoclassicism was actually able to influence public opinion in favor of a revolutionary program.

As a result, the revolutionary implications of neoclassicism have usually been taken for granted. The era of the Revolution was regarded as a period of artistic regeneration which corresponded to the ideological and social resurgence of the French nation. According to this view, the artistic medium of the rising bourgeoisie was the severe and monumental style which supplanted the erotic decorations of Boucher and Fragonard.

Recently an opposite interpretation has been advanced. It is argued that neoclassicism became associated with the revolutionary doctrine for purely incidental and external reasons. The fact that most of the artists of the time who became revolutionaries—and these were decidely in the majority—were also partisans of the neoclassic movement, has been attributed by some to an accident of chronology. It is pointed out by them that these movements happened to become popular at the same time and that they were both regarded as "new" in 1789. Others would even go so far as to insist that neoclassicism, because it imposed rules upon the individual artist, was a reactionary, even a counter-revolutionary style. The proponents of this newer view believe that the true revolutionary art developed only after the Bourbon Restoration in the romanticism of Gros, Géricault and Delacroix. While there is evidence to support all these statements, such sweeping generalizations are bound to oversimplify the true situation. Actually the facts are far more complex than these arguments indicate.

Since scholars have been unable to agree upon the meaning of terms such as "classicism" and "romanticism," the division of the history of art into periods and styles has tended to become almost meaningless. As a result, a substantial portion of the arguments regarding the revolutionary implications of "neoclassicism" is purely verbal, and the contradictions of the traditional "classical-revolutionary" thesis and the more recent "romantic-revolutionary" antithesis are more apparent than real.

The form of David's painting was "classical" in the sense that it was characterized by an emphasis upon line rather than color, upon static composition rather than upon movement, and upon the imitation of Greek and Roman sculpture. On the other hand, the treatment of his subject matter was highly "realistic" in its imitation of nature. Finally, the content of his art was essentially romantic, if by "romantic" we mean, in part, an admiration of an enviable and idealized past, and an emphasis upon an emotional message. The "romantic" character of David's art is reinforced by a statement he made in 1793 that the artist must draw his inspiration from "all the springs of the human heart."[124] Even a superficial examination of David's productions during the Revolutionary period indicates that he practiced his own dictum. While the form of French "classicism" in the last part of the eighteenth century may be regarded as reactionary because it looked backward to earlier canons of taste, still its "romantic" content imbued it with a spirit that was truly revolutionary.

In support of the revolutionary implications of neoclassicism, it can be pointed out that fundamental moral purposes, certain ideal characteristics such as rationalism, human dignity and secularism, and various legislative or legal concepts are common to both neoclassicism and Revolution. In the first place, David's art and revolutionary thought attempted to inculcate heroic and civic virtues. The "noble" subjects favored by neoclassic artists were intended to serve, not merely the regeneration of painting, but also the moral instruction of society. Thus the didactic character of the new art may be compared to revolutionary ideology and legislation which aimed at nothing less than the regeneration of mankind.

Then too, certain abstract ideas can be detected in the art and thought of the revolutionary generation. Rationalism is one of the distinguishing features of classical art and certainly the revolutionaries appealed to reason as the criterion of their legislation and as the justification for their deeds. The clear proportions, rhythmic composition and application of optical, geometrical and anatomical laws are characteristic of the highly rational organization of David's paintings. Neoclassicism and the revolutionary ideals breathed the spirit

[124] *Moniteur*, no. 57 (27 Brumaire, an. II; November 17, 1793), p. 231.

of secularism. That is to say both tended to draw away from traditional Christianity and both had a tendency to glorify the state. It is not without significance that David's few attempts at religious art were remarkable for their pagan and secular qualities. In his paintings the Horatii, Socrates and Brutus place the welfare of the state above their own and patriotically sacrifice themselves for the good of the fatherland.

Finally, both neoclassicism and revolutionary ideology were convinced of the importance and utility of law, order and logic. The ideal of "beautiful" nature "discovered" by classic artists was to be applied in accordance with certain logical proportions as infallible as the mathematical laws upon which they were based. Similarly the revolutionary legislators believed that natural laws and self-evident truths could be applied to government and society in the form of logical principles, wise decrees, and rational institutions. While the neoclassicists expected to regenerate the decadent art of the old regime, the revolutionaries hoped to reform existing political, social and economic conditions and to abolish all the old irrational practices and abuses. In one case they sought a perfect art and in the other, a perfect society; the means anticipated was the same in both: the rational application of "the laws of Nature and of Nature's God."

Both were in effect different manifestations of the same age, an age which conceived the universe as a vast and intricate mechanism of severe and mathematical beauty, governed by eternal and unchanging laws, capable of being understood by the mind of man, and capable of being controlled by him if these laws could be discovered and applied. While the problem of the essential nature and inter-relationship of art styles and revolutionary upheavals in general must remain within the domain of the philosophers, it would seem, in the light of the similarities suggested above, that the two specific movements under discussion are closely related. It can be said that neoclassicism and the French Revolution were intrinsically related in the sense that they both were products of the same climate of opinion, expressions of the same Weltanschauung. But much more than this can be stated: Neoclassic art *was* a powerful propaganda weapon of the Revolution. This weapon was wielded with great effect by David in the struggle to overthrow the old order and establish a bourgeois regime. If neoclassicism had been alien to the revolutionary spirit, the artist would never have been able to use it so effectively in the control of public opinion.

CHAPTER II

An Artist Becomes A Propagandist

At the outset, David became a whole-hearted partisan of the Revolution. Instead of emigrating to become a successful court painter of foreign kings and émigré nobles, or withdrawing to provincial seclusion to paint innocuous scenes of classical mythology, he remained in Paris to defend the interests of his fellow artists, to destroy the artistic institutions of the old order, and to become the propagandist of the Revolution. He dared to follow the dictates of his conscience; he served the First Republic and thereafter was damned forever by royalists and Bonapartists. As a friend of Marat and Robespierre he has been execrated by the more conservative republicans as well.

After Thermidor he was imprisoned, and when no basis could be found for the charges of terrorism made against him, he was released, to be hounded by his enemies for the remainder of his career. Following the restoration he went into exile, and when he died the Bourbon government refused to allow his body to be returned to France for burial. Since then his political antagonists have not ceased to defame his character, his career, and his art.[1]

Why did David, the greatest artist of his day. thus jeopardize his reputation, his security, his liberty, and even his life, by using his talents to help overthrow the monarchy and establish a bourgeois republic? In short, why did the master of the Neoclassic School become "the Robespierre of the brush"? David was no discontented, maladjusted failure unable to win success under the monarchical system. On the contrary, he had a considerable stake in the Old Regime: socially, financially, and professionally he would presumably stand to lose far more than he might hope to gain by a radical revolution.

The aristocracy was proud to receive and entertain such a talented artist as David on a basis of perfect equality, and the salons of the highest society were open to him. Spirited Countess Angiviller graciously entertained the famous painter and his colleagues with dazzling

[1] For the influence of political passions upon David's reputation *see* the Bibliographical Essay pp. 143–61.

magnificence.[2] More important than having wined and dined him, the Count himself had watched over and aided David's artistic advancement, and with his celebrated tact and courtesy he had salved the artist's acute personal sensibilities in a manner which was truly remarkable.[3] The painter frequented Saint-Leu, the seat of the Duke of Orleans. Not only was he an intimate friend of the household,[4] but he probably imbibed there the liberal ideas of Barnave, the Lameths, Volney, and others. David mingled with the Chéniers, the Abbé Delille, "Pindar" Lebrun, the critic Suard, and other literary and social lights at the brilliant and fashionable salons of the Chéniers, the Trudaines, the Ducreux, and of Mme. Vigée-Le Brun.[5]

In addition to a high social position, the old regime also offered David wealth, since he could be certain of good prices and a steady market for his pictures. Most artists could look forward to a comfortable living, but exceptional painters such as David might expect to amass a considerable fortune. As previously stated, his wife had brought him financial security, and the King furnished "palatial" quarters free of rent together with lucrative annual commissions. Finally, the patronage of the aristocracy and wealthy amateurs and the speculations of collectors and dealers provided a growing market at excellent prices.

Above all, professional honors and prestige would accrue to an artist of David's calibre. He had already reached the height of popular acclaim, but he could still look forward to that symbol of royal approbation, the ribbon of the Order of St. Michel. As has been in-

[2] *See* the contemporary memoirs, *e.g.*, Count Ségur, *Mémoires,* II, 34; A. F. Sergent, *Reminiscences,* ed. Simpson (London: Chapman and Hall, 1889), p. 5. J. G. Wille, *Mémoires et Journal,* II, 152; Ségur, *loc. cit.;* Miette de Villars, *Mémoires de David,* pp. 97–99; J. F. Marmontel, *Mémoires,* ed. Tourneux (Paris: Librarie des Bibliophiles, 1891), I, 46.

[3] Many instances besides those mentioned above might be given. *See,* for example, the postscript the Count added in his own hand: Angiviller to David, July 21, 1787, *N.A.A.F.,* ser. 1, III (1874–75), 396–97. This interpretation is quite contrary to the usual one as given by Goncourt (*Histoire de la société française,* pp. 41–43). It is strengthened by Angiviller's *Mémoires* (ed. Bobé, Copenhagen: Levin & Munksgard, 1933).

[4] Mme. S. F. D. de Genlis, *Mémoires inédites* (Paris: Advocat, 1825), III, 156–57.

[5] P. Dimoff, *André Chénier* (Paris: Droz, 1936), I, 80; A. J. Bingham, *M.-J. Chénier* (New York: Priv. Print., 1939), p. 5; Mme. M.E.L. (Vigée) Le Brun, *Souvenirs* (Paris: Charpentier, 1869), I, 64, II, 267; A. Péron, *Examen des Horaces,* p. 28; cf. C. Lacretelle, *Dix années d'épreuves* (Paris: Allouard, 1841), pp. 82–83.

dicated, the coveted post of Director of the French Academy at Rome would no doubt one day be his. Possibly he might even acquire a title of nobility before he died.[6]

Already he enjoyed the benefits of membership in that ancient and honorable body, the Royal Academy of Painting and Sculpture. Its Salon every two years gave him a unique opportunity to obtain publicity—so essential for a successful career. Its meetings enabled him to foregather with his more illustrious colleagues and bask in the sunshine of his monarch's favor. Shortly he would become one of its officers[7] and help control the artistic life of France; in time he might even become Director of the Royal Academy.

Why, then, did David rally to the new order? What converted the fashionable artist enjoying royal favor into a "radical revolutionary" who glorified Le Peletier, Marat, and Robespierre, and condemned Louis XVI to the guillotine? In one way or another this important question has been considered by almost all of David's biographers. In many cases the answer given is an index of the author's political or artistic opinions rather than an explanation of the artist's motives. It is possible that a completely satisfactory answer cannot be found; it is certain that no single factor will suffice to clarify this complex problem. A number of elements must be considered before attempting to answer the question.

In the first place, some contemporaries assumed that David's neoclassic art somehow inspired him with a patriotic desire to re-establish republican institutions as well as the artistic glories of ancient Greece and Rome.[8] That is to say, his "vision of antiquity" produced his "revolutionary spirit."[9] Those who regretted David's devotion to the Revolution commonly explained his attachment to its leaders by his preoccupation with the idealized heroes of Plutarch: "He saw Phocion in Marat, and in Robespierre a new Marius."[10] It may well be that Winckelmann's ideas convinced David that classical republican institutions were essential to a revival of the artistic greatness of the an-

[6] *See* p. 18 and p. 3.

[7] He was appointed Associate Professor July 7, 1792: *P. V. Acad.*, X, 167–70.

[8] E.g., Thomé, *Vie de David,* p. 93; A. V. Arnault, *Oeuvres* (Paris: Bossange, 1827), VIII, 19; Coupin, "Notice sur David," p. 56; David, *Le Peintre David,* p. 111; Delécluze, *Louis David,* pp. 136–37; *Biographie nouvelle des contemporaines,* V, 231.

[9] Parker, *Cult of Antiquity,* pp. vii, 1–7.

[10] Thomé, p. 93.

cients. Just as he wanted to reform the decadent art forms of his day by a return to nature and to classical models, so he joined the movement to replace the outmoded political and social institutions of the French monarchy with others inspired by the more democratic features of the Greek and Roman republics.

Others believed that they found the key to the artist's revolutionary career in his personality.[11] Undoubtedly, David's artistic sensibility, mercurial temperament, volatile emotions, ardent enthusiasm, and fierce independence might have been expected to help turn him against the established order but they did not fully explain his devotion to the republican regime. Nor did the vague statements of those who insisted upon his "powerful ambition . . . and unusual energy of will" actually account for his revolutionary connections.[12] Those who knew him maintained that "generous ardor," high-minded idealism and well-meaning, though sometimes fanatical, enthusiasm rather than selfishness and jealousy, motivated his activities during this period.[13]

Be that as it may, professional and class interests as well as personal factors must be taken into account. As an *habitué* of the prerevolutionary salons of the bourgeois intellectuals and liberal nobles (such as the Duke of Orleans) David was familiar with English and American constitutional theories and with the enlightened ideas of the *philosophes*. It is reasonable to assume that he shared the aspirations of his class for destruction of the old feudal structure and control of a reformed national state. Moreover, the status of the arts under the old regime convinced him that the artists must be emancipated from the inequalities and abuses of the existing cultural institutions, and that art must take its rightful place in a new social order. Undoubtedly David's deep-rooted conviction that the Academy must be reformed gave added impetus to his desire to participate in the Revolution.

While David's fellow revolutionists led the fight against the remnants of political, social, and economic feudalism, the chief of the Neo-

[11] E.g., Meyer, *Fragments sur Paris,* (Hamburg, 1798), II, 206; L. Rosenthal, *Louis David* (Paris: Librarie de l'art ancien et moderne, 1905), p. 42; B. Hauréau, *La Montagne* (Paris: Bréauté, 1834), pp. 65–66; Saunier, *David,* p. 39.

[12] K. Brun, *J. L. David und die französische Revolution* (Zurich, 1890), p. 10.

[13] Meyer, *op. cit.,* II, 207–08; Coupin, p. 56; Thomé, p. 93; P. C. F. Daunou, *Mémoires,* ed. Barrière and Lescure (Paris: Firmin-Didot, 1848), p. 417; M. A. Baudot, *Notes historiques* (Paris: Jouaust, 1893), p. 14; Le Brun, p. 179; David, p. 111. Lenoir (p. 1) attributes his political role to "domestic disappointments," meaning his separation from his wife.

classic School rallied the artists in a battle against the aristocratic cultural institutions of the old regime. A brief examination of the organization of the fine arts before the Revolution reveals why the Royal Academy of Painting and Sculpture which monopolized the artist's means of publicity, fame, and fortune, was regarded by David as a symbol of reaction.[14]

Virtually a closed corporation of about sixty members, this organization, protected by the King, was, like the social structure of the old regime itself, a hierarchy of three classes: Officers, Academicians and *Agréés.* All authority, initiative, and control were vested in the first class, which formulated policies and made all decisions; the second class merely had a voice in the deliberations; and the third class had no rights at all. Members were seated and their paintings were hung in accordance with this rigid hierarchy. Only the Academy's members could exhibit at the biennial Salon, and they alone were honored by government commissions. Under Angiviller and Pierre the Academy became more aristocratic and despotic than ever. By 1787, it had succeeded in suppressing all exhibitions organized by non-members so that the Academic monopoly was complete. Such absolute powers, class distinctions, and special privileges were manifestly incompatible with the new spirit abroad in France. When David embraced the revolutionary principles of his class, a battle with the Academy became all but inevitable.[15]

In addition to condemning the corporation as a monopolistic stronghold of privileged aristocrats, David bitterly attacked the Academy as a school of fine arts. Its students copied a model, under the successive direction of twelve professors who changed every month; and competed for various prizes. David, on the other hand, was a firm believer in the atelier method of the old masters; and he had built up a large and successful art school in his own studio. Though his pupils were outstandingly successful in winning academic honors such as the *Prix de Rome,* he unceasingly urged them to express their own in-

[14] Mairobert, *L'Espion Anglais,* VI, 60–62; *Almanach royal, année* [1789] (Paris: D'Houry, n.d.), pp. 517–23; J. A. Dulaure, *Description des curiosités de Paris* (2.ed.; Paris: Lejay, 1787), I, 34; L. P. Deseine, *Notices historiques sur les anciennes académies* (Paris: Le Normant, 1814), pp. 1–55.

[15] Deseine, pp. 56–57; Count Paroy, *Précis historique de l'origine de l'Académie royale de peinture* (Paris: Gratiot, 1816), pp. 31–32. Cf. J. Renouvier, *Histoire de l'art pendant la révolution* (Paris: Renouard, 1863), p. 8.

dividuality, and to avoid the academic tradition as they would the plague. Its "virus" would, he believed, poison their style, destroy all originality, and reduce them to formalism, decadence, and bad taste.[16] On September 17, 1789, David complained that "the Academy no longer likes the antique."[17] The aristocrats of the Academy had no intention of allowing the dissemination at *their* Salon of the revolutionary propaganda associated with David's neoclassic paintings.[18]

The underlying hostility between David and the Academy, which had already been expressed on a number of occasions, though probably caused primarily by the incompatibility of rationalistic classicism and privileged decadence, was irritated by a personal opposition as well. The irascible temperament of the exasperated innovator clashed with the aristocratic pride of the academic conservatives. David's smoldering resentment against the opposition of the royal corporation was fanned into open rebellion by an affront at the hands of its officers.[19]

During the first week of September, 1789, the growing discontent of the younger artists attached to David's new principles was expressed in a pamphlet, *Voeu des Artistes,* which called for posthumous admission of Drouais to the Academy, exclusion of the professors' protégés from the special classes reserved for medal winners, and permission to sketch from classical antique models. This brochure, which openly attacked Angiviller and the "blind protectors of rampant mediocrity," was praised by the revolutionary journalist Feydel as the work of "a good citizen." The Academic officials completely and publicly disavowed this publication through the pages of the *Journal de Paris.*[20] Though they granted the last two demands of the pupils, they

[16] E. J. Delécluze, p. 57; Lenoir, pp. 3–4; Pierre to Angiviller, January 27, 1787: *Correspondance d'Angiviller,* II, 194–95; David, p. 57; Jal, p. 478.

[17] Letter of David to Wicar: Schneider, *Quatremère de Quincy,* p. 159.

[18] For the ban on David's *Brutus* at the Salon of 1789, *see* p. 19.

[19] Paroy, who maintained at first (1816) in his *Précis historique,* pp. 31–32, that it was "the false principles of liberty and equality" which led David to fight the Academy, later in his *Mémoires* (ed. Charavay, Paris: Plon-Nourrit, 1895) declared that he did so out of a desire for revenge for the King's refusal to be painted by him. *See* p. 139–41, regarding the alleged portrait of Louis XVI.

[20] *Voeu des Artistes* [Paris: Gueffier, 1789], the opening gun in the campaign, is conveniently forgotten by David's opponents (Deseine, p. 65) and overlooked by Brown, (p. 38). *L'Observateur* (Feydel), no. 19 (September 22, 1789), pp. 137–39. Meeting of September 12, 1789: Wille, II, 218; *P. V. Acad.,* X, 24–26. *Journal de Paris,* no. 260 (September 17), p. 1180. The *Observateur* (no. 19 [September 22], p. 139) insists that Angiviller forced the disavowal.

seem to have revoked their decision. In a violent argument at the meeting of October 3, David's insistent demands for the honors of the Salon for his beloved pupil Drouais and for consideration of the *Voeu* of the young artists were denied by the officers.[21]

The irate maestro soon found an ally against them in the engraver Miger, who was also agitating for reform. Twenty other progressive Academicians joined them on December 5 in presenting a formal demand for democratic revision of the statutes, reform of abuses, and drafting of a *"constitution fraternelle."*[22] Recognizing the seriousness of this "declaration of war" in such troubled times, the officers asked the rebels to forward their demands. Thus requested for memorials, the dissident Academicians met to formulate their program. David, their leader by fame and principles, was elected president. On January 30, 1790, they presented their claims for a revision of the statutes by all three classes of the Academy. Meanwhile, the officers, realizing that change was inevitable, had begun their own revision. Now, enraged by David's democratic proposals and perhaps alarmed by his joining the Jacobin Club (on February 4), the officers determined to challenge the legality of his pretensions. At the February 6 meeting they arrogantly rejected the claims of the dissidents as "irregular," insinuating that they were the fabrication of a few malcontents, and excluded them from the use of the halls of the Academy. Determined to oppose what they regarded as "privileged despotism," the dissidents met at David's apartment to plan their campaign. They invited the *agréés* of the Academy to join with them in a united front for "justice and equality." [23]

[21] Meeting of September 26: Wille (II, 222) says that the *first* two were accorded but not the last. The official *P.V. Acad.* (X, 28), indicated that the first would be discussed and that the others were granted. The old engraver is sometimes mistaken as to dates. Meeting of October 3: Wille, II, 222–23. This meeting is not mentioned by *P.V. Acad.* Cf. David, p. 65.

[22] S. C. Miger, *Lettre à M. Vien . . . 20 novembre 1789* (n.p., n.d.), and *Discours . . . à l'Académie royale de peinture . . . 28 novembre 1789 . . .* (n.p., n.d.). J. L. David and others, *Demande faite à l'Académie . . . du 5 décembre 1789* (n.p., n.d.).

[23] Meeting of officers, December 5, 1789: *P.V. Acad.*, X, 39. Meetings of dissidents, December 14: David, p. 67. General meeting, January 30, 1790: *P.V. Acad.*, X, 44; Wille, II, 236; David, p. 68. Meetings of officers, January 9 and following: *P.V. Acad.*, X, 42 ff. Meeting of officers, February 5: *P.V. Acad.*, X, 45–46; Wille, II, 237; David, pp. 68–69. General meeting February 6: *P.V. Acad.*, X, 47; Wille, *loc. cit.*; David, p. 69. Meetings of dissidents, February 22 and 24: David, p. 70; Paroy, *Mémoires*, p. 263.

Then David and his followers appealed to the Paris Commune. The Municipality applauded and voted to support their struggle for revolutionary principles. Worried by the overture to the *agréés,* Vien had written to Angiviller for instructions and had been told to temporize. Abandoned by his superior, the Director was forced by the invocation of the political authorities to try to restore harmony by conciliation.[24] A joint committee of the upper two groups, including David and his confrères, was elected on March 6 to reform the statutes, but the demands of the *agréés* for equality were denied. The minority group, however, were pledged to win the rights of the *agréés,* and therefore they met at the home of their leader to draft a protest against the "illegal exclusion."[25] Their memorial, presented to the Academy on March 27, was rejected on instructions from Angiviller, and David was deprived of his place on the statutes commission. In April a similar note was received in "absolute silence." During the succeeding months the Academy disputed over the reform of its statutes without David, and even won over a few of his adherents.[26]

Having discovered that it was impossible to reform the Academy in accordance with the principles of the new order, David apparently determined to destroy it and replace it with a democratic organization. To this end he now tried to capture both public attention and government support. On June 28, 1790, a deputation which he led before the Constituent Assembly was very favorably received by President Le Peletier and the legislators, who ordered that David's address be printed.[27] Thus encouraged, David and his supporters sent addresses

[24] Commune meeting, February 25, 1790: S. Lacroix, ed., *Actes de la Commune de Paris* (Paris: Cerf, 1896), ser. 1, IV, 205. Vien to Angiviller (with reply) February 25: *Cor. Ang.,* II, 279–80. Speech of Vien, meeting of February 27: *P.V. Acad.,* X, 47–49; David, 75–76. The attempt failed, for Wille (II, 241) indicates that the dispute continued.

[25] Meeting of March 6: *P.V. Acad.,* X, 50–52; Wille, II, 242–43; David, pp. 77–78. Cf. the hostile and distorted accounts of Paroy, *Précis, passim,* and Deseine, p. 60. Meetings of dissidents: David, p. 82. *Mémoire sur l'Académie royale de peinture et de sculpture par plusieurs membres de cette Académie* [Paris: Valade, 1790], signed by David and others March 6.

[26] Angiviller to Vien, Versailles, March 26, 1790: *Cor. Ang.,* II, 281. Meeting of March 27: *P.V. Acad.,* X, 54–55; Wille, II, 244, merely speaks of "a kind of revolt" of the students of the Academy at this meeting. Meeting of April 10: *P.V. Acad.,* X, 57; Wille, p. 245. *P.V. Acad.,* X, 62–65; Wille, pp. 251–53. Vien kept Angiviller informed: *Cor. Ang.,* II, 294–95. *See* letters of *agréés*: *P.V. Acad.,* X, 57–58, 69.

[27] Michel Le Peletier de Saint-Fargeau (1763–1793), a wealthy noble turned revolutionist, was later glorified by David as a Republican martyr. *See* pp. 78, 99 ff.

to the National Assembly and the King, and presented copies of their memorial to the Jacobin Society, and eleven Paris newspapers.[28]

Their address emphasized three points: first, the importance of the arts to the Revolution by their inculcation of civic virtues; second, the incompatibility of the old Academy with the new spirit of reason and the constitution; and finally, the establishment of a new regime by the creation of a Commune of the Arts. Distributed in pamphlet form, the *mémoire* provoked heated discussion. It inaugurated David's campaign against the Academy and represents one of the earliest formulations by the revolutionary artists of the theory of the political and social utility of the arts.[29]

Thereafter, the Royal Academy knew no peace. As a result of David's publicity campaign, the National Assembly denounced the privileged body as an aristocratic despotism and ordered it to revise its statutes within one month to conform with the principles of the new constitution.[30] In September the violent dispute over the proposed reforms led to a factional struggle within the Academy. The officers wished to preserve the *status quo*; certain Academicians desired moderate reforms from within; but David and his followers aimed at total reorganization on a democratic basis.[31]

Procès-verbal de l'Assemblée nationale [*Constituante*] (Paris: Baudouin, 1790), XXIII, 40 (hereafter cited *P.V.Nat.*); *Journal des débats et des décrets,* no. 327, [n.d.], pp. 1–2 (hereafter cited as *J.D.D.*);*Le Point du jour,* XI, no. 349 (June 30, 1790), pp. 299–300. *Adresse des représentants des beaux-arts à l'Assemblée nationale dans la séance du 28 juin 1790* [Paris: Imp. nat., 1790], signed by David as president and others.

[28] July 1, 1790, texts: David, pp. 85–86. At least one of these journals, the *Chronique de Paris,* no. 216 (August 4, 1790), p. 861, analyzed it for its readers.

[29] *Mémoire sur l'Académie royale de peniture* . . . [Paris: Valade, 1790]. *See* the rebuttals by Deseine and others: M. Tourneux, *La Bibliographie de l'histoire de Paris pendant la révolution française* (Paris: Imp. nouvelle, 1900), III, 879. *See* pp. 78–84.

[30] August 20, 1790: *P.V.Nat.,* no. 386, p. 12; *Archives Parlementaires de 1787 à 1860 . . ., 1. sér, (1787–1799),* (hereafter cited as *A.P.*) ed. J. Mavidal, E. Laurent and others (Paris: Dupont, 1876), XVIII, 173–76; *Moniteur,* no. 229 (August 23, 1790), p. 962; *Point du jour,* no. 404 (August 2), p. 223; *Journal gratuit,* no. 13 [n.d.], p. 202. Vien to Angiviller, August 23: *Cor. Ang.,* II, 297.

[31] Wille, II, 265–66, 269, 275, 278–79; *P.V. Acad.,* X, 79–81. Letter of Officers, September 23, 1790: *ibid.,* pp. 80–81. Letter of Renou to President of Legislative Assembly: *Procès-verbaux de la Commune générale des Arts,* p. xxiii (hereafter cited as *C.G.A.*). Renou to Huet de Froberville, January 29, 1792: David, p. 102. Vien to Angiviller, Paris, September 10, 1790: *Cor. Ang.,* II, 298–99.

The majority of the Academicians drew up a new set of regulations, embodying David's pedagogical principles but excluding the *agréés* and, on September 21, presented them to the National Assembly.[32] Though Vien made his peace, most of the officers remained adamant and continued their vendetta with David.[33] The latter, disgusted with the interminable wrangling and convinced that the time had come for the establishment of a democratic art society, created the Commune of the Arts of 300 members on September 27, 1790.[34]

Though the old Academy managed to prolong its existence for two more years, David was successful in substituting his new ideas of liberty and equality for the traditional concepts of privilege. Under his withering attacks new statutes were adopted, the name was changed to "Central Academy," the *agréés* were taken in, the Salon was thrown open to all, and its halls were finally stormed by the Commune of the Arts.[35] From then on the Academy was living on borrowed time.

Though the Goncourts' statement that "scarcely a week passed without a popular outcry for 'suppression of all the academies,'" is based on a misreading of their source,[36] the assertion is not without a certain amount of truth. Opponents as diverse as the academician Chamfort, the journalist Mercier, the radical Marat, and the mad baron

[32] *A.P.*, XIX, 121–35. *Adresse et projet de statuts et règlements pour l'Académie centrale . . . présentée à l'Assemblée nationale par la majorité des membres* (Paris: Valade, 1790); Wille, II, 265–66; *P.V. Acad.*, X, 81–82. Cf. Paroy, *Précis*, pp. 13–14, who insists that these artists were "never more than a minority;" also Deseine, p. 61.

[33] Vien to Angiviller, November 24, 1790: *Cor. Ang.*, II, 303–04; Wille, II, 267–68. A. Renou and others, *Esprit des statuts et règlements de l'Académie royale . . .* ([Paris]: Hérissant, November 11, 1790), and *Adresse à l'Assemblée nationale par la presque totalité des officiers* ([Paris]: Hérissant, November 30, 1790). Paroy, *Précis*, p. 14; Deseine, p. 6.

[34] *C.G.A.*, p. xix. Cf. *Chronique de Paris*, no. 318 (November 14, 1790), sup. p. 3; *Courrier de Paris dans les 83 départements* (Gorsas) XVIII, no. 16 (November 16), p. 254 (hereafter cited as *Courrier de Gorsas*).

[35] New statutes, March 5, 1791: *P.V. Acad.*, X, 97. New name, November 15, 1790: Wille, II, 278. *Agréés* admitted, November 8, 1791: *P.V. Acad.*, X, 138–39; Wille, II, 326–27; *Almanach royal . . . année [1792]* (Paris: Testu, n.d.), pp. 485–86. Salon opened, August 21, 1791: *see* pp. 38–39. Invasion, July 18, 1793: *C.G.A.*, p. 4; *see* p. 92.

[36] Goncourt, *op. cit.*, p. 180, misquoting *Mercure de France*, no. 43 (October 23, 1790), p. 140. The cry was that of a *colporteur* selling a pamphlet calling for suppression, (probably the one listed by Tourneux, no. 17862). Several writers such as S. Blondel, *L'Art pendant la révolution* (Paris: Laurens, [1887]), p. 34, and Brun, *J. L. David*, p. 9, follow Goncourt instead of checking the passage in the *Mercure*.

Cloots[37] kept up a running fire against the "remnants of aristocracy,"[38] until David was ready to destroy them. In the meantime (1791) Quatremère de Quincy, David's companion on the Naples trip, intruded his pomposity and pedantry into the "academic brawl." Though he upheld study of nature and the antique, Quatremère, unlike David, advocated state control of art education and pointed the way to a new and sterile academicism.[39]

Besides undermining the traditional regime of the arts, David's leadership of the dissident Academicians prepared him for his role of propagandist of the Revolution. Already known for his neoclassic principles and liberal sympathies, his organization of the revolt of the artists made him a popular figure. Stubborn opposition to his demands for reform enraged the artist and forced him to appeal to the politicians in the Commune, the National Assembly, and the Jacobin Club. These men gladly embraced the opportunity to attach this "champion of liberty" to their party.

David had become a member of the Jacobin Club early in 1790. He attended its meetings assiduously and was already becoming known for his advanced political views.[40] Furthermore, the power of David's classic art as a propaganda weapon had been demonstrated at the Salon of 1789 where his *Brutus* had captured the popular imagination. His portrayal of the virtuous Roman consul was so well known that its very appearance symbolized the triumph of good citizenship. The

[37] *Des Académies* (Paris: Buisson, 1791). *Le Nouveau Paris* (Paris: Fuchs, [1798]), III, 46. *L'Ami du Peuple* (Marat), no. 194 (August 17, 1790), p. 8. "Défi aux académies royales, imperiales et gothiques," (in) *Etrennes de l'orateur du genre humain* (Paris: au chef-lieu du Globe, 1793), pp. 15–20.

[38] *Mercure de France,* no. 43 (October 23, 1790), p. 139.

[39] *Considérations sur les arts du dessin en France, suivi d'un plan d'Académie ...* (Paris: Desenne, 1791), *Suite aux considérations . . .* (Paris: Desenne, 1791), *Seconde suite . . .* (Paris: Desenne, 1791); Paroy, *Précis,* pp. 15–17, *Mémoires,* pp. 263–64; Deseine, pp. 177–78. R. Schneider (*Quatremère de Quincy*) violates history to give Quatremère the prior and preponderant role in the struggle (p. 152) and contradicts himself by claiming that Quatremère, who, he says, remained above parties, was "chief of the democratic party of the artists" (p. 162).

[40] Aulard, *Jacobins,* I, xiv; P.J.B. Buchez and P. C. Roux, eds., *Histoire parlementaire de la révolution française* (Paris: Paulin, 1835), XIV, 448; David, pp. 108–09. Contrary to many writers, David was not a member of the more conservative *Société de 1789.* The official *Règlemens de la Société de 1789 et liste de ses membres* (Paris: Lejay, 1790), p. 35, reveals that the member of that name lived on the Rue des Frondeurs; David inhabited the Louvre throughout the period.

performance of Voltaire's play of the same name in the fall of 1790 was a striking demonstration of the effectiveness of David's *Brutus* as a weapon of the new order.

The theater was obviously a powerful means of swaying public opinion in the direction of the Revolution, and some radicals called for a "Theater of the People" which would present only "patriotic plays."[41] Political dramas such as M.-J. Chénier's *Charles IX* introduced revolutionary propaganda to the French stage. All the successful plays of the period had at least a touch of this revolutionary propaganda, and the theater became an arena for rival political groups. Probably David, an avid playgoer, regularly attended the uproarious performances of revolutionary Paris.[42] During 1790 the patriots suffered with growing exasperation the demonstrations of the aristocrats at various "counter-revolutionary" plays. "The people's answer" was to demand Voltaire's tragedy of *Brutus*.[43] Its first production since the beginning of the Revolution (on November 17, 1790) was inaugurated in a highly charged atmosphere.[44] The première was largely a royalist victory, but at the second performance aristocratic demonstrators were ousted from the theater under the stern gaze of a Roman bust of Brutus placed on the stage by David.[45] As the last lines of the play were spoken, the painting of the Salon of 1789 was presented as a living tableau. "Every Parisian knows David's picture," said a German eyewitness. "Everyone instantly recognized the intention of publicly honoring the artist before the nation. The unanimous

[41] *Jean Bart, ou je m'en fouts*, no. 36 [n.d.], p. 8. Cf. R. Rolland, *Le Théâtre du peuple* (Paris: Rue de la Sorbonne, 1903).

[42] Bingham, *op. cit.*, pp. 1–3, 8–9, 30–34; B. Hyslop, "The Theater during the Terror," *Journal of Modern History*, XVII (December, 1945), 334. J. J. Guiffrey, "David et le théâtre," *G.B.A.*, ser. 3, XXX (September, 1903), 202; Delécluze, p. 372.

[43] *L'Intérêt du peuple*, no. 1 (November 22, 1790), p. 12; *Courrier de Gorsas*, XVIII, no. 9 (November 9), p. 133; *Moniteur*, no. 323 (November 19), p. 1336; *Chronique de Paris*, no. 300 (October 27), pp. 1197–98.

[44] R. O. Rockwood, *The Cult of Voltaire to 1791* (unpublished Ph.D. thesis, University of Chicago, 1935), p. 108. Violence was expected so weapons and even canes were prohibited at the performance, and special police precautions were taken.

[45] *Chronique de Paris*, no. 329 (November 25), p. 1314; *Mercure de France*, no. 49 (December 4), pp. 40–44; *Moniteur*, no. 323 (November 19), p. 1336; *Patriote françois*, no. 468 (November 19), pp. 2–3; *Intérêt du peuple*, no. 1 (November 22), p. 13; *Le Postillon par Calais*, VI, no. 264 (November 21), pp. 3–4; *Journal des clubs ou sociétés patriotiques*, no. 1 (November 20), p. 56. Duke of Orleans, *Correspondance*, ed., Roussel (Paris: Marchant, 1800), p. 227.

applause was like that of a national festival."[46] It was considered most appropriate that David, "whose patriotism is worthy of his genius," should share the triumph of Voltaire's "revolutionary" tragedy.[47]

The master of the Neoclassic School, always an indefatigable worker, did not neglect his brushes during 1789 and 1790. He executed several beautiful portraits and was invited by the municipality of Nantes to come and paint its patriotic mayor.[48] These works were unimportant compared to the great commission given David by the Jacobin Club and confirmed by the Constituent Assembly. The aspiring politicians with whom the artist associated were not slow in utilizing his celebrated talents to advance their cause. Nor did David require much urging to employ his brush for the glorification of the events of the Revolution,

On June 20, 1790, the anniversary of the first act of resistance of the deputies of the nation to the royal will—the Oath of the Tennis Court—was celebrated by a society formed for this purpose.[49] David, who was present at this brilliant commemorative fête, promised to "transmit to posterity the features of the inflexible friends of the public weal."[50] The Jacobins decided that the pictorial representation of "the act of formal disobedience to the King" should be executed under their auspices. At the meeting of October 28, Dubois-Crancé made the following announcement: "To immortalize our thoughts we have chosen the painter of *Brutus* and the *Horatii*, the French patriot whose genius anticipated the Revolution." The proposal was greeted with "loud and repeated applause," and David accepted "with enthusiasm." A public subscription was to be started for an enormous

[46] G.A. von Halem, *Paris en 1790*, ed. and trans. A. Chuquet (Paris: Chailley, 1896), p. 312; *Chronique de Paris*, no. 329 (November 25), p. 1314; Georges Duval (*Souvenirs de la Terreur* [Paris: Werdet, 1841], I, 242), says it "produced a mediocre effect."

[47] *Mercure de France*, no. 49 (December 4, 1790), p. 43.

[48] C. Saunier, "Voyage de David à Nantes en 1790," *Revue de l'art ancien et moderne*, XIV (July, 1903), 33–41.

[49] F. A. Aulard, "Le Serment du jeu de paume," *La Révolution Française* (hereafter cited as *R.F.)*, XVII (July, 1889), 18; [F.M. de Kerverseau and others], *Histoire de la révolution de France par deux amis de la liberté* (2. ed.; Paris: Garnery, 1792), V, 122–23.

[50] *Description du serment et de la fête civique célébrés au Bois de Boulogne par la Société du jeu de paume de Versailles, des 20 juin 1789 et 1790* [Paris: Garnery, 1790], quoted by A. Mathiez, *Les origines des cultes révolutionnaires, 1789–1792* (Paris: Bellais, 1904), p. 49.

painting of the historic scene. When completed the picture was to be engraved and distributed for propaganda purposes, and the original was to be presented to the National Assembly.[51] Mirabeau drew up an address which was read to the legislative body by a Jacobin deputation on November 6 and distributed in pamphlet form by order of the Assembly.[52] Thus sanctioned by the nation, the Club opened its subscription on January 1, 1791, and from the beginning individuals and patriotic societies hastened to send in the required sums.[53]

In the meantime David began the enormous task of recording the memorable meeting which had opened the Revolution. The canvas was to be the first of the great works in which David immortalized important moments of French history. His task, as he saw it, was to eternalize a contemporary scene within a classical composition. The preparatory drawings which have survived and a fragment of the unfinished canvas make it possible to trace the artist's steps in the composition of this picture. First, he made a large number of quick sketches, roughly indicating his figures in chalk or pencil, brushing in the light and shade with a wash, and adding the accents in ink to produce a vibrating atmosphere of flickering light, space and movement expressing the visual exactness of an agitated crowd.[54] The pictorial charm and baroque freedom of these drawings recall the style of Ga-

[51] October 28 according to Tourneux, nos. 9100–01, Aulard, *Jacobins,* I, 333, and David, p. 38; October 31 according to Halem, *op. cit.,* p. 250 and the *Patriote françois,* no. 451 (November 2, 1790), p. 2; November 1 according to *Courier de Provence,* XI, no. 214 (November 9), p. 294. Edmond-Louis Alexis Dubois de Crancé (1747–1814) had been one of the *jurants.* The German traveler von Halem provides the most vivid description of the event: Letter of November 5: *Paris en 1790,* pp. 250–252. The accounts of Brissot (*Le Patriote françois,* no. 451 [November 2, 1790], pp. 2–3) and Mirabeau (*Courier de Provence,* XI, no. 214 [November 9], pp. 294–95) are essential.

[52] *Adresse des Amis de la constitution à l'Assemblée nationale* (Paris: Imp. nat., 1790); *P.V. Nat.,* no. 463, p. 25; *J.D.D.,* no. 497 [n.d.], p. 9; *Moniteur,* no. 313 (November 9, 1790), pp. 1294–95; *Courier de Provence,* no. 214 (November 9), pp. 295–99.

[53] *Prospectus* and *Projet de Souscription,* nos. 9100–01, Tourneux, II, 383–84. *Journal des Amis de la constitution,* no. 13 (February 22, 1791), p. 577. F. Courboin, "A propos du jeu de paume" in *Mélanges offerts à M. Jules Guiffrey* (Paris: Champion, 1916), p. 283.

[54] These are discussed in the Essay on Sources, pp. 194–95. David left three albums of drawings for his painting (nos. 67, 71, 72, *Catalogue, des tableaux* [*etc.*] *de M. Louis David . . . 19 avril 1826,* p. 17); one is at Versailles; the others are scattered. Five such sketches studied at Fogg Museum of Art and two others at Wildenstein and Co., are from lot no. 71 of the David sale. Ohers aret reproduced by K. Holma, *David: son évolution et son style* (Paris: Lejay, 1940), pl. XVIII–XX.

briel de Saint-Aubin and give the effect of eyewitness sketches.[55] Next David appears to have made more precise linear drawings of the groups he selected from his preliminary studies.[56] These detached figures were classical in spirit and meticulously drawn in the nude from models. Then they were organized into a perfectly balanced composition. Finally they were transferred to the sheet on which the linear perspective had been traced.[57] The result was a magnificent finished drawing, motionless and monumental in character, in a scale of an inch to the foot.[58]

While David busied himself with this great project, he continued his attacks upon the academic "Bastille" by actively campaigning for freedom of exhibition. He had no great difficulty in interesting his politician-friends in the cause of artistic liberty. His "non-privileged" followers of the Commune of the Arts prepared petitions requesting the abolition of Academic privileges and the opening of the Salon to all artists. These they presented to the Constituent Assembly on March 22 and August 9, 1791. Their leader supported them by publishing an approving letter, which the *Chronique de Paris* declared "did honor to the patriotic principles of this great artist."[59] Through the medium of his friend and fellow Jacobin, Barère, David carried his idea to the Assembly which decreed, on August 21, that the National Exposition at the Louvre should be open to all artists without distinction.[60] The "patriotic" press rejoiced that "the chains with which the

[55] One of the greatest of French draftsmen and illustrators of the eighteenth century (1724–1780). On the basis of the eighteenth century and "romantic" character of these drawings some art critics claim David suppressed his "natural vision" in favor of classicistic discipline for ideological reasons. C. Stirling, "Art and the Revolution" in *The French Revolution: A loan exhibit* (New York: Wildenstein, 1943), pp. 15–16. *See* plate VIII, above.

[56] *See*, e.g., the drawing at Fogg Museum of Art (no. 1943.800). *See* plate IX.

[57] Such an unfinished sheet approximately the size of the completed drawing is at Fogg Museum of Art (no. 1943.799). *See* plate VIII, below.

[58] Louvre no. 1914 R.F. Pen, ink, and bistre wash, 25.59" by 41.34". Signed and dated "J. L. David faciebat anno 1791." no. 3197 in *Inv. dess.*, IV, 76–79. *See* plate VII.

[59] Memorial of March 12: *C.G.A.*, p. xxi. Petition of June 21: no. 1297 in A. Tuetey, *Répertoire générale des sources manuscrites* (Paris: Imp. nouvelle, 1894), III, 117. *P.V.Nat.*, LXVI, 40; *A.P.*, XXIX, 305; *Mercure de France*, no. 229 (August 17), p. 924. Letter of David, August 16: *Chronique de Paris*, no. 229 (August 17), p. 924.

[60] *Le Logographe*, no. 146 (September 19, 1791), p. 712; *Journal des Etats-généraux, ou journal logographique* (Le Hodey), XXXIV [n.d.], pp. 82–85; *Point*

VII. OATH OF THE TENNIS COURT

Finished Drawing by David

Courtesy of Le Musée du Louvre

VIII. OATH OF THE TENNIS COURT

Courtesy of the Fogg Museum of Art

Above: Preliminary Study by David   Below: Working Drawing by David

IX. OATH OF THE TENNIS COURT

Preliminary Sketch by David *Courtesy of the Fogg Museum of Art*

X. OATH OF THE TENNIS COURT

Original unfinished Canvas by David

Courtesy of Le Musée du Louvre

despotic . . . Academy . . . loaded budding genius . . . have been broken."[61]

The Salon of 1791, which inaugurated a new era for artists, was a triumph for David in several respects. First of all, the Academy lost control of the exhibition to its archenemy, who was appointed one of the commissioners.[62] Furthermore, David's attainment of freedom of publicity for artists increased his reputation as a liberal leader. As at previous shows, the style and subject matter of the pictures clearly indicated the victory of the Neoclassic School. Finally, the master's own works dominated the exposititon. Benefitting by a new rule, David once more showed his renowned *Brutus, Socrates,* and *Horatiii* to an enthusiastic audience, which included the simple peasant who had been so moved by the artist's Roman masterpiece.[63] The sensation of the exhibit, however, was his sepia drawing for the *Oath of the Tennis Court.*[64] This design, a marvel of unity of spirit and action, and diversity of figures and movement, was praised in the highest terms by the poet André Chénier, the critic Suë, and other contemporaries.[65] Its striking success prompted the Constituent Assembly on Barère's proposition, to decree as one of its last acts, that:

> The National Assembly, considering that the 20th of June, 1789, is the epoch which assured France a free constitution, decrees that . . . David's picture will be completed at the expense

du jour, no. 773 (August 22), pp. 382–88; *Courier de Provence,* no. 332 (August 23), pp. 343–46; *Moniteur,* no. 234 (August 22), pp. 968–69; *A.P.,* XXIX, 611–14; *Collection générale des décrets rendus par l'Assemblé nationale* (Paris: Baudouin, 1791), XVII, 322–23 (hereafter cited as *Col. Baud.*).

[61] *Annales patriotiques et littéraires,* no. 689 (August 22), p. 1847; cf. *Courier de Provence,* no. 179 (August 23), pp. 90–91.

[62] David's letter of acceptance, August 28, 1791: *A.A.F.,* ser. 1, IX (1857–58), 350.

[63] *Ouvrages . . . exposés au Louvre par ordre de l'Assemblée nationale au mois de septembre, 1791 . . .* (Paris: Imp. Bâtimens du Roi, [1791]), nos. 134, 274, 299, 719. *Chronique de Paris,* no. 271 (September 28, 1791), p. 1092; *Lettre bougrement patriotique du véritable Père Duchêne,* no. 212 [n.d.], pp. 3–4. Cf. the royalist and hostile *Journal de la cour et de la ville,* VI, no. 1 (November 1, 1791), p. 490. *See* pp. 1–2.

[64] *Ouvrages . . . exposés,* no. 132; *Chronique de Paris,* no. 271 (September 28), p. 1092. *See* p. 38 note 58.

[65] A. Chénier, "Sur la peinture d'histoire": *Journal de Paris,* no. 84 (March 24, 1792), sup. no. 35, pp. 1–2; cf. *Feuille du jour,* no. 87 (March 27), pp. 690–92. J. J. Suë, "Rapport sur les tableaux de David," *op. cit.,* pp. 278–79.

of the public treasury and that it will be placed in the meeting place of the National Assembly.[66]

Through the newspapers, David requested the participants to send him their likenesses, or to sit for him, and he made a series of remarkably fine portrait sketches of the various deputies.[67] Then he began to work on the 35 by 26 foot canvas[68] in the Church of the Feuillants which the government assigned to him as a studio. All the details of the composition were transferred to the canvas by a light line. Then in accordance with Renaissance practice, the life-size figures were brushed in from living nude models. In the final overpainting these academic studies would have been clothed.[69] Though David worked industriously for over a year, only four heads and some of the hands were finished. Then political events intervened, and in September, 1792, David went to sit among the *Montagnards* of the Convention, leaving the painting incomplete. Under the Directory the painter offered, without success, to finish the *Oath,* substituting famous men of the day for the then "insignificant" members of the Constituent Assembly.[70] Finally, in 1801, David announced in the newspapers that the failure of the subscription forced him to abandon forever his picture of the *Jeu de Paume.*[71]

[66] September 28, 1791: *Logographe,* no. 156 (September 29), p. 770; *Point du jour,* no. 812 (September 29), pp. 509–10; *Moniteur,* no. 272 (September 29), p. 1134; *Courier de Provence,* no. 367 [n.d.], p. 224; *A.P.,* XXXI, 438; *Col. Baud.,* XVIII, 720.

[67] David, p. 108; A. Brette, *Le Serment du jeu de paume* (Paris: S.H.R.F., 1893), p. xxxvii. Some of these oil sketches on canvas have been preserved; Bailly (Louvre), Barère (Versailles), Dubois-Crancé (Priv. col.), Père Gérard, Grégoire, Prieur de la Marne (Besançon), etc.: Cantinelli, nos. 65–71; Holma, nos. 71–77.

[68] Memorandum of Denon, 6 Thermidor, an XI [July 25, 1803] (when the canvas was stored in the Louvre): *Inv. dess.,* IV, 79. The finished size was to be 30′ by 20′ French measure (i.e., 32′10″ by 22′11″ English measure).

[69] G. Opresco, "En regardant peindre David et Gros," *Revue de l'art ancien et moderne,* XVI (December, 1929), 234–36; J. G. Goulinat, "La technique de David," *L'art vivant,* I (December 15, 1925), 27–28.

[70] Memorial of David to the Minister of Interior (1797): David, pp. 344–46.; Brette, pp. xxxvi–xxxvii.

[71] *Moniteur,* no. 67 (7 Frimaire, an X), p. 266; *Le Publicist,* no. 68 (8 Frimaire), p. 266. For the subsequent history of the unfinished canvas, *see* no. 1462 (in) F. L. Bruel, and others, comps., *Un siècle d'histoire de France par l'estampes 1770–1871; Collection de Vinck; inventaire analytique* (Paris: Imp. nat., 1914) (hereafter cited as *Col. Vinck*), II, 18; *Inv. dess.,* IV, 79. *See* plate X, opposite p. 39.

Since the actual canvas remained unfinished, the drawing exhibited at the Salon of 1791, though not intended by its author as an exact likeness,[72] has been the basis of almost all the representations of the event and has been accepted as an "irrefutable document." The French scholar, Armand Brette, has shown that the painter's allegorical sense, artistic taste, political beliefs, and response to public opinion —in other words, his propaganda acumen—caused him to modify the historical facts.[73] Nevertheless, David has captured and recorded for the historian the spirit which the Constituents wished to convey to posterity.[74] For better or for worse, David's *Oath of the Tennis Court* reproduced in all the textbooks, on public monuments and even on a commemorative postage stamp (June, 1939), and lauded as an "official report,"[75] has become a republican legend which still exerts its influence upon Frenchmen.

In its own day this revolutionary delineation demonstrated David's "civism," strengthened his personal ties with the political leaders, and confirmed his abilities as a propagandist. It was engraved and widely distributed, becoming in fact a typical feature of the meeting places of the Jacobin Clubs.[76] The importance of Barère and his newspaper, the *Point du Jour,* is often attributed to David's composition. David and his latest work were not only acclaimed by public opinion, but were also honored by the first published ode of the greatest poet of the period—André Chénier.[77] Such anti-royalist symbolism as the thunderbolt striking the Palace of Versailles (seen through the open windows of the Tennis Court), which alienated the more conservative monarchists, caused his Jacobin colleagues to idolize him more than ever.[78]

[72] "L'auteur n'a pas eu l'intention de donner la ressemblance aux members de l'Assemblée": *Ouvrages . . . exposés . . . 1791,* no. 132.

[73] Brette, *op. cit.,* pp. xxxvii-xlii; "Le Serment du jeu de paume et ses signataires: la légende et l'histoire," *R.F.,* XX (1891), 385–417, 524–49.

[74] B. Barère de Vieuzac, *Mémoires* (Paris: Labitte, 1844), IV, 176–77.

[75] Louis Blanc, *Histoire de la révolution française* (Paris: Langlois, 1847), II, 297.

[76] Because the subscription failed, the Gerdret engraving never appeared (Courboin, *op. cit.,* pp. 281–85) ; however, at least five others were executed (*Col. Vinck,* II, 17–19; *Inv. dess.,* IV, 79). L. de Cardenal, *La Province pendent la révolution; histoire des clubs jacobins (1789–1795)* (Paris: Payot, 1929) , p. 90.

[77] "Le Jeu de Paume, à Louis David, peintre" (in) *Oeuvres complètes,* ed. Dimoff (Paris: Delagrave, 1920) , III, 230–43.

[78] Genlis, *Mémoires,* IV, 103; *Thomé,* p. 48; *Biographie moderne* (2. ed.; Leipzig: Besson, 1806), II, 32.

David's popularity already seemed to foreshadow a political career. During the elections to the new legislative body, his artist clients of the Commune of the Arts petitioned the Paris Electoral Assembly to elect an artist who would revive the arts and regenerate France thereby.[79] The president of the electoral body, of which David was a member, lauded his genius which "seems always to forsee the Revolution which broke our chains, for while others degraded their brushes to flatter indolence, David painted Socrates, he painted Brutus."[80] Even though he was not a candidate, the artist received a number of votes for deputy.[81]

David now used his favored position and powerful friends to obtain subsidies for his fellow artists. A month after decreeing freedom of exhibition, the Constituent Assembly voted 100,000 livres for "works of encouragement."[82] The judgment of the awards was delayed, however, because of the fear of the non-privileged artists that the Academy would dictate the decision, and the hostile and uncooperative attitude of that aristocratic body.[83] Romme, of the Committee of Public Instruction, after an investigation recommended formation of a joint commission of both groups. A decree of December 3, 1791, established the first Jury of the Arts—another great innovation—which naturally included David.[84] However, the artist excused himself to design the patriotic festival in honor of the soldiers of the Châteauvieux Regi-

[79] September 10, 1791: *Pétition des artistes* (in) E. Charavay, ed., *Assemblée électorale,* II, 195.

[80] September 21: *Assemblée électorale,* II, 260.

[81] *Ibid.,* pp. 204, 258, 260, 265.

[82] September 17, 1791: *P.V. Nat.,* no. 768, pp. 40–42; *Logographe,* no. 146 (September 19), p. 712; *Journal des Etats-généraux,* XXXIV, no. 8 (September 19), pp. 342–44; *Col. Baud.,* XVIII, 376.

[83] Petition of nonacademic artists to Legislative Assembly, October 19, 1791: *Procès-verbal de l'Assemblée nationale* [*législative*] (Paris: Imp. nat., 1791), I, 167 (hereafter cited as *P.V. Leg.*) ; *A.P.,* XXXIV, 281–82. Petition of Academic artists read November 5: *P.V. Leg.,* I, 327; J. Guillaume, ed., *Procès-verbaux du comité d'instruction publique de l'Assemblée législative* (Paris: Imp. nat., 1889), p. 16. Renou, secretary of the Academy, wrote numerous letters to the legislators complaining of the procedure of judgment and accusing David of catering to the mob for dictatorial ends: David, pp. 101–04; *C.G.A.,* pp. xxii–xxv; *Cor. Ang.,* II, 312.

[84] Report of Romme, November 29, 1791: *A.P.,* XXXV, 451–53; *Projet de décret . . . sur les réclamations des artistes qui ont exposé au Salon du Louvre* [Paris: Imp. nat., 1791]. Decree: *P.V. Leg.,* II, 243–45; *Col. Baud.,* XIX, 180; *P.V. Acad.,* X, 143–45.

ment.[85] When the Jury awarded him first prize, he insisted that the sum be divided among three young artists who had competed unsuccessfully for an award. This disinterested conduct won him "honorable mention" in the National Assembly.[86]

In addition to helping preserve the artistic and scientific treasures of the nation by serving on the Commission of Monuments, and campaigning for contests for the construction of public works to help his fellow artists,[87] David continued his propaganda activities. The popular public festivals which he organized at this time (1791–92), sounded the keynote and established the pattern for all ensuing *fêtes nationales* of the Revolution. Meanwhile the experience which he acquired in theatrical productions prepared him for the role of *ordonnateur* of festivals.

David's passionate interest in the theater has already been mentioned.[88] His designs for costumes for Talma had produced a complete revolution in this field of art. Instead of wearing plumed hats and silken doublets, Greek and Roman heroes now strode the boards in tunics and helmets designed by David.[89] Early in 1792, he took time from the atelier of the *Jeu de Paume* to use his talents for the *mis en scène* of a purely propaganda opus: the *Caius Gracchus* of his friend Marie-Joseph Chénier, brother of the famous poet. He is said to have attended the private reading of the play by its author,[90] and apparently was persuaded to help produce it.

This political drama, though laid in Republican Rome, was actually "an assault on the privileged aristocracy" of France.[91] The first performance was a test of strength between the *sans-culottes* who wildly demonstrated in favor of its revolutionary sentiments and the aristo-

[85] *See* pp. 56 ff.

[86] Letter of David to the President of the National Assembly, May 2, 1792: *Musée des Archives nationales: documents . . .* (Paris: Plon, 1872), p. 733; *A.P.*, XXXXII, 668–69; David, pp. 107–08; *P.V. Leg.*, VIII, 50.

[87] David was one of the original members appointed November 8, 1790: L. Tuetey, ed., *Procès-verbaux de la Commission des Monuments, 1790–1794* (Paris: Charavay, 1902), I, 4, but he seldom attended its meetings. Guillaume, *op. cit.*, p. 48.

[88] *See* pp. 16, 35.

[89] Lenoir, p. 10; Delécluze, pp. 220–23; Duval, *Souvenirs*, I, 242; J. G. Millingen, *Recollections of Republican France* (London: Colburn, 1848), p. 110.

[90] [S. E. Monnel], *Mémoires d'un prêtre régicide* (Paris: Mary, 1829), I, 254.

[91] Bingham, *M.-J. Chénier*, p. 60.

cratic claque who failed in their attempts to cry it down.[92] As the Parmesan ambassador remarked "the two parties seem to have chosen the theaters for their scuffling."[93] Although there were many criticisms of the play itself, the costumes and decorations designed by David were appreciated by the audience and praised by the press.[94]

One journal remarked that "these heroic morals of the Roman Republic do not appear at all strange . . . to the spectators. . . . The hatred of all tyrannies is in every heart, and the fire of liberty needs only to be fed."[95] And David, whose classic paintings had invoked for Frenchmen the heroic morality of the ancients, was now ready to feed the fires with a new propaganda technique—the revolutionary festival.

[92] *Thermomètre du jour,* [ser. 2], no. 42 (February 11, 1792), pp. 348–49; *Révolutions de Paris,* XI, no. 136 (February 18), pp. 314–16; *Journal de Paris,* no. 42 (February 11), p. 174; *Folies d'un mois,* 5e mois, no. 12 [n.d.], pp. 3–4.

[93] Dispatch of Bailli de Virieu to Count Ventura, Paris, February 26, 1792: Grouchy and Guillois, eds., . . . *Correspondance* (Paris: Flammarion, 1903), p. 334.

[94] *Thermomètre du jour,* no. 42 (February 11, 1792), p. 349; *Folies d'un mois,* 4e mois, no. 20 [n.d.], p. 1. *Révolutions de Paris,* no. 136 (February 18), pp. 313–17; *Journal de Paris,* no. 42 (February 11), p. 174; *Feuille du jour,* no. 40 (February 9), pp. 313, 318–19.

[95] *Révolutions de Paris,* no. 136 (February 18, 1792), p. 316.

CHAPTER III

Festivals: A Propaganda Technique

After the destruction of the old regime, the supporters of the Revolution sought to consolidate their position and to re-establish the moral unity of the nation on a new basis. The growing feeling of national patriotism might be employed to attain that unity, and the revolutionary gospel might be spread among all groups if a suitable propaganda technique were perfected. "Patriotic" clubs, newspapers, and the theater molded popular opinion in favor of the new order, but the most characteristic expression of the revolutionary spirit lay in the national festivals.

These manifestations of revolutionary solidarity and patriotic fraternity were spontaneous in their origin,[1] but they were soon adopted and consciously employed by a relatively small group of political leaders for propaganda purposes. They were found to be particularly effective in appealing to the illiterate masses and those who could not afford the relatively expensive club memberships, newspapers, and theater tickets.

A series of spontaneous Federation festivals which culminated in the Fête of Federation in Paris, July 14, 1790 had begun during the "Great Fear." These popular gatherings which pledged mutual aid against a common enemy had spread from village to province to region and had gradually taken on a deeper significance. The participants swore to support the new order and to unite in the common cause of liberty. Mass was said, and the banners of the National Guard were blessed at these ceremonies.

The National Assembly decided to participate in the movement by organizing a national festival at Paris on the first anniversary of the fall of the Bastille. In an electric atmosphere of expectancy and good feeling great crowds of volunteers of all classes constructed a colossal amphitheater on the Champ de Mars. Here on the appointed day a vast throng awaited the procession of *fédérés* from the newly created Departments, the deputies of the National Assembly, and the King and

[1] Mathiez, *Origines des cultes révolutionnaires,* pp. 38–39.

Queen. The banners of the National Guard were blessed; Talleyrand celebrated Mass on the great altar of *la patrie;* and Lafayette, the master of ceremonies, administered the oath to the assembled throng "to be faithful forever to the nation, the law and the king;" and Louis XVI swore to maintain the Constitution. Contemporary accounts all agree that the spectacle was profoundly moving. The Federation symbolized the new consciousness of patriotic allegiance to the nation and to the Revolution and promised that Frenchmen in fraternal union would defend the revolutionary cause with religious fervor.

This impressive ceremony seemed to mark the unity of all Frenchmen and symbolized the loyalty of the nation to the monarch and the faith of the people in the Catholic Church. Within less than a year, however, the spread of revolutionary sentiment, the flaring up of bitter religious strife over the Civil Constitution of the Clergy, and the flight of the King had completely disrupted the happy concord of the Federation. Monarchy and Catholicism could no longer be used to cement the spiritual unity of the nation, and other symbols had to be found to win the allegiance of the people to the new Constitution. The Festival of July 14 had demonstrated how potent festivals could be in capturing the popular imagination. To replace devotion to the King and the Church with loyalty to the nation and the growing cult of the Revolution, the festivals became more and more pagan in character. Greece and Rome were enlisted to rally the emotions of the people to the ideals of the new order. The first important completely lay celebration was the interment of Voltaire in the Panthéon in 1791.

When Voltaire died in 1778, the Paris clergy had denied him Church burial; therefore he had been interred at the monastery of Scellières. After Church property was nationalized in 1789, Voltaire's old friends, led by his nephew, the Marquis Charles de Villette, and the *philosophe,* Condorcet, opened a campaign to bring his body to Paris and provide a solemn demonstration of gratitude to "the Father of the Revolution." On December 21, 1789, Villette, in a letter to the *Chronique de Paris,* first proposed the pantheonization of Voltaire, but without immediate result.[2]

[2] Marquis de Ferrières, *Mémoires,* ed. Berville and Barrière (Paris: Baudouin, 1821), I, 493–95. Rockwood, *The Cult of Voltaire to 1791,* a scholarly analysis of "public" opinion of "the symbol Voltaire," is the best work on the apotheosis. The author's principal source was the newspapers at the Bibliothèque Nationale. Of those quoted on the apotheosis only two were unavailable to this writer who employed several others not used by Rockwood.

Efforts were renewed in November, 1790, when a law was passed requiring all priests to take the oath to the Constitution and the first performance of the Revolution of Voltaire's *Brutus* was announced.[3] The *Société de 1789,* a club of moderate reformers to which Villette and Condorcet belonged, sent a delegation to the Commune to demand that official steps be taken to reclaim Voltaire's body. At the same time, Villette carried his proposals to the Paris Jacobins and asked their aid.[4] Though new recruits such as the radical Baron Cloots, the writer M.-J. Chénier, Palloy, the "Patriot wrecker of the Bastille," and Camille Desmoulins[5] joined the movement, the National Assembly showed no interest until after the Papal denunciation of the Civil Constitution of the Clergy (March-April, 1791). Confronted with the news that Voltaire's body must be moved, they agreed to consider the advisability of bringing it to Paris and finally decreed his glorification on May 30, 1791.[6] The announcement was favorably received by the "patriotic" press, particularly by the *Chronique de Paris.*[7] This decree was regarded by the counter-revolutionaries as a direct affront to religion, but their protests could not stop the preparations.[8]

The flight of the King on June 20 broadened the significance of the celebration, for it now became a rallying point for antiroyalist

[3] *See* pp. 35–36.

[4] November 9, 1790: Lacroix, *Actes de la Commune,* ser. 2, II, 121, 209; cf. *Adresse aux parisiens* in *Courrier de Gorsas,* XVIII, no. 7 (November 7, 1790), pp. 100–02. Jacobin Club: *Chronique de Paris,* no. 316 (November 1, 1790), pp. 1261–62. The German observer Halem (*Paris en 1790,* p. 297) gives the date as November 3; Lacroix (*op. cit.,* ser. 2, I, 233) gives November 9; while Aulard (*Jacobins,* I, 367) claims November 10. The evidence of Gorsas proves that Villette's address was delivered before November 7: *Courrier de Gorsas,* no. 10 (November 10), pp. 151–52. Cf. J.F.E. Robinet, *Le Mouvement religieux à Paris (1789–1801)* (Paris: Cerf, 1896), I, 530.

[5] *Révolutions de France et de Brabant,* no. 57 [n.d.], pp. 228–31.

[6] May 8, 1791: *Col. Baud,* XIV, 83; *A.P.,* XXV, 661; *Le Point du jour* (Barère), XXII, no. 666 (May 9), pp. 82–84; *Le Logographe,* no. 13 (May 9), p. 56. Decree of May 30: *A.P.,* XXVI, 610; *Point du jour,* XXII, no. 688 (May 31, 1791), p. 532; *Logographe,* no. 35 (May 31), p. 166; *Col. Baud.,* XIV, 354.

[7] Vol. IV, no. 152 (June 1, 1791), p. 605. Cf. *Révolutions de Paris,* no. 100 (June 11), p. 445, n.1; *Bouche de fer,* IV, no. 62 (June 1), p. 16; *Courier de Provence,* XVI, no. 274 [May 30], p. 532.

[8] Mlle. de Givry to her brother, Paris, June 1, 1791: P. de Vaissière, ed., *Lettres d'"aristocrates"* (Paris: Perrin, 1907), p. 287; *L'Ami du roi* (Montjoie and Crapart), no. 151 (May 31), pp. 601–02; *L'Ami du roi* (Royou), (June 1), pp. 1–2.

groups.[9] The ceremony first set for July 4 ultimately had to be delayed until the 11th. Meanwhile the propaganda of the conservatives attempted to take advantage of the difficult economic situation to rouse the poorer classes against the squandering of public funds on a useless fête.[10] Publication of the details of the celebration precipitated a violent pamphlet war for and against the apotheosis.[11] It was attacked by various individuals and groups such as the Jansenists who feared the establishment of a new civic religion, and defended warmly by pro-Voltaireian journalists and pamphleteers.[12] A group headed by Quatremère posted an expostulatory petition and tried to carry off the philosopher's remains the night before the ceremony.[13]

On July 10 and again on the morning of July 11, 1791, heavy rains caused postponement of the fête. But restless crowds and threatening labor difficulties in the Faubourg Saint Antoine forced a revision of plans, and the procession left the Bastille in mid-afternoon.[14] Its most striking characteristic was the influence of antiquity. The purpose of the planners of the fête had been to "emulate the pomp [and] grandeur of the Greek apotheoses and the Roman consecrations."[15] The

[9] *Chronique de Paris,* IV, no. 174 (June 12, 1791), p. 668; *Bouche de fer,* no. 88 (July 10), pp. 2–3.

[10] *Le Spectateur national et le modérateur,* II, no. 225 (July 13, 1791), pp. 959–60; *Le Babillard du Palais-Royal,* no. 29 (July 12), pp. 7–8; *Gazette de Paris* (July 12), p. 3; *Journal général* (Fontenai), no. 161 (July 11), p. 671; *Actes des apôtres,* no. 183 [n.d.], p. 13.

[11] *Courier de Provence,* no. 303 [June 20, 1791], pp. 239–40; *Journal de Paris,* no. 171 (June 20), pp. 686–89; *La Feuille du jour,* no. 172 (June 21), p. 699. The pamphlet *Ordre de marche de la translation de Voltaire à Paris le lundi 11 juillet . . .* [Paris: Cercle Social, 1791] which Rockwood cites in this regard must have appeared after July 8 rather than in June (see *Moniteur, Chronique de Paris,* and *Journal de Paris* of July 8.)

[12] Robinet, *op. cit.,* I, 540–42. Camille Desmoulins (*Révolutions de France et de Brabant,* no. 85 [n.d.], p. 288) implied that the Jansenist names were a mere blind. *Journal de Paris,* no. 199 (July 18), p. 811; *Journal du Club des Cordeliers,* no. 5 [n.d.], pp. 43–47.

[13] *Chronique de Paris,* no. 193 (July 12, 1791), p. 781. Prompt action by the neighboring sections repulsed the foray. In May, 1814, another group of reactionary fanatics was successful, and Voltaire's bones disappeared without a trace in the city dump.

[14] Letter of F. L. Bouchette, Paris, July 10, 1791: C. Looten, ed., *Lettres . . .* (Paris: Champion, 1909), p. 609. *A.P.,* XXVIII, 112; *Feuille villageoise,* no. 43 (July 21), p. 294; *Journal de Paris,* no. 193 (July 12), p. 775.

[15] *Lettres choisies de Ch. Villette* (Paris: Clousier, 1792), p. 190; *Chronique de Paris,* no. 186 (July 5, 1791), p. 745.

paraphernalia, costumes, and musical instruments were specially constructed on classical models after designs by David. The master's years of study in Rome—the long nights spent sketching the casts of Trajan's column, the painstaking hours employed in transferring the treasures of the museums to his notebooks, the careful tracings of the engraved plates of the monumental volumes of the antiquarians, the reveries among the ruins of Herculaneum and Pompeii[16]—all these were placed at the service of the Revolution for the décor of the festival. These as well as the erudite Abbé Barthélemy's best seller—*Le Voyage du jeune Anacharsis en Grèce*—and various illustrated works—notably that of Banier and Le Mascrier—helped inspire the general *mis en scène*.[17] Probably the processions of the Church suggested the "stations," banners, sacred images, and other features. David collaborated with Célerier for the organization of the procession. Every detail was designed to stimulate the patriotic ardor of the masses and its completely lay character expressed the anticlerical sentiments of the times.[18]

Prominent among the participants were National Guards and other military units; the Jacobins, market porters, and workers of the Faubourg Saint Antoine; Palloy and his Bastille wreckers; the electors of 1789 and 1790; deputies of the sections, of the schools and theaters, and of the National Assembly; officials of the Districts, the Commune,

[16] *See*, pp. 9–12.

[17] (Paris: De Bure, 1788), 4 vols. *Cérémonies et coutumes religieuses de tous les peuples du monde . . . figures . . . de Bernard Picart* (Amsterdam: Bernard, 1728–43), 9 vols. Cf. Locquin, *op. cit.*, p. 171.

[18] For descriptions, see *Journal de Paris*, no. 194 (July 13, 1791), pp. 778–80; *Feuille villageoise*, no. 43 (July 21), p. 295; *Ami du roi* (Montjoie and Crapart), no. 31 (July 30), pp. 182–91; *Révolutions de Paris*, no. 105 (July 16), p. 10; *Bouche de fer*, IV, no. 90 (July 12), pp. 1–6; *Journal général* (Fontenai), no. 166 (July 16), pp. 691–92; *Moniteur*, no. 193 (July 13), p. 802; *Chronique de Paris*, V, no. 193 (July 12), p. 780; *Ami de la révolution, ou philippiques*, IV, no. 53 (July 13), p. 53; *Journal général de l'Europe*, I, no. 14, morning edition (July 14), p. 114. The following were not used by Rockwood: *Courrier de Gorsas*, XXVI (July 13), pp. 179–80, 188–89; *Gazette universelle*, no. 192 (July 11), p. 767; *Journal historique et politique*, no. 29 (July 16), p. 262; *Annales patriotiques et littéraires de la France* (Mercier), no. 350 (July 14), p. 1682 (hereafter cited as *Annales patriotiques*); *Courier de Provence*, XV, no. 315 [July 12], pp. 510–11; Dispatch of Virieu to Ventura, July 18: Grouchy, *op. cit.*, pp. 285–87; Millingen, *Recollections*, pp. 64–67; J. A. Dulaure, *Esquisses historiques des principaux événemens de la révolution française* (Paris: Baudouin, 1823), I, 472–80. For the hymns sung, *see* C. Pierre, *Les Hymnes et chansons de la révolution* (Paris: Imp. nat., 1904), pp. 205–13, and *Musique executée aux fêtes . . .* (Paris: Imp. nat., 1894), pp. 3–4.

and the Department, and other functionaries. Various groups carried banners inscribed with suitable mottoes, a model of the Bastille, medallions of Rousseau, Franklin, Mirabeau, and Desille.[19] The impressive central feature was the huge triumphal *char,* designed by David. Towering above the rest of the procession, it bore the sacred remains. This magnificient vehicle was drawn by twelve white horses led by attendants in Roman costume. According to all accounts,[20] observers were struck by its neoclassical perfection, and even hostile critics of the fête found David's *char* "very fine."[21]

This revolutionary pageant, purely lay in character and classical in spirit, proceeded with its symbols of civism, and its host of officials and private organizations devoted to the new regime, through the rain-swept streets of Paris from the Bastille to the Panthéon. It halted at intervals for various demonstrations which had been arranged at the Opéra, the Comédie Italienne, Villette's home, and the Comédie Française. An unscheduled stop was made at the Tuileries beneath the windows of the royal prisoners. As night descended, rain again dampened the spirits of many, but the others plodded on through the gathering darkness by the torches of art students from David's studio.[22] At about half past nine, the sarcophagus was installed in the Panthéon next to Mirabeau.

As to the extent and enthusiasm of the crowd, sources vary, depending upon the degree of hostility to Voltaire. Villette's figure of 100,000 participants and 100,000 spectators[23] may be too high, but

[19] *See,* p. 55.

[20] The exception who proves the rule is that English pedant and antiquary [Stephen Weston], *Letters from France during the summer of 1791* (London: Debrett, 1792), pp. 106–07.

[21] "Diary of the second Viscount Palmerston in France during July and August 1791" (in) Duke of Sutherland, *Despatches of Earl Gower,* ed. Browning (Cambridge, [Eng.]: University Press, 1885), p. 289. For contemporary engravings, see *Collection de Vinck,* nos. 4171–80; S.R.N. Chamfort and others, eds., *Collection complète des tableaux historiques de la révolution française* (Paris: Didot, 1802), I, 220 (hereafter cited as *Tableaux historiques*), see plate XI opposite p. 50; *Révolutions de France et de Brabant,* no. 86 [n.d.], frontispiece; and *Révolutions de Paris,* no. 105, (July 16, 1791), frontispiece.

[22] G. Touchard-Lafosse, (*Souvenirs d'un demi-siècle* [Paris: Dumont, 1836], II, 121) who gives a highly amusing but most inaccurate account of the fête, claims that a thunderstorm nearly ruined David's decorations and that on M.-J. Chénier's suggestion the *char* proceeded to the Panthéon at a gallop which rattled Voltaire's bones lugubriously and precipitated the head of his effigy into the gutter.

[23] *Lettres choisies de Ch. Villette,* p. 188.

XI. FESTIVAL OF VOLTAIRE, JULY 11, 1791

Triomphe de Voltaire Engraving by Berthault after Prieur

No. 55 in *Collection complète des tableaux historiques de la révolution française*

contemporary accounts agree that there were huge crowds. People swarmed in gardens, at intersections, at the windows, and on the roofs of buildings along the route. Sympathetic descriptions speak of the enthusiasm of the people, but reports of hostile witnesses, such as the journalist Fontenai and the Marquis de Ferrières, are to the contrary. On the other hand, the *Chronique de Paris* contrasted the enthusiasm of the crowd "which seemed to deify its liberator" with the greater reserve of the aristocrats of the Quai de Voltaire. The *Moniteur* emphasized the popularity of the fête and said that criticisms of the luxury of the pantheonization were reduced to silence by "the reasoning of sensible people." An "air of joy and serenity" prevailed according to the *Gazette universelle.* An English observer, Stephen Weston, declared that "the show . . . gave universal satisfaction." Trouble had been anticipated by the authorities, and extraordinary police precautions were taken, but there was no disorder.[24]

The procession was described either as a deeply moving, popular, and truly antique spectacle; or a grotesque and ridiculous farce, depending upon the personal views of the writer. The eulogies of the prorevolutionary press were unstinted. As was to be expected, the *Chronique de Paris* declared it to be "the most beautiful and most imposing of festivals." According to Mirabeau's *Courier de Provence,* "never was a pomp more brilliant or more solemn," and the *Moniteur* declared it to be a truly national festival in all its details. The ceremony was described by the *Correspondance nationale* as "religious and civic." Camille Desmoulins declared that "no saint of the old calendar could boast of having made as brilliant an entrance into heaven as . . . Saint Voltaire." A Greek eyewitness was actually moved to tears by this "magnificent" revival of the customs of his ancestors. While Count Fernán Nuñez, the Spanish ambassador, was reminded of the days of ancient Rome, the student Edmond Géraud believed that this "imposing ceremony" marked an epoch in modern history.[25]

[24] *Journal général* (Fontenai), no. 166 (July 16, 1791), pp. 691–92; Letter of Ferrières to his wife, Paris, July 13, 1791: H. Carré, ed., *Correspondance inédite . . .* (Paris: Colin, 1932), p. 385. *Chronique de Paris,* V, no. 193 (July 12), p. 781. *Moniteur,* no. 193 (July 13) , p. 802. *Gazette universelle,* no. 194 (July 13), p. 774. Weston, *loc. cit.* Letter of Bouchette, Paris, July 10: Looten, *op cit.,* p. 609.

[25] *Chronique de Paris,* no. 193 (July 12, 1791), p. 782. *Courier de Provence,* XV, no. 315 (July 13), p. 511. *Moniteur,* no. 193 (July 13), p. 802. *Correspondance nationale,* no. 44 (July 16), pp. 138–42. *Révolutions de France et de Brabant,* no. 85 [n.d.], pp. 290–91. Koraës to Dimitrios Lotos, Paris, November 15: *Lettres . . .*

Adverse observers characterized the fête as shabby, lacking in pomp, dignity and order, and grotesque in the mixture of modern and antique motifs.[26] The Marquis de Ferrières declared it to be "a kind of farce," and another aristocrat called it "a foolish carnival." Similar views were expressed by the English and American envoys, and Lord Palmerston's father, then traveling in France, condescendingly spoke of the "very shabby, ill-dressed people" who participated. David never forgave Madame de Genlis for ridiculing the fête which she insisted, "was in fact the most foolish, abominable and ridiculous absurdity that was ever seen in Paris prior to the festival . . . of Reason."[27]

It is not difficult to see why the celebration moved some to enthusiasm and others to ridicule. For sympathizers of Voltaire and of the new regime, the apotheosis had a meaning which antagonistic spectators could not appreciate. The festival was regarded by many patriots as a personal victory for Voltaire over his persecutors. Others, however, such as the *Mercure* interpreted the glorification of the philosopher as the virtual triumph of the ideals of the Revolution. It was hailed as the triumph of reason over superstition, philosophy over theology, and of justice and tolerance over tyranny and fanaticism. "It was not merely the funeral of Voltaire, it was that of prejudice and abuse; they celebrated there the annihilation of tyrants and the immortality of Voltaire." A writer in the *Journal des Clubs* graphically depicted the death of fanaticism under the wheels of David's neoclassical juggernaut. The Girondin journalist Carra said he heard people exclaim, "Fanaticism is dying! At last we have a fatherland; we will die in its defense." The apotheosis of Voltaire, who had come to be the incarnation of the Revolution, was hailed as a symbol of the triumph of the new regime over the old. The unsuccessful flight of

(1782–1783), trans. and ed., Marquis de Queux de Saint-Hilaire (Paris: Firmin-Didot, 1880), pp. 15–16. Fernán Nuñez to Floridablanca: A. Mousset, ed.,*Un Témoin ignoré de la révolution: Comte Fernán Nuñez* (Paris: Champion, 1924), p. 134; Letter of Géraud, July 19: G. Maugras, ed., *Journal d'un étudiant (1789–1793)* (Paris: Lévy, 1890), pp. 187–89.

[26] *Journal général de France,* no. 194 (July 13, 1791), p. 780; *La Rocambole des journaux,* no. 8 (July 13), p. 138; *Ami du roi* (Montjoie and Crapart), no. 194 (July 13), pp. 775–76. *Feuille du jour,* no. 193 (July 12), p. 92.

[27] Ferrières to his wife, July 13, 1791: Carré, *op. cit.*, p. 385; Dutailly to Faivre, July 10–12: Vaissière, *op. cit.*, p. 297. *Despatches of Earl Gower,* p. 105; *Diary and Letters of Gouverneur Morris* (New York: Scribners, 1885), I, 430; "The Diary of the second Viscount Palmerston," p. 289. Mme. de Genlis, *Mémoires,* IV, 103.

the King made it seem even more a triumph of the Revolution. The *Bouche de fer* saluted the republican festival which indicated ". . . the enormous distance . . . between an imbecile king and the [defender] of the oppressed." The fires of liberty were about to destroy the last traces of despotism, it was believed, and citizens were to complete the work of the Precursor by consecrating themselves to the public cause.[28]

Nevertheless, all pro-revolutionary elements probably did not support the festival. Marat was opposed; the Constitutional clergy did not participate; and the hungry proletariat may have grumbled at the expenditure. The celebration was promoted by a small group of Voltaire's old friends and literary supporters who were greatly aided by favorable circumstances—confiscations of Church property and growing anticlericalism. This little clique could not have succeeded without the growing support of the pro-revolutionary press. However, newspaper opinion and public opinion must be distinguished, although in view of the wide variety of papers available a writer can be found to reflect almost every shade of opinion. The Constitutional journals united in hailing the apotheosis as the vindication of Voltaire and as the triumph of tolerance and liberty over fanaticism and tyranny. While all patriots did not share this view, it probably reflected the feeling of most supporters of the Constitution of 1791.[29]

The festival may have been laughed at by the orthodox as a ridiculous burlesque, but the serious import of the celebration was not lost on them. They protested that Voltaire was unworthy of such honors, that they were too costly for the nation and came at an inappropriate time.[30] Underneath, however, was the realization that the Revolution had from the clerical point of view turned its back on religion.[31] The festival had certainly drawn the line more sharply between the Revolution and the Church. Because of the purely lay char-

[28] J.-B. Brissot, *Mémoires,* ed. Perroud (Paris: Picard, [1911]), II, 85. *Mercure de France,* no. 31 (July 30, 1791), p. 182. Mme. M.J.P. Roland [de la Platière], *Lettres,* ed. Perroud (Paris: Imp. nat. 1902), II, 327. *Courier de Provence,* XV, no. 315 (July 1), p. 510–11. *Journal des clubs,* III, no. 39 (August 10), pp. 674–75. *Annales patriotiques* (Carra), no. 350 (July 14), p. 1682. *Bouche de fer,* IV, no. 90 (July 12), pp. 1–2. Brissot, *Mémoires,* p. 326; *Ami de la révolution,* IV, no. 53 (July 13), p. 56

[29] Rockwood, *op. cit.,* pp. 214–16.

[30] *Nouvelles ecclésiastiques* (September 20, 1791), pp. 149–53; Letter of Fougeret to Lecoy de la Marche, July 11: Vaissière, *op. cit.,* p. 404; Dutailly to Faivre: *ibid.,* p. 297.

[31] *Journal historique et politique,* no. 29 (July 16, 1791), p. 262; *Ami du roi* (Royou), (July 13), p. 3; *Feuille du jour,* no. 182 (July 11), p. 3.

acter of the ceremony the clergy saw it as an attack on religon—the inauguration of a new civic cult. It was this indication of the existence of a new religion which alienated the devout and was probably the fundamental cause of the protests against the festival.

For the friends of the Revolution, the "Triumph of Voltaire" had an even greater significance. It was a clever political maneuver of the "patriot" party which, by converting a popular figure into a revolutionary saint, provided a symbol around which reformers might rally. It marked another step in the development of revolutionary religion: the introduction of neoclassical art and atmosphere into civic celebrations. It set the pattern for the subsequent propaganda festivals of the Revolution. Finally, it was the first of several such ceremonies realized through the collaboration of leading artists of the day: Gossec for the music, M.-J. Chénier for the lyrics, and above all, David for the decorations and organization.

Less than a week after the Voltaire ceremony, the Massacre of the Champ de Mars (July 17, 1791) raised a bloody barrier between the constitutionalists and the republicans. The shooting down by Lafayette and the National Guard of unarmed petitioners who demanded trial of the King and a new government, may have represented a deliberate effort on the part of conservatives to crush the growing republican movement.[32] If this was the hope of the Constitutional Monarchists, their success was only momentary. Except for the conservative members such as Barnave, Lameth, and Lafayette who left to form the Feuillant Club, the Jacobins tended to become more republican in their sentiments. The radicals were provided with a symbol, and a legacy of hatred was left in the hearts of the Parisian masses. While the constitutionalists were in power a festival to honor the victims of the massacre was of course out of the question, but there was at hand another group of martyrs—victims of a similar slaughter, the year before, in the name of "law and order"—around whom a propaganda demonstration could be organized.

"That fête [i.e., the Federation of July 14, 1790] poisoned the spirit of the troops," wrote General Bouillé, Commander of the Army of the East.[33] The celebration had indeed helped spread revolutionary senti-

[32] G. Michon, *Essai sur l'histoire du parti Feuillant; Adrien Duport* (Paris: Payot, 1924), pp. 266, 277; A. Mathiez, *Le Club des Cordeliers et la massacre du Champ de Mars* (Paris: Champion, 1910), p. 192.

[33] *Mémoires* (London: Cadell & Davies, 1797), I, 134.

ment among the troops, but their discipline was already severely undermined. Mutinies broke out in various garrisons, but at first moderate measures had restored order. Then several regiments at Nancy, including the Swiss of Châteauvieux, had rebelled against their aristocratic and abusive officers who met their demands for back pay with acts of brutality (August, 1790). The National Assembly, on Lafayette's recommendation, voted to send his cousin, General Bouillé, to suppress the mutiny by force. Those of the Swiss Regiment who survived Bouillé's decimation were condemned to the galleys at Brest.

At first, the brutal measures were applauded by the Assembly; and Desille, a young National Guard officer who had been killed in the fracas, became a martyr.[34] But the Parisians of the Cordeliers and the Faubourgs raged, for the proletarians remembered that in July, 1789, the Regiment had refused to fire on the people.[35] Châteauvieux became the battle cry of those who believed that the Revolution was coming to nothing through the weakness of the wealthy bourgeoisie. Marat, Fréron, Hébert, Danton, and others denounced the Nancy affair as a counter-revolutionary plot,[36] and David's associate, Collet d'Herbois, championed the cause of the Swiss in pamphlets, articles, and speeches at the Jacobin Club.[37] Gradually, public opinion turned in favor of the survivors; especially when Bouillé deserted after the Varennes fiasco, and Lafayette, after the Champ de Mars tragedy. Many agreed with Brissot that though none of the parties were innocent, the soldiers were the least culpable.[38] On November 1, 1791, Collot had a subscription opened to raise funds to help free the galley

[34] *See*, p. 50; *Col. Vinck*, no. 3550–60, II, 570–73.

[35] *Histoire de la révolution par deux amis de la liberté*, V, 271–72.

[36] *L'Ami du peuple* (Marat), no. 208 (September 1, 1790), p. 1 through no. 213 (September 6), p. 12; *L'Orateur du Peuple* (Fréron), no. 22 [n.d.], p. 173 through no. 25 [n.d.], p. 193. *Je suis le véritable Père Duchêne* (Hébert), no. 60 [n.d.], p. 1; *Journal du diable*, no. 83 [n.d.], pp. 7–8. Curiously enough the royalist Rivarol agreed: *Journal politique-national*, III, no. 5 [n.d.] pp. 58–60.

[37] Jean-Marie Collot d'Herbois (1750–1796) was an ex-comedian who became a member of the Committee of Public Safety during the Terror. *See* his *Rapport fait à la Société des amis de la constitution . . . le 26 juin 1791 . . . en réclamation de justice pour quarante-un soldats du régiment de Châteauvieux* [Paris: Imp. nat., 1791]; *La Vérité sur les soldats de Châteauvieux . . . 30 mars* [Paris: Imp. Patriote françois, 1791]; Aulard, *Jacobins*, II, 555–63; III, 223, 232, 298. Cf. J. N. Billaud-Varennes, *Mémoires inédites*, ed. Begis (Paris: Nouvelle Revue, 1893), p. 372.

[38] *Le Patriote françois*, no. 488 (December 9, 1790, pp. 1–2.

convicts at Brest. A decree of the National Assembly of December 31 resulted in their inclusion in the amnesty of September 14, and plans were made for a public festival in honor of the "martyrs of liberty and the fatherland."[39]

On March 24, 1792, a delegation headed by "our most illustrious patriots"—David, M.-J. Chénier, Collot d'Herbois, Tallien and Mlle. Theroigne de Méricourt, a famous revolutionary Amazon—presented a petition to the Municipality requesting its permission for, and participation in, a celebration honoring the soldiers of Châteauvieux.

> This touching festival [ran the petition] will be everywhere the terror of tyrants, the hope and consolidation of patriots. This festival which civism and the fine arts are going to render imposing and memorable . . . [will be] the triumph of the martyrs of the cause of the people.

The Commune applauded the proposal, and Pétion, the Girondin mayor, promised to attend with municipal officials. David was asked to be the master of ceremonies of this demonstration in honor of the "martyrs of the Revolution."[40]

The Feuillant and counter-revolutionary press were furious. André Chénier, who a few days before had praised David's genius, now led the assault on the festival and its promoters in the pages of the *Journal de Paris.* While his brother Marie-Joseph wrote lyrics in their honor, André attacked the Swiss as "insubordinate and rebellious . . . murderers . . . public enemies;" called their champion, Collot d'Herbois, a liar; and abused the Municipality for sanctioning the demonstration. He was joined by his friends, the poet Roucher, the deputy Chéron, and other Feuillants, in vain efforts to discredit the coming Fête of Liberty.[41] Collot d'Herbois' reply from the tribune of the Jacobin

[39] The phrase is Marat's: *Ami du peuple,* no. 209 (September 2, 1790), p. 6; *Moniteur,* no. 2 (January 2, 1792), p. 7; *A.P.*, XXXVI, 357, 721; *Journal de Paris,* no. 260 (September 17, 1791), p. 1059; *P.V. Leg.,* III, 271.

[40] *Courier français,* no. 89 (March 29, 1792), pp. 4–5; *Révolutions de Paris,* no. 142 (March 31), p. 586; *Journal de Paris,* no. 87 (March 27), p. 353; *Moniteur,* no. 88 (March 28), p. 361; *Folies d'un mois,* 5e mois, no. 23 [April, 1791], p. 2. *L'Instituteur du peuple,* no. 2 [n.d.], p. 7. For the program of the fête, *see* L. M. Ternaux, *Histoire de la Terreur* (3.ed.; Paris: Lévy, 1868), I, 349–52.

[41] March 20, 1792: *Journal de Paris,* no. 84 (March 24), sup. no. 35, pp. 1–2. *Ibid.,* no. 89 (March 29), sup. no. 38, pp. 1–2. *Ibid.,* no. 95 (April 4), sup. no. 41, pp. 1–2. *Ibid.,* no. 101 (April 10), pp. 409–10. *Ibid.,* no. 92 (April 1) through no. 106 (April 15), *passim;* Lacretelle, *Dix années d'épreuves,* p. 84.

Club was widely distributed.[42] Although the Constitutional Monarchists insisted that public opinion was indifferent or hostile, the patriotic press maintained that there was great popular enthusiasm for the Swiss.[43]

This "expiatory ceremony for the massacre of the Champ de Mars" was castigated by the Lafayette faction of the National Guard as an insult to their honor and as an incitement to revolt, but it was supported by the Girondin Municipality of Paris and by the Cordeliers and other radicals.[44] David, its organizer, was likewise a target for the opponents of the festival. Rumors were spread which aimed at discrediting him; he was accused of working for both sides, for they claimed he had painted a picture of the King accepting the Constitution.[45]

The atmosphere was highly charged with revolutionary spirit and war fever. Ugly rumors spread regarding the coming festival. Royalist journalists maintained that it would be used by the Jacobins as the occasion for a *coup d'état* against the monarchy, and some patriots feared a violent dissolution of the Assembly and a general massacre of *sans-culottes*.[46] The Municipality warned that counter-revolutionaries intent on creating trouble had arrived in Paris disguised as National Guards. In an open letter Pétion defended the fête and censured the "evil intentioned" who "fanned the flames of discord." Militant royal-

[42] *Journal des débats et de la correspondance de la Société des amis de la constitution, séante aux Jacobins à Paris,* debates, no. 172 (April 6, 1792), p. 21 (hereafter cited as *Journal des Jacobins*). Text: *Réponse . . . à des notes barbares envoyées à divers journaux contre les soldats de Châteaux-Vieux . . . le 4 avril . . .* (Paris: Imp. Patriote françois, 1792). Extract: *Moniteur,* no. 101 (April 10), pp. 415–16.

[43] *Journal de Paris,* no. 95 (April 4, 1792), sup. no. 41, pp. 1–2. *Feuille villageoise,* no. 31 (April 6), p. 109; *Annales patriotiques,* no. 97 (April 6), p. 430; *Révolutions de Paris,* no. 142 (March 31), pp. 582–87.

[44] *Révolutions de Paris,* no. 143 (April 7, 1792), pp. 9–10. *Journal de Paris,* no. 96 (April 5), sup. no. 42, pp. 1–2, no. 98 (April 7), p. 397, and sup. no. 44, pp. 1–3; *Despatches of Earl Gower,* pp. 172–73; *Folies d'un mois,* 5e mois, no. 13 [n.d], p. 4, and no. 28 [n.d.], p. 2; *Courier français,* no. 89 (March 29), pp. 4–5; *Rocambole,* no. 5 (April 14), pp. 82–83; *Ami du Peuple* (Marat), no. 637 (April 22), pp. 4–8. Dispatch of A. Pisani, Paris, April 8, 1792: M. Kovalevskii, ed., *I Dispacci degli ambasciatori Veneti alla corte di Francia durante la rivoluzione* (Turin: Bocca, 1895), I, 429.

[45] *See* pp. 49, 87.

[46] *Folies d'un mois,* 5e mois, no. 2 [n.d.], pp. 2–3; *Rocambole,* no. 5 (April 14, 1792), p. 82. *Annales patriotiques,* no. 104 (April 13), p. 458.

ists such as Du Rozoy urged the King to forbid the celebration, to *"montez à cheval"* and to place himself at the head of the National Guard. David and his fellow Jacobins, particularly Robespierre, were determined that the fête should be held as scheduled.[47]

In this superheated atmosphere the Swiss were voted the honors of the Legislative Assembly by a narrow margin on April 9. Led by Collot d'Herbois and accompanied by National Guards and armed citizens, they filed through the hall with flags flying and drums beating to the deafening applause of the gallery. Feuillant orators were helpless in the face of this overpowering demonstration. Meanwhile, the royalist press ridiculed the performance and chuckled at the disunity in the ranks of its enemies.[48]

Outside the Assembly the constitutionalists had no better success. Though they continued up to the very day of the festival to attack the celebration, its promoters, and its object, their efforts were fruitless. Petitions, placards, letters to the press, caricatures, and even a satirical ode by André Chénier, were unable to block the festival.[49] Though certain officers insisted that the fête was an insult to the National Guard, the rank and file did not seem to share their view.[50] Mayor Pétion insisted that it would be both unconstitutional and dangerous to forbid the celebration. Journals friendly to the festival supported the Mayor's contention that no legislative permission was necessary. Hostile papers and pamphleteers attacked him for "toadying" to the mob by supporting this "manifestation of republican-

[47] *Journal de Paris,* no. 101 (April 10, 1792), p. 409. Letter of Pétion dated April 6, posted April 8: *Moniteur,* no. 101 (April 10), p. 415. *Gazette de Paris* (Du Rozoy) (April 12), p. 3. *Journal des Jacobins,* debates, no. 173 (April 8), no. 174 (April 10), no. 175 (April 11), *passim.*

[48] *P.V.Leg.,* VII, 138–39; *Journal de Paris,* no. 101 (April 10, 1792), p. 407. *Journal historique et politique,* no. 16 (April 21), pp. 159–63; *Révolutions de Paris,* no. 144 (April 14), pp. 54–55. Foreign observers such as the envoy of Parma interpreted this incident as a proof of Jacobin strength: Virieu to Ventura, April 15: Grouchy, *op. cit.,* p. 342. *Ami du roi* (Royou), (April 11), p. 103; *Ami du roi* (Montjoie), no. 101 (April 10), p. 401. Later in the day the Jacobins accorded them a similar welcome: *Journal des Jacobins,* debates, no. 175 (April 11), pp. 1–2.

[49] *Journal de Paris,* no. 92 (April 1, 1792), through no. 106 (April 11), p. 330; *Feuille du jour,* no. 88 (March 28), p. 698, no. 90 (March 30), p. 715, no. 91 (March 31), p. 722; *Les Sabats Jacobites,* III, no. 64 [n.d.], pp. 209–14; *Col. Vinck,* no. 3572, II, 576; Letter of Géraud, April 15: Maugras, *op. cit.,* p. 272.

[50] *Journal universel* (Audouin) no. 872 (April 12, 1792), p. 1559, no. 873 (April 13), pp. 1563–64; *Révolutions de Paris,* XII, no. 143 (April 7), pp. 8–16.

ism."[51] Many were convinced that the fête would be an occasion for armed violence.[52]

April 15, 1792, the anxiously awaited day of the celebration, unlike that of Voltaire's apotheosis, was clear and beautiful. A vast procession left the Faubourg Saint-Antoine between ten and eleven in the morning.[53] In it David had combined neoclassic art with the symbols of revolutionary religion. Gossec provided appropriate music, and M.-J. Chénier was responsible for the republican lyrics and in-

[51] *Journal de Paris,* no. 105 (April 14, 1792), p. 425; *Rocambole,* no. 5 (April 14), pp. 82–83; *Le Spectateur national et modérateur,* no. 137 (April 15), pp. 180–81; *Chronique de Paris,* no. 106 (April 14), pp. 418–19. *Le Thermomètre du jour* (Dulaure), [ser. 2], no. 106 (April 15), pp. 114–15 (hereafter cited as *Thermomètre*). *Spectateur,* no. 137 (April 15), p. 181. Cf.P.S. du Pont de Nemours, *Lettre . . . à M. Pétion* [Paris, 1792], and *Second lettre à M. Pétion* [Paris, 1792]. The royalists attacked him just as viciously: *Ami du roi* (Royou), (April 12), pp. 1–2; *Ami du roi,* (Montjoie), no. 102 (April 11), p. 405.

[52] Letter of M. Lefebvre d'Acy to M. Vanderberghe, Paris, April 12, 1792: Vaissière, *op. cit.,* p. 455; *Ami du roi* (Royou), (April 12), p. 2; *Journal universel* (Audouin), no. 873 (April 13), pp. 1563–64; Letter of Mme. Jullien to her husband, Paris, April 16: E. Lockroy, ed., *Journal d'une bourgeoise, 1791–93* (2. ed.; Paris: Lévy 1881), p. 67; Du Pont, *Lettre à M. Pétion; Thermomètre,* no. 106 (April 15), p. 114; Dispatch of Pisani, Paris, April 8: Kovalevskii, *op. cit.,* p. 429.

[53] For contemporary descriptions: *Détail et ordre de la marche de la fête en l'honneur de la liberté donnée par le peuple à l'occasion de l'arrivée des soldats de Château-Vieux . . . 15 Avril, 1792 . . .* [Paris, 1792]. The accounts in the *Mercure de France,* no. 16 (April 21, 1792), pp. 204–06, and *Journal historique et politique,* no. 16 (April 21), pp. 204–06, are identical. *Annales patriotiques,* no. 108 (April 16), pp. 475–76, no. 109 (April 17), pp. 478–79; *Journal général de France,* no. 108 (April 17), pp. 430–31; *Moniteur,* no. 108 (April 17), p. 444; *Feuille villageoise,* no. 31 (April 26), pp. 110–14; *L'Auditeur national,* no. 107 (April 16), pp. 5–6; *Révolutions de Paris,* no. 145 (April 17), pp. 265–66; *Gazette universelle,* no. 108 (April 17), p. 431; *Journal universel* (Audouin), no. 878 (April 18), p. 1606–08; *Mercure universel,* XIV, no. 414 (April 17), pp. 265–66; *Courier français,* no. 109 (April 18), pp. 5–7; *Courrier de Gorsas,* ser. 2, VII, no. 16 (April 17), pp. 242–52; *Sabats Jacobites,* III, no. 67 [n.d.], pp. 257–72; *Chronique de Paris,* no. 109 (April 17), pp. 431–32; *Courrier extraordinaire ou le premier arrivé* (Duplain), (April 16), p. 8; *Patriote françois,* no. 981 (April 17), pp. 432–33; *Thermomètre,* no. 107 (April 16), pp. 125–26, no. 108 (April 17), pp. 130–33. Letter of Mme. Jullien to her husband, Paris, April 16: Lockroy, *op. cit.,* pp. 62–68. Letter of Géraud, Paris, April 15: Maugras, *op. cit.,* pp. 275–77; Eyewitness description: L.S.J. Salamon, *Correspondance secrète,* ed. Richemont (Paris: Plon-Nourrit, 1898), pp. 500–04; Dulure, *Esquisses,* II, 45–52. For contemporary engravings, see *Col. Vinck,* nos. 3567–70, II, 574–75; no. 59 of *Tableaux historiques,* I, 236; *Révolutions de Paris,* no. 145 (April 21), p. 98. For music, *see* Pierre, *Musique des fêtes,* pp. 348–50; *Hymnes et chansons,* pp. 221–22. *See* plate XII, above, opposite p. 60.

scriptions. The Swiss, freed from the galleys of the old regime, represented humanity's emancipation from the shackles of tyranny, and nothing was omitted which could remind observers that this was the Fête of Liberty. Aside from the classical influence, its most striking characteristic was popular participation. As Brissot expressed it, "The people were the regulator, the executor, the ornament, and the object of the celebration."[54]

Although all classes were represented, the bulk of the participants were the common people of Paris—especially those from the poorer sections. The radical popular societies were out in full force. Great numbers of National Guards, unarmed and off duty, students, veterans, and market porters were included in the vast throng. Mosaic tables inscribed with the Declaration of the Rights of Man; the flags of France, England, and the United States; busts of great men; two antique sarcophagi, one dedicated to the Swiss killed at Nancy and the other to the National Guards who died there; and a model of a galley—all these figured in the procession. A huge triumphal *char* bearing a statue of Liberty and adorned with partiotic bas-reliefs dominated this living panorama of the Revolution. This time David's neoclassical chariot was drawn by twenty-four brewery horses.[55] The forty Swiss, led by Collot d'Herbois and escorted by French Guards and *sans-culottes,* marched together. They were preceded by young girls in white who carried the chains of the released prisoners. A jester on "a long-eared courser," symbolizing the "blockheads" who had tried to prevent the fête, brought up the rear.

After a pause at the Bastille to dedicate a statue of Liberty, the procession advanced to the Mayor's palace where Pétion—in a strictly private character to be sure—joined Robespierre and Danton next to the *char*. Subsequently, deputies from the Legislative Assembly and the band of the National Guard took their places in the huge cortège. Royalists were scandalized and *sans-culottes* delighted when the statue of Louis XV was crowned with a red cap and blindfolded at the passage of Liberty's chariot.

Progress was slow since the crowd halted frequently to dance the *ronde nationale* and sing the *ça ira*. It was evening before the Champ de Mars was reached. Here was celebrated the ritual purification of the Altar of the Fatherland upon which patriots had been killed. After

[54] *Patriote françois,* no. 981 (April 17, 1792), p. 432.

[55] The wheels and platform were those used for Voltaire's *char*.

XII. FESTIVALS OF LIBERTY AND THE LAW

Above: *Première fête de la liberté à l'occasion des Suisses de Château-Vieux*
Engraving by Berthault after Prieur — No. 59 in *Tableaux historiques*

Below: *Pompe funèbre en l'honneur de Simoneau maire d'Estampes*
Engraving by Berthault after Prieur — No. 61 in *Tableaux historiques*

singing a hymn to Liberty, the great throng embraced each other and danced around the altar in a spontaneous demonstration of "patriotic gaiety, perfect equality and civic fraternity." [56]

The contemporary accounts do not agree as to the extent and enthusiasm of the crowd. Though Carra's figure of 400,000 and Audouin's of 500,000 spectators may be too high, there seem to have been at least 100,000 participants.[57] All the accounts speak of enormous crowds, except the hostile Genevese, Mallet du Pan, who maintains that there were "very few spectators," and Dupont de Nemours who says these few were mostly women. One fact seems clear: the working class was out in full force, but the opponents of the celebration were conspicuously absent. According to all except Mallet and the anti-Jacobin *Sabats Jacobites,* the people were in high spirits. The "patriots" speak of the naive joy and fraternal exaltation of the crowd; reactionaries imply that the merrymaking was stimulated by quantities of *eau de vie*.[58]

Friendly and hostile observers agreed that, despite the universal anticipation of trouble, a remarkable state of order prevailed. It was a noteworthy fact that marshals of the festival, poetically armed with sheaves of wheat instead of riot sticks, took the place of the public police. Patriotic journals maintained that order and decency reigned because of the peaceful and fraternal sentiments and civic restraint of the participants. Conservatives declared that the good behavior of the crowd was due to certain National Guard detachments standing to arms in their barracks. However, the bayonets of these eager defenders of law and order do not seem to have been visible to the crowd.[59]

[56] *Annales patriotiques,* no. 108 (April 17, 1792), p. 478.

[57] *Annales patriotiques* (Carra), no. 108 (April 17, 1792), p. 478. *Journal universel* (Audouin), no. 876 (April 16), p. 1597. *Thermomètre,* no. 108 (April 17), p. 131; *Gazette universelle,* no. 108 (April 17), p. 431.

[58] Mallet says he was at the Champ de Mars at 6:30 and found it "almost solitary;" actually the crowd did not arrive there until almost 8:00: *Mercure de France,* no. 16 (April 21, 1792), p. 205; *Seconde lettre de M. du Pont à Pétion,* p. 4; *Sabats Jacobites,* no. 67 [n.d.], pp. 264–65. *Journal général de France,* no. 108 (April 17), p. 431. The *Feuille villageoise* (no. 31 [April 26], p. 114) says there were no drunks to be met that night.

[59] Cf. *Révolutions de Paris,* no. 145 (April 21, 1792), p. 103 and *Sabats Jacobites,* no. 67 [n.d.], p. 26 with *Courier français,* no. 109 (April 18), p. 7; *Journal universel,* no. 878 (April 18), p. 1607; Letter of Géraud, April 15: Maugras, *op. cit.,* p. 275; and *Thermomètre,* ser. 2, no. 108 (April 17), p. 132.

As was to be expected, this festival of the people was described as either a profoundly touching, joyously popular, and fraternally patriotic ceremony; or a scandalous, shabby, and shameful saturnalia, depending upon the writer's attitude toward the masses. The pro-revolutionary journalists waxed enthusiastic. Dulaure declared that "nothing was lacking to give the fête all the magnificence compatible with a popular festival." According to Brissot, "Nothing could be more beautiful than this festival because nothing is more beautiful than a great mass of men animated by the same sentiments of patriotism and of fraternity. . . ." The *Moniteur* was "profoundly impressed by this spectacle," while the *Feuille villageoise* became eloquently effusive. Robespierre found it "simple and sublime." "A profound feeling of patriotic gaiety and of fraternal love prevailed," said Carra, in his newspaper, the *Annales patriotiques,* and produced "a picture of perfect equality and of civic fraternity." [60]

Counter-revolutionists and constitutionalists characterized the celebration as a shabby, grotesque, and unrestrained carousal. It "resembled perfectly the triumph of crime," said one royalist paper; and the Duchesse de Tourzel disparaged it as a "ridiculous and indecent promenade of miserable deserters." One word sufficed for Earl Gower's unimaginative observation: "absurd." In the opinion of the *Journal générale de France,* "nothing could be as shabby or as miserable as this . . . noisy and picturesque mob . . . of the very poorest inhabitants." "It was only a bad farce and *chienlerie* carried out by the *sans-culottes*" said one aristocrat, while the *Journal de la cour et de la ville* assured its readers that "the scandalous fête" was "ridiculous." In general, the Constitutional Monarchists seemed to have shared M. Pitra's opinion that this "odious scandal" was an ineffaceable stain on the Revolution.[61]

[60] *Thermomètre* (Dulaure), no. 107 (April 16, 1792), p. 125. *Patriote françois* (Brissot), no. 981 (April 17), p. 432. *Moniteur,* no. 108 (April 17), p. 444. *Feuille villageoise,* no. 31 (April 26), p. 110. *Le Défenseur de la constitution* (Robespierre), no. 4 [n.d.], p. 187. *Annales patriotiques* (Carra), no. 108 (April 17), p. 478.

[61] *Folies d'un mois,* 5e mois, no. 27 [n.d.], p. 4. Tourzel, *Mémoires* (2. ed.; Paris: Plon, 1884), II, 80. *Despatches of Earl Gower,* p. 172. *Journal général de France,* no. 108 (April 17), pp. 430–31. Letter of M. Lefebvre d'Acy to M. Vanderberghe, April 17: Vaissière, *op. cit.,* p. 456. *Journal de la cour et de la ville,* no. 49 (April 18), p. 390, no. 50 (April 19), p. 400. Letter of M. Pitra, elector of 1789, June, 1792: F. M. Grimm and others, *Cor. lit.,* XVI, 139.

What was the effect upon the spectators of this popular demonstration organized by the Jacobins? According to the patriotic press, all the "good citizens" of Paris entered into the spirit of the occasion and were deeply moved by the celebration. Other sources confirm this evidence. For example, Mme. Jullien wrote to her husband that she was raised to "a rapture of pleasure."[62] The conservative journals do not agree. Some insist that the spectators were few and apathetic; others, that they absented themselves out of indignation and contempt. Some of those who admit the presence of large crowds say that they were inspired with "scorn and horror," watched with "silent contempt," or turned away with "mocking laughter."[63]

This apparent contradiction probably results partly from lack of observation (many of the reactionary reporters obviously had not witnessed the whole of the celebration),[64] partly from wishful thinking which led to overgeneralizations from individual incidents, and partly from a desire to minimize the success of the demonstration. The basic reason was, however, that opponents of the festival could no more appreciate the ceremonies of the new cult than a Protestant can fully understand the Mass. Though the sympathizers of these "martyrs of the Revolution"[65] tended to exaggerate the favorable influence of the fête upon the minds of their contemporaries, there can be no doubt that many were deeply moved by it. "You cannot imagine," wrote young Géraud to his parents, "how much this fête has raised the thermometer of the public temper."[66]

Most republicans regarded the festival as far more than the vindication of innocent patriots unjustly condemned by a tyrannical government. For them it was a festival of liberty, of equality, of fraternity; a mass demonstration of the people against their oppressors; a manifesto that the existing order must be replaced by a republic

[62] *Feuille villageoise,* no. 31 (April 26, 1792), p. 110; *Moniteur,* no. 108 (April 17), p. 444; *Courier français,* no. 107 (April 16), pp. 5–6; *Défenseur de la constitution,* no. 4 [n.d.], p. 187; *Annales patriotiques,* no. 108 (April 16), p. 479. Letter of April 16: Lockroy, *op. cit.,* p. 62.

[63] *Mercure de France,* no. 16 (April 21, 1792), p. 205. *Journal de Paris,* no. 107 (April 16), p. 433. *Rocambole,* no. 6 (April 19), p. 99; *Spectateur et modérateur,* no. 139 (April 17), p. 189. *Sabats Jacobites,* no. 67 [n.d.], p. 266n. *Gazette universelle,* no. 108 (April 17), p. 431.

[64] *Ami du roi* (Montjoie), no. 107 (April 16, 1792), p. 428, frankly admits the fact.

[65] *Instituteur du peuple,* no. 2 [n.d.], p. 7.

[66] Letter of April 15, 1792: Maugras, *op. cit.,* p. 277.

based on universal suffrage. Camille Desmoulins proclaimed it "the fête of insurrection" where "despotism and aristocracy were crushed under the wheels of the chariot of [liberty]." Marat felt that it consecrated "the holy doctrine of resistance" to bad government. According to Robespierre, the celebration was the "triumph of liberty and patriotism." Others regarded it as proof that "patriotism and humanity were stronger than malevolence and incivism." The *Moniteur* and the *Journal universel* believed that it gave the people a new consciousness of their strength and showed that they were worthy to be free; the *Courier français* remarked on "the astonishing force" of the "development of the authority of liberty." Prudhomme may have merely expressed their thought more concretely when he described it as a demonstration against Lafayette and the King and declared that it proved that "a free people has no need of bayonets to restrain themselves." In a word it was "the complete triumph of the people over their enemies and calumniators."[67]

The "friends of law and order" considered the fête a scandalous exaltation of foreign mutineers who had defied their officers and murdered National Guardsmen; a criminal glorification of the spirit of rebellion, and a rallying of the rabble against their rulers. The reactionary press ridiculed the festival and boasted that the National Guard had prevented the anticipated attack on the Tuileries. "The King still lives," exulted Royou's *Ami du roi,* "and his faithful subjects breathe again." Earl Gower told his government that the purpose of the fête was "to render Mr. de la Fayette [sic] and the Feuillants unpopular." He and others believed that it had discredited the Jacobins rather than their opponents.[68] Nevertheless, some conservatives realized the deeper implications of the demonstration. Aristocrats and Feuillants were both wounded and worried by its republicanism, and the

[67] *Feuille villageoise,* no. 29 (April 12, 1792), p. 72. *Tribune des patriotes* (Desmoulins), no. 2 [n.d.], pp. 64–65. *Ami du peuple* (Marat), no. 637 (April 22), p. 8, *Défenseur de la constitution* (Robespierre), no. 4 [n.d.], p. 187. *Feuille villageoise,* no. 31 (April 26), p. 109. *Moniteur,* no. 108 (April 17), p. 444; *Journal universel,* no. 878 (April 18), p. 1608; *Courier français,* no. 109 (April 18), p. 5. *Révolutions de Paris* (Prudhomme), no. 145 (April 21), pp. 104–108. *Annales patriotiques,* no. 108 (April 17), p. 479.

[68] *Rocambole,* no. 6 (April 19, 1792), p. 99; *Journal de Paris,* no. 107 (April 16), p. 434; *Mercure de France,* no. 16 (April 21), p. 205; *Sabats Jacobites,* no. 67, [n.d.], p. 271. *Ami du roi* (Royou), (April 19), p. 1. *Despatches of Earl Gower,* p. 172. Dispatch of Pisani, Paris, April 16: Kovalevskii, *op. cit.,* p. 433.

conservative *Journal historique et politique* assures us that "consternation reigned in the Tuileries." At least one editor remarked on the disquieting emergence of a new revolutionary cult—that of liberty. The *Rocambole* felt that the "honoring of the assassins of the virtuous Desille" indicated "the degree of abasement to which the nation has sunk." The astute Mallet du Pan observed that "the mere execution [of the fête] fulfilled one of the principal ends of the promoters."[69]

What, then, were these ends? It is doubtful that the radicals contemplated storming the royal palace at this time. Unarmed men, women, and children, even several hundred thousand of them, are unlikely to throw themselves upon the bayonets of twenty thousand determined enemies. What the Jacobins probably intended was a demonstration aimed at assembling their forces and rallying the weaker brethren to their cause. Their avowed aim was to intimidate the "tyrants" and encourage the "patriots" by honoring "the martyrs of the cause of the people."[70] The purpose of David, M.-J. Chénier and perhaps Gossec, appears to have been to use their talents to instill in the hearts of the participants their own hatred of the old regime and their own fanatical devotion to the principles of the Revolution.[71]

The fête in honor of the soldiers of the Châteauvieux Regiment was the first of the series of similar republican festivals of which David was sole organizer. As in the case of Voltaire's apotheosis, the ceremony was partly inspired by David's Roman studies, the *Voyage de la Jeune Anacharsis*,[72] and other works, and the processions of the Church and the monarchy. Now the master added two other elements which were to become characteristic of the revolutionary festivals: Republican symbols such as the statues of Liberty, tables of the Rights of Man and the *bonnet rouge;* and popular participation. Physical prototypes of the figure of Liberty can be found in David's sketchbooks, and the concept of the personification of ideas is as old as time. Inscribed tablets were undoubtedly Biblical in inspiration. The *bonnet rouge*

[69] *Courier français*, no. 109 (April 18, 1792), p. 5; *Journal de Paris*, no. 107 (April 16), p. 433; *Patriote françois*, no. 982 (April 17), p. 1. *Journal historique et politique*, no. 24 (June 16), p. 177. *Courrier extraordinaire* (April 16), p. 8; *Rocambole*, IV, no. 6 (April 19), p. 99. *Mercure de France*, no. 16 (April 21), p. 206.

[70] *See* the petition of March 24, p. 56.

[71] Bingham, *M.-J. Chénier (1789–1794)*, p. 70. The case for Gossec's revolutionary sentiments appears rather dubious in the light of his collaboration in the Fête of the Law, *see* p. 71.

[72] Particularly II, 43, 47–48, 593; III, 167.

worn by the liberated galley slaves was adopted by the Jacobins as being, like the Phrygian cap of antiquity, the emblem of enfranchisement and liberty.[73] David carefully selected, and where necessary, labeled his allegorical symbols so that their meaning was clear to his audience. If we may believe the "patriotic" journalists, the crowd was moved to revolutionary fervor by these emblems.[74] The artist's preoccupation with classical symbolism as a vehicle for republican ideology is illustrated by a fine pencil drawing which he made at about this time, the *Allegory of Liberty and Tyranny*.[75]

The art of processions was not an innovation at the outbreak of the Revolution, but with it the festivals changed entirely in their meaning and in their form. They became the living expression, the external manifestation of the cult of the Revolution, organized in accordance with the formula "of the people, by the people, for the people." In the words of David himself, "National festivals are instituted for the people; it is fitting that they participate in them with a common accord and that they play the principal role there."[76] Rousseau had recommended that the spectators be made participants and had cited Spartan and Genevese precedents,[77] but David seems to have been the first to apply the principle on a large scale and with a purpose which was primarily political propaganda.

David's contemporaries appreciated his abilities as a propagandist. "Profoundly moved by this spectacle," at least two journals suggested that such fêtes "which have already made a new people" be multiplied to propagandize the cause of the Revolution. "Popular festivals are the best education for the people." The royalists, too, seem to have been impressed. The day after the fête, the *Journal de la cour et de la ville* declared that if David would exercise his talents in the interests of the monarchy "we would soon be reconciled with our [chief of] the French

[73] Although the liberty cap appeared in France as a symbol as early as 1789, it was not worn until 1791 and did not become fashionable until the spring of 1792.

[74] *Courrier de Gorsas,* no. 16 (April 17, 1792), p. 246, *Thermomètre,* no. 108 (April 17), p. 131.

[75] Collection of Dr. W. R. Valentiner. Reproduced: *The Art Quarterly,* IV (Summer, 1941), 191. Cf. E. Scheyer, "French drawings of the Great Revolution," *ibid.,* pp. 189–93.

[76] Lenoir, "David, Souvenirs historiques," p. 7.

[77] "Lettre à d'Alembert sur les spectacles," *Oeuvres complètes,* ed., Musset-Pathay (Paris: Dupont, 1824), II, 176.

school."[78] Unfortunately for the Feuillants, their spokesman André Chénier had, on the very day of the celebration, published his sarcastic *Hymn on the Triumphal Entry of the Swiss of Châteauvieux* in which he expressed his animosity toward the liberated soldiers, Collot d'Herbois, and the Festival of Liberty.[79] Although they could not command the services of the organizer of the Fête of Liberty, they recognized the effectiveness of his technique and determined to promote a "Fête of the Law" to counteract the Jacobin pageant in honor of "Liberty."

The Constitutional Monarchists found the occasion for their party demonstration in the funeral honors accorded to Jacques Guillaume Simonneau, the mayor of Étampes, who had been killed on March 3, 1792, by rioting peasants who wanted him to fix the price of grain. When the lynching became known, all factions, including the Jacobins, decried this violence done to the law, and funeral ceremonies in his honor were celebrated in a number of cities.[80] A movement was started within the National Assembly to erect a monument to his memory in the market place of Étampes "to teach the people their duty."[81] In the murdered mayor, the Feuillants saw a martyr of the law who might be used as a weapon against their political opponents and at the same time as a symbol to overawe the masses among whom the spirit of insurrection was spreading. They planned a "triumph of the law" to neutralize the effects of the *sans-culotte* Festival of Liberty.

From the start the Jacobins were blamed for the Simonneau affair despite the fact that the victim was one of their own members. Their political antagonists soon opened a campaign for a state funeral for

[78] *Thermomètre,* no. 108 (April 17, 1792), p. 131; *Courrier de Gorsas,* no. 18 (April 19), pp. 275, 281. *Moniteur,* no. 108 (April 17), p. 414. *Journal de la cour et de la ville,* no. 47 (April 16), p. 374.

[79] *Journal de Paris,* no. 106 (April 15, 1792), pp. 429–30; *Oeuvres complètes,* III, 259–61.

[80] *Moniteur,* no. 67 (March 7, 1792), p. 263, no. 76 (March 16), p. 312; *Révolutions de Paris,* no. 139 (March 10), p. 443; *Feuille villageoise,* no. 34 (May 17), p. 183; *Journal de l'église constitutionelle de France,* III, no. 5 (May 10), p. 71.

[81] March 6, 1792: *P.V. Leg.,* VI, 75, 78. *See* J. Guillaume, ed., *Procès-verbaux du Comité d'instruction publique de l'Assemblée législative,* (Paris: Imp. nat., 1889), pp. 141, 152 (hereafter cited as *C.I.P. Leg.*). The Monument was voted March 18: *P.V. Leg.,* VI, 258; J.A.J. Debry, *Rapport sur les honneurs à rendre à la mémoire de J. G. Simonneau . . . et décret du 18 mars . . .* [Paris: Imp. nat., 1792], p. 3; *Col. Baud.,* XXI, 64.

the martyred mayor as a demonstration against the radicals. Agents of the court were said to have joined the Feuillants in circulating petitions and collecting funds for a counterblast to the Châteauvieux festival.[82] Naturally, David and his colleagues presently abandoned the cause of Simonneau and opposed the ceremonies ostensibly planned in his honor. The very day that the Châteauvieux survivors were honored by the Assembly and the Jacobins, Robespierre blocked a proposal within the Club for a fête glorifying the mayor of Étampes. On April 15, Marat made a vicious attack on Simonneau and those who used him, and other Jacobins such as Camille Desmoulins and Robespierre joined in.[83]

In the midst of this acrimonious campaign, war came with the declaration of hostilities against Austria on April 20, 1792. More than ever an antidote to the Fête of Châteauvieux, which had tended to encourage insubordination among the troops and insurrection among the people, seemed essential to the conservatives. They energetically continued their campaign, and the King himself is supposed to have contributed heavily.[84]

On April 21 some National Guards petitioned the Paris Commune for a public funeral for Simonneau. The Municipality consented, but the ceremony was to be financed by private subscription.[85] Nevertheless, the promoters wanted a "truly national festival" (i.e., sanctioned and paid for by the government and held in the Champ de Mars). On April 30 came the first military reverses, which the generals blamed on the lack of discipline among the troops; therefore, on May 6, the petitioners informed the national legislature that it was "time to prove that the inflexible reign of law had finally come." Their ceremony would be a "death blow" to the "enemies of the Constitution" and a

[82] *Moniteur,* no. 67 (March 7, 1792), p. 263. *Journal de Paris,* no. 134 (May 13), p. 539 through no. 157 (June 5), p. 634. A. Fantin-Desodoards, *Histoire philosophique de la révolution* (4. ed.; Paris: Belin, 1801), II, 134; Letter of M. Pitra, Paris, June, 1792: *Cor. lit.,* XVI, 141.

[83] April 9, 1792: *Journal des Jacobins,* no. 175 (April 11), pp. 1–2; *Journal de Paris,* no. 104 (April 13), sup. no. 48, p. 4. *L'Ami du peuple,* (Marat), no. 630 (April 15), pp. 2–8. *La Tribune des patriotes* (Desmoulins), no. 2 [n.d.], pp. 65–66. *Défenseur de la constitution,* no. 4 [n.d.], pp. 179–208.

[84] Fantin-Desodoards, *loc. cit.;* C. de Lacretelle, *Histoire de la révolution française* (Paris: Treuttel et Wurtz, 1824), III, 106.

[85] *Pétition . . . présentée . . . 21 avril au . . . Commune par un nombre de citoyens-soldats de la garde nationale parisienne,* [Paris: Potier, 1792].

"signal of victory" to their comrades at the front. The deputies applauded, gave their authorization, and voted to send a delegation to the rites.[86]

Quatremère de Quincy, David's former companion and collaborator, now a staunch Feuillant but still a pedant, drew up a report on the festival which he read to the Assembly on May 12. National festivals, he intoned, "can excite disorder or calm it, command obedience and enforce respect for the law." Their sanction of the Simonneau fête was "a call to order more powerful, I dare say, than the most menacing laws." Despite the opposition of the radicals to the authoritarian character of the celebration, his proposal was adopted "with urgency."[87]

The Department of Paris was charged with the details of the procession. It is usually stated, though on insufficient evidence, that Quatremère was the author of the program. Nor is it certain that the classicistic doctrinaire was the master of ceremonies of the fête. However, it is not unlikely that he may have inspired its archaeological allegories, its "grave and silent" spirit, and its pedantic imitation of a "frieze in motion." The generally accepted account also attributes a leading role to David. Nevertheless, it is clear that, as will presently appear, David had nothing whatever to do with the procession nor with its *décor*.[88]

The day set for the festival, June 3, 1792, was overcast and threatening, but at the appointed time the procession left the Boulevard Saint-Antoine from which the Fête of Liberty had started. Its neoclassic trappings were somewhat overpowered by the undisguised accoutrements of modern militarism. National Guard uniforms con-

[86] *P.V. Leg.*, VIII, 126; *Col. Baud*, XXII, 30; *Moniteur*, no. 128 (May 7, 1792), pp. 529–30.

[87] *P.V. Leg.*, VII, 231; *J.D.D.*, no. 229 [n.d.], pp. 206–08; *Col. Baud.*, XXII, 52; *Moniteur*, no. 134 (May 13, 1792), pp. 539–41.

[88] Letter of Pitra: *Cor. lit.*, XVI, 141; Letter of Roland, Minister of the Interior, to the National Assembly: *A.P.*, XLIV, 348. *Programme arrêté par le directoire du département de Paris, pour la fête de Simonneau* [Paris: Ballard, 1792]. Tourneux (*Cor. lit.*, XVI, 141n) cites the *Journal de Paris*, but the latter (no. 134 [May 13, 1792], p. 539) merely states that Quatremère was the reporter of the decree of May 12. R. Schneider (*Quatremère de Quincy*, pp. 58–59) cites a letter of Roucher (who wrote the lyrics for the fête) in *Journal de Paris* (no. 157 [June 5], p. 634), but it there states that Molinos and Legrand were the *ordonnateurs*. It is the *Révolutions de Paris* (no. 152 [June 9], p. 452) which awards this dubious honor to Quatremère. On David's role *see* p. 75.

trasted in startling fashion with ancient Roman togas, but they somehow clarified the message which the authors of the demonstration expected to convey: Law, order, and property were sacred and would be maintained not only by the symbolic "sword of the law" but by the bayonets of the troops. The Revolution was over; further insurrection would be crushed by force. The element of popular participation so characteristic of the Fête of Liberty was entirely lacking. However, in addition to its classical spirit, it had one other quality in common with its two predecessors: it was purely lay in character.[89]

Preceded by trumpeters of the national cavalry, the great military parade moved along the boulevards, through the Place Louis XV, where it was joined by a large number of national deputies, and across the Seine to the Champ de Mars. Cavalry, gendarmerie, grenadiers, light infantry, sappers and other national guard, and regular army units marched by in overwhelming strength. The only other considerable group which participated in this Festival of the Law was the host of government functionaries. The popular societies were conspicuously absent. Thus dignified by the presence of its agents, the law was further represented in symbolic form: banners, an enormous sword, its book open on a golden throne, tables of the law, antique altars and candelabra, and a colossal statue of the Law holding a sceptre were carried by slaves clad in classical tunics. A bust of Simon-

[89] *Chronique de Paris,* no. 155 (June 2, 1792), pp. 614–16, no. 158 (June 5), pp. 626–27; *Journal de Paris,* no. 157 (June 5), pp. 633–34, no. 159 (June 7), pp. 641–42; *Gazette universelle,* no. 156 (June 14), p. 288; *Annales de la religion et du sentiment,* III, no. 22 [n.d.], pp. 458–61; *Révolutions de Paris,* no. 152 (June 9), pp. 450–55; *Mercure de France,* no. 23 (June 9), pp. 128–30; *Journal général* (Fontenai), no. 155 (June 3), pp. 626–27; *Journal de la cour et de la ville,* III, no. 37 (June 6), pp. 291–92; *Défenseur de la constitution,* no. 4 [n.d.], pp. 187–193; *Thermomètre,* no. 155 (June 3), pp. 506–09, no. 157 (June 5), pp. 523–24; *Mercure universel,* no. 462 (June 4), pp. 58–60; *Patriote françois,* no. 1031 (June 6), p. 630; *La Rocambole, ou journal des honnêtes gens,* IV, no. 20 (June 7), pp. 323–25; *Le Consolateur,* II, no. 46 (June 8), p. 316; *Courrier extraordinaire* (June 3), pp. 1–4 and sup. (June 4), p. 12; *Courrier de Gorsas,* IX, no. 4 (June 4), pp. 53–63; *Feuille du jour,* II, no. 165 (June 3), pp. 1222–25; *Ordre, marche et détail de la cérémonie décretée par l'Assemblée . . . dans . . . la mémoire de J. G. Simonneau* [Paris: Ballard, 1792]. Dispatch of Virieu to Ventura, June 10: Grouchy, *op. cit.,* p. 350; Dulaure, *Esquisses,* II, 52–58. For contemporary engravings, see *Col. Vinck,* nos. 3599–3600, II, 584; no. 61 of *Tableaux historiques,* I, 244; *Révolutions de Paris,* no. 152 (June 9, 1792), p. 450. For the music, *see* Pierre, *Musique des fêtes,* p. 357; *Journal de Paris,* no. 155 (June 3), p. 625; *Mercure universel,* no. 462 (June 4), p. 60; *Chronique de Paris,* no. 158 (June 5), p. 267. *See* plate XII, below, opposite p. 60.

neau, his sash of office, a model of his monument, and a bas-relief depicting his death were also exhibited in the cortège. Lugubrious and triumphal hymns were provided by the Feuillant poet Roucher with music by Gossec.[90] The procession ended at the Champ de Mars with a ceremony shut off from the public by a solid phalanx of soldiers. A downpour of rain and the outburst of the *ça ira* interrupted the crowning of Simonneau's bust. The ritual closed with the crash of artillery and the flicker of bayonets as the troops presented arms. People cried "*vive la loi*" or "*vive la liberté*," according to their sympathies.

As in the case of the previous festivals, the contemporary accounts vary somewhat with regard to the extent and enthusiasm of the crowd. Though "patriots" such as Dulaure and Gorsas say there were few spectators, more conservative writers state that considerable crowds were attracted.[91] Witnesses agree, however, that there was no enthusiasm for the fête among the spectators.[92] Rejoicing was certainly not to be expected at a funeral, but there seems to have been no real grief either. The *Mercure universel* speaks of a "respectful silence," which Roucher interpreted as sorrow, but during most of the program the people seem to have watched without marked emotion of any kind. It was only when Mayor Pétion went by that the *sans-culottes* registered feeling by giving him an ovation. The "patriots" showed their true sentiments by singing revolutionary songs when rain interrupted the ceremony and by drowning the cries of the "aristocrats" with shouts of "*vive la liberté*" at the close. On the whole, however, the crowds were outwardly quiet and orderly—overwhelming armed force insured tranquillity—but below the surface the radical sections of Paris seethed.[93]

[90] *See* p. 65 note 71.

[91] *Thermomètre* (Dulaure), no. 157 (June 5, 1792), p. 523; *Courrier de Gorsas*, IX, no. 9 (June 9), p. 132. *Mercure universel*, no. 462 (June 4), p. 59; *Annales de la religion et du sentiment*, no. 22, [n.d.], p. 461; *Rocambole*, no. 20 (June 7), p. 324; *Feuille du jour*, no. 167 (June 5), p. 1247.

[92] In addition to citations in note 89 see: *Annales patriotiques*, no. 157 (June 5, 1792), p. 693; *La Trompette du Père Duchêne* (Lemaire), no. 21 [n.d.], p. 1; Letter of Mme. Jullien to her son: Lockroy, *op. cit.*, pp. 108–09.

[93] *Ami du roi* (Montjoie), no. 156 (June 4, 1792), p. 623. *Mercure universel*, no. 462 (June 4), p. 59. Roucher in *Journal de Paris*, no. 151 (June 5), p. 633. *Thermomètre*, no. 157 (June 5), p. 523. *Courrier de Gorsas*, no. 4 (June 4), p. 61; *Patriote françois*, no. 1031 (June 6), p. 630. *Courrier extraordinaire* (June 4), sup., p. 12. Letter of M. Lefebvre d'Acy to M. Vanderberghe: Vaissière, *op. cit.*, p. 108.

As was to be expected, the controversial nature of the festival led to constrasting characterization. It tended to be either a solemn, majestic, and tasteful ceremonial, or a militaristic and bureaucratic pseudo-antique mummery. One of its participants declared it to be "a spectacle worthy of the beautiful days of antiquity." Roucher modestly proclaimed, "We no longer have anything to envy the triumphal festivals of ancient Rome." "A most imposing spectacle," said the conservative *Mercure universel.* The *Feuille du jour* voiced similar sentiments and agreed with the *Consolateur* that it was "majestic." In the opinion of the royalist *Journal de la cour et de la ville,* the fête was "noble, decent and imposing." Girondin journals such as the *Annales patriotiques* were likewise rather favorable in their comments.[94]

Rightist papers compared it with the Fête of Châteauvieux—to the great disparagement of the latter. For the moderate *Feuille villageoise,* however, it was "very intertesting . . . though less animated, less touching than the popular festival of liberty." Even Brissot, who favored the fête, said that he thought it was "very pompous," and that unlike the former festival, it was "only a ceremony." And a "long and boring" one at that, insisted Fontenai, who added that there was "nothing great or imposing in the ensemble." Dulaure said that the "bad taste" of the *décor,* "the military uniforms, the threatening bayonets, and the cannon gave this ceremony an air of sadness, of despotism, which was not found in the Festival of Liberty." Almost every feature of the demonstration was ridiculed by the *Révolutions de Paris,* which declared that "this jumble of antique religious ceremonies and modern military evolutions resembles nothing so much as a rehearsal for the Corpus Christi procession." As a "man of the people," David disparaged the "odious allegories" which "dishonor this funeral celebration," and as an artist he criticized the "hodgepodge of bizarre and grotesque costumes, which a Visigoth of the twelfth century would not have had the bad taste to put together."[95]

[94] Letter of Pitra, *Cor. lit.,* XVI, 141. Letter of Roucher in *Journal de Paris,* no. 157 (June 5, 1792), p. 634. *Mercure universel,* XVI, no. 462 (June 4), p. 59. *Feuille du jour,* no. 167 (June 5), p. 1246. *Consolateur,* no. 46 (June 8), p. 316. *Journal de la cour et de la ville,* no. 37 (June 6), p. 291. *Annales patriotiques,* no. 157 (June 5), p. 692.

[95] *Feuille villageoise,* no. 38 (June 14, 1792), p. 288. *Patriote françois* (Brissot), no. 1031 (June 6), p. 630. *Journal général* (Fontenai), no. 157 (June 5), p. 634. *Thermomètre* (Dulaure), no. 157 (June 5), p. 523. *Révolutions de Paris,* no. 152 (June 9), pp. 450–55. Letter of David to Gorsas: *Courrier de Gorsas,* no. 9 (June 9),

Nor was raillery a monopoly of the left. Mallet du Pan's mockery is strikingly similar to that of the *Révolutions de Paris* and of David. The ultra-royalist Montjoie said that the symbolic paraphernalia of the fête showed that "these gentlemen have lost their balance." One social-minded "aristocrat" denounced the procession as "an insult to our misery and to that of the People, on whom it would have been more civic to have spent the money which it must have cost." That other groups were displeased with the expense of the celebration is indicated by Fontenai.[96]

The anticlericalism of this rite of the Revolutionary religion was obvious, and it was the paganism rather than the ostentation of the festival which irritated most reactionaries. Some were content to sneer quietly at the "fête of Saint Simonneau, constitutional martyr." Others, such as Montjoie, saw that the festival was a "veritable cult" which marked the growth of a revolutionary religion. The *Annales de la religion et du sentiment* was even more disturbed by the pagan and idolatrous features of the ritual of the new faith. Thus the Fête of the Law takes on an added significance as an episode in the dechristianization movement. Its promoters expressed their hope of attaching the people to their regime through a new "kind of religious cult so necessary to maintain the force and authority" of the government. Other funeral rites in honor of Simonneau in the departments "were intentionally laic and more or less accompanied by antireligious manifestations."[97]

In Paris this anticlerical demonstration took the form of a municipal decree directed against the Corpus Christi procession.[98] The religious processions of the Catholic Church were too effective in win-

pp. 131–32. The master, with his usual fairness, praised the execution of certain portions of the *décor*.

[96] *Mercure de France*, no. 23 (June 9, 1792), pp. 128; *Ami du roi* (Montjoie), no. 156 (June 4), p. 624. *Folies d'un mois*, 7e mois, no. 4 [n.d.], pp. 2–3. *Journal général* (Fontenai), no. 155 (June 4), p. 631.

[97] *Ami du roi* (Montjoie), no. 156 (June 4, 1792), p. 624; *Rocambole*, no. 20 (June 7), p. 323; *Mercure de France*, no. 23 (June 9), p. 128. Letter of M. Lefebvre d'Arcy to M. Vanderberghe: Vaissière, *op. cit.*, p. 459. Ami du roi (Montjoie), no. 146 (June 4), p. 624. *Annales de la religion et du sentiment*, no. 22 [n.d.] pp. 458–61. Letter of Pitra, *Cor. lit.*, XVI, 145. Cardenal, *La Province*, p. 289.

[98] Text: Robinet, *Le Mouvement religieux à Paris*, II, 203–04; *Annales patriotiques*, no. 157 (June 5, 1792), p. 693 and in *Patriote françois, Courrier extraordinaire, Journal général* (Fontenai), and other journals.

ning proselytes to escape the attention of the leaders of the new order. Some of these wished to deprive the clergy of this potent device for influencing the masses. Manuel, the Municipal agent, inspired by the anticlericalism expressed in the Simonneau rites and reassured by the attitude of the Assembly, had the Paris Commune publish a decree on June 4, discouraging the usual decorations, military escort, and business holiday occasioned by the procession of the Holy Sacrament. The measure was lauded by some and assailed by others, but the celebration took place as usual despite the official restrictions.[99] Far from being the masters of the street, the anticlericals were insulted and beaten for refusing to uncover.[100] As a manifestation of revolutionary religion, then, the Fête of Simonneau, lacking popular support, was unable to prevent the triumph of the Church on June 7, Corpus Christi Day.

For the Constitutional Monarchists, the fête may have been a "triumph of the law," but it is fairly certain that the Paris masses regarded it as a "triumph of the aristocrats—an insult to patriotism." The absence of national and civic symbols was noted with disapprobation, and the people, we are told, supplied this lack by cries of *"vive la nation! vive la liberté!"*[101] On the other hand, Jacobins were insulted or enraged by the presence of counter-revolutionary emblems displayed in the procession.[102] Most offensive of all to the patriots was a painted bas-relief depicting the murder of Simonneau by men armed with pikes. Now the latter weapon was regarded as the characteristic arm of the *sans-culotte*—the veritable symbol of the revolutionary masses. When the news of the uprising reached Paris, it was said that pikemen had participated, but immediately "patriot" eye-

[99] *Tribune des patriotes,* no. 3 (June 15, 1792), pp. 148–50; *Trompette du Père Duchêne,* no. 21 [n.d.], pp. 3–6, through no. 24 [n.d.], p. 3; *Journal général* (Fontenai), no. 157 (June 5), pp. 129–31; *Mercure de France,* no. 23 (June 9), pp. 129–31; *Gazette de Paris* (June 13), pp. 1–2; *Jean Bart, ou je m'en fouts,* no. 32 [n.d], pp. 1–7; Tourzel, *Mémoires,* p. 124.

[100] *Courrier de Gorsas,* no. 9 (June 9, 1792), pp. 128–29, no. 10 (June 10), pp. 137–44.

[101] *Feuille du jour,* no. 167 (June 5, 1792), p. 1246; *Journal de Paris,* no. 155 (June 3), p. 625; *Défenseur de la constitution,* no. 4 [n.d], p. 193. *Thermomètre,* no. 157 (June 5), p. 524; *Mercure universel,* no. 462 (June 4), p. 60.

[102] *Journal des Jacobins,* no. 207 (June 6, 1792), pp. 1–2; *Défenseur de la constitution,* no. 4 [n.d.], p. 190; *Journal de la cour et de la ville,* no. 37 (June 6), p. 291; *Consolateur,* no. 46 (June 8), p. 316; *Feuille du jour,* no. 167 (June 5), p. 1246; *Révolutions de Paris,* no. 152 (June 9), pp. 450–55.

witnesses had denied the allegation.[103] Contemporaries felt that by flaunting such a "slanderous representation" or "lying picture," the promoters of the festival had "insulted the people" and thereby branded themselves as counter-revolutionaries.[104]

Somehow the rumor started that David had executed this bas-relief, and René Schneider's unsupported statement to that effect has been generally accepted as true. The facts are quite different: David published an open letter in the press which settled the matter for his contemporaries and which should clarify the question for modern historians. Not only did he deny having "traced the deceitful bas-relief" or given the "monstrous idea of the allegories which dishonored this funeral celebration," but he roundly abused the promoters of the fête. Quatremère seems to indicate that the bas-relief was by Roland, the sculptor who executed the colossal figure of the law for the same ceremony.[105]

In the eyes of contemporaries, far from being a personal triumph for Simonneau, the celebration was merely the excuse for a "counter-demonstration" by the Feuillants against the Festival of Châteauvieux, a "reprisal" for the Fête of the People. It has since been characterized as "a maneuver of the court and of the counter-revolutionaries who wanted at any price a revenge for the Fête of Liberty."[106] It was also a part of the bitter campaign waged by the Feuillants against the Jacobin Society for control of the latter's network of affiliated clubs, for domination of public opinion, and for direction of the government. This propaganda war eventually ended in a victory for the left-wing Jacobins. In this war the Fête of the Law was of course only one

[103] *Moniteur,* no. 67 (March 7, 1792), p. 263, no. 68 (March 8), pp. 277–78, no. 69 (March 9), p. 281; *Courrier de Gorsas,* no. 9 (June 9), pp. 130–31; *Trompette du Père Duchêne,* no. 21 [n.d.], pp. 1–3.

[104] *Révolutions de Paris,* no. 152 (June 9, 1792), pp. 451, 455. *Trompette du Père Duchêne,* no. 21 [n.d.], pp. 2–3. *Courrier de Gorsas,* no. 9 (June 9), p. 133.

[105] Schneider, *Quatremère de Quincy,* p. 58. Tourneux (*Cor. lit.,* XVI, 141n and *Bibl.,* III, 492), claims on the strength of a note by Meister on "Lettre de Pitra" that David executed the emblems, decorations and bas-relief. Letter of David to Gorsas: *Courrier de Gorsas,* no. 9 (June 9, 1792), pp. 131–32. A. C. Quatremère de Quincy, "Notice historique sur Roland," (1819) (in) *Recueil des notices historiques* (Paris: le Clere, 1834), p. 109.

[106] Camille Desmoulins in *Tribune des patriotes,* no. 2 [n.d.], p. 66. Robespierre in *Défenseur de la constitution,* no. 4 [n.d.], p. 193. Cf. Delaure in *Thermomètre,* no. 157 (June 5, 1792), p. 523. G. Laurent, ed., in *Oeuvres complètes de Robespierre,* (Paris: Alcan, 1939), IV, 119n. Cf. Fantin-Desodoards, *loc. cit.*

battle, but it was lost because the Constitutional Monarchists had not mastered the festival technique.

As has been indicated, aside from purely partisan motives, the organizers of the Simonneau demonstration intended to "teach the people a lesson in respect for the law."[107] To what degree were they successful in impressing the crowd with the sanctity of law and order, or even with the threat of their armed might? Obviously in the light of the "days" of June 20 and August 10 they failed completely. But after all, one may object, does not propaganda have its limitations? An immediate answer came the very next day. In spite of the laws against armed petitioners, fifteen hundred *sans-culottes* with pikes, clubs, sabres, and rifles in their hands came to make demands on the National Assembly. They filed through the legislative meeting place for three-quarters of an hour to the sound of drums, revolutionary songs, tremendous applause, and repeated cries of *"vive la nation! vive la liberté!"* while the lawmakers sat impotent and overwhelmed.[108]

Nor did the authors of the pageant have any illusions as to the effectiveness of their propaganda demonstration. Quatremère said that his neoclassical images "did not produce any great moral effect on the minds of the public." Even the sanguine M. Pitra admitted that "the Fête of the Law . . . is far from being able to repair all the harm they caused by the impious and scandalous farce which they did not fear to honor with the sacred name of Fête of Liberty."[109] Grudgingly the promoters of the Simonneau festival were forced to admit that David had succeeded where they had failed.

Why was David's demonstration crowned with success while that of the Feuillants was ineffective? Both utilized the forms of antiquity to convey their messages. Probably Mallet du Pan put his finger on the answer when he pointed out that at the funeral of Simonneau "the people seemed to ask one another the meaning" of these neoclassic symbols.[110] David, on the contrary, made certain that his allegories were intelligible to his audience. A "man of the people," he under-

[107] Quatremère de Quincy, "Notice historique sur Roland," *op. cit.*, p. 108; Letter of Pitra, *Cor. lit.*, XVI, 145; *Révolutions de Paris*, no. 152 (June 9, 1792), p. 450; *Mercure de France*, no. 23 (June 9), p. 128.

[108] *A.P.*, XLIV, 551; *Thermomètre*, no. 157 (June 5, 1792), p. 524; *Mercure de France*, no. 23 (June 9), pp. 129–30.

[109] "Notice historique sur Roland," p. 108. Letter of Pitra, *Cor. lit.*, XVI, 108.

[110] *Mercure de France*, no. 23 (June 9, 1792), p. 129.

stood the masses, and he had no sympathy for erudite pedants like Quatremère who, in striving for imitation of antiquity, lost contact with the human realities of their own day. David never adopted Quatremère's "magistral and sententious tone which characterizes pedagogues full of conceit."[111]

Instead he learned how to handle crowds on a large scale, a technique which was to become invaluable to him later. As has been shown, he consciously instituted festivals "of the people, by the people, for the people" in the first modern large-scale use of political pageantry. Thus it was to the French Revolutionary precedent established by David that the leaders of the twentieth-century revolutionists could turn when they were confronted with a problem similar to his, namely, the inculcation of the masses with the ideology of a new regime.

[111] *Révolutions de Paris,* no. 152 (June 9, 1792), p. 450.

CHAPTER IV

An Artist Serves The Republic

The destruction of the Bourbon monarchy by the insurrection of the people on August 10, 1792, produced a spontaneous attack upon the symbols of the old order. Everywhere emblems of royalty were torn down and the images of kings were overthrown. The movement was not entirely, or even primarily, vandalistic in nature. In the minds of the revolutionists the great bronze statues of Louis XIV in the Place Vendôme and of Henry IV on the Pont Neuf, for example, breathed the spirit of despotic government. Desirable though they might be from the point of view of art, as royalist propaganda they must be destroyed. The artists rallied to the new regime, and counter-revolutionary representations were replaced by republican symbols and *sans-culottes* monuments. Under the First Republic a statue of Le Peletier Saint-Fargeau, revolutionary martyr, was planned for the site of the monument to Louis XIV,[1] and another colossal statue symbolizing "The French People" was projected for the Pont Neuf.[2] Both were undertaken at the initiative of David and both gave rise to contests which aided the artists of the time.

David expressed the purpose of such propaganda art projects when he proposed the Pont Neuf monument. This colossus, he said, was to be erected on the fragments of the statues of the kings so as to "transmit to posterity . . . the triumph of the French people over despotism and superstition." It was to be cast from captured cannon so that

[1] Proposed by David on January 25, 1793: *Procès-verbal de la Convention* [Paris: Imp. nat., 1793], V, 403 (hereafter cited as *P.V. Conv.*); *Col. Baud.* XXVII, 99; *L'Auditeur national,* II, no. 127 (January 26, 1793) , p. 4; *Bulletin des Amis de la vérité,* no. 27 (January 26) , p. 1; *Journal des amis* (Fauchet) , I, no. 5 (February 2), p. 224; *Journal de France,* no. 154 (February 23), p. 1; *Courier de l'égalité*, III, no. 161 (January 26), p. 29; *Le Défenseur de vérité*, no. 5 (February 2), p. 78.

[2] Proposed by David 17 Brumaire, an II [November 7, 1793]: *J.D.D.*, no. 415 [n.d.], p. 243; *Révolutions de Paris*, XVII, no. 217 (18 Frimaire) , pp. 288–89; *Journal de l'instruction publique,* IV, no. 19 [n.d.], pp. 74–75; *Moniteur,* no. 49 (November 9) , p. 200; *Auditeur national,* no. 412 (November 8) , p. 6; *Mercure universal* (18 Brumaire), p. 125; *Discours prononcé . . . 17 Brumaire* . . . [Paris: Imp. nat., 1793].

"victory will furnish the bronze," he declared.[3] He further developed his concept of the role of the revolutionary artists when he presented a painting of Le Peletier to the Convention:

> Each of us is accountable to the fatherland for the talents which he has received from nature; if the form is different, the end ought to be the same for all. The true patriot ought to seize with avidity every means of enlightening his fellow citizens, and of presenting ceaselessly to their eyes the sublime traits of heroism and of virtue . . . . Citizens, the Supreme Being who shared his gifts among all his children wishes that I express my thought by the organ of painting. . . .[4]

He would be satisfied, he continued, if the children of future generations would be inspired to emulate Le Peletier, to "fight or die" for the principles of the Revolution.[5]

On another occasion he declared:

> The arts . . . . ought to help to extend the progress of the human spirit, to propagate and to transmit to posterity the striking examples of the efforts of an immense people, [who], guided by reason and philosophy, are bringing forth on earth the reign of liberty, equality, and the law. The arts then ought to contribute powerfully to public instruction. [They] are the imitation of nature in its most beautiful and its most perfect aspects; a sentiment natural to man attracts him toward the same object. It is not only by charming the eyes that the monuments of art have fulfilled this end; it is by penetrating the soul, it is by making on the mind a profound impression, similar to reality. It is thus that the traits of heroism, of civic virtues offered to the regard of the people will electrify its soul, and will cause to germinate in it, all the passions of glory, of devotion to the welfare of the fatherland.[6]

Thus during the era of the Revolution the philosophical concept of the relation of art to the state and society was developed to its

[3] Report of 27 Brumaire, an II: *P.V. Conv.*, XXV, 287. *See* p. 131 note 12.

[4] *See* pp. 101–102.

[5] March 29, 1793: *P.V. Conv.*, VIII, 344–46; *Moniteur*, no. 90 (March 31, 1793), p. 400; *Journal de France*, no. 189 (March 30), pp. 2–3. *Annales patriotiques*, (April 6), p. 81; *Bulletin des Amis de la vérité*, no. 90 (March 30), p. 1; J. L. David, *Discours prononcé à la Convention nationale le 29 Mars 1793 . . . en offrant un tableau de sa composition représentant Michel Lepelletier* [*sic*] *au lit de mort* [Paris: Imp. nat., 1793].

[6] November 15, 1793: *P.V. Conv.*, XXV, 233, 241; *Moniteur*, no. 57 (27 Brumaire), p. 231; *Journal de l'instruction publique*, IV, no. 21 [n.d.], pp. 232–37; J. Guillaume, ed., *Procès-verbaux du Comité d'instruction publique de la Convention nationale* (Paris: Imp. nat., 1891), II, 830–31 (hereafter cited as *C.I.P.*).

logical conclusion. Thinkers and legislators agreed in effect that the arts were not merely the "ornaments" of the social structure but on the contrary were "parts of its bases." They were regarded as one of the most powerful means of attaching the people to the state by satisfying their spiritual needs, educating them, enriching their lives, and by stimulating their patriotism and encouraging a love of liberty. The contemporary political situation, the current cult of antiquity, and the philosophical speculation of the eighteenth century, all contributed to the development of the theory of a democratic, moralizing art which would serve as an auxiliary to the legislators.[7]

The idea that art might be used by the state as a means of arousing feeling favorable to the regime had been familiar to the French monarchy at least since the reign of Louis XIV. Count Angiviller's efforts to make the fine arts "an emanation of the throne" have already been mentioned.[8] It is worth noticing that in the critical days before the fateful "day" of August 10, the King was instructing Academic artists to paint subjects of French history for the Salon of 1793.[9] Charles Le Brun (1619–1690), first painter of the "Sun King," had already demonstrated that such propaganda in order to be effective, must be organized into a kind of dictatorship. Since his time the government had exercised control through the monopolistic Royal Academy.[10] The opinion that historical painting was superior to all other branches of the art had been firmly established. All these ideas, then, which became the weapons of the Revolution were bequeathed to it by the old regime, but they were to receive an extraordinary extension at the hands of David.

The concept of the political and social importance of the arts was inherent in the doctrines of the German aesthetician Winckelmann.[11] In classical antiquity there had been an organic relationship between the fine arts, government, and the life of the people. Greece and, to a lesser extent, Rome furnished admirable examples for the eighteenth

[7] For a clear, contemporary formulation of the theory, see *Décade philosophique,* I, no. 7 (10 Messidor [an II]), pp. 401–411. Cf. *Journal de l'instruction publique,* VII, no. 34 [n.d.], pp. 32–50.

[8] *See* pp. 3–4.

[9] List of artists chosen by His Majesty, May 7, 1792: Engerand, *Inventaire,* pp. xxxiv–xxxv.

[10] *See* pp. 3, 28.

[11] *Gedanken über die Nachahmung der griechischen Werke in der Malerei und Bildhauerkunst* (Dresden: Walthy, 1755) *passim. See* pp. 5, 8, 10–11.

century legislator. Just as classical antecedents helped to mold their constitutional, educational, social, and economic reforms, so, too, the cult of antiquity helped to shape their propaganda program.

Among the *philosophes* the belief was current that art had a social significance and should serve to spread a civic philosophy. Like the aestheticians, they pointed to Greek and Roman precedents, particularly in connection with the use of the fine arts as propaganda.

In *L'Esprit des Lois,* Montesquieu had called attention to the universal belief of the Greeks regarding the power and influence of music and its essential position in the state.[12] Voltaire repeatedly stressed the importance of the fine arts to the state and to the individual.[13] He was aware of the use to which they could be put by an absolute government, for he placed in the mouth of Genghis Khan the words: "[The arts] occupy the people and render them more docile." [14] On the other hand, he maintained that "the culture of the arts always renders souls more honest and more pure." [15] He denied that they were prejudicial to morality and insisted that they tamed the manners even of "tyrants." On the eve of David's departure for Rome the Patriarch of Ferney complained of the decadence of the arts and wailed, "Adieux to the arts in our century . . . the great days of France are passed." "The good times are gone, the best wine is drunk." [16] If he had been granted another decade of life to witness the triumph of David's revolutionary *Horatii* and *Brutus,* which restored French artistic supremacy, he might perhaps have taken heart.

Even Rousseau, who attacked the arts as demoralizing, depicted in glowing colors the political and social utility of festivals. After criticizing the theater in his *Lettre à d'Alembert sur les spectacles* (1758), he continues:

> What! Must there be no spectacles in a Republic? On the contrary, there must be many. It is in the Republic that they are born, it is in its bosom that one sees them sparkle, with a veritable air of fête. . . . It is in the open air, it is beneath the sky that you must assemble and give yourself up to the sweet senti-

[12] Book IV, Chap. VIII (n. ed.; Geneva: Barrillot, 1749), II, 87.

[13] *Oeuvres complètes,* ed. Moland (Paris: Garnier, 1877), II, 544–45, III, 373.

[14] *Ibid.,* V, 320. "L'Orphelin de la Chine," Act II, scene v. These lines were at first suppressed by the royal censor.

[15] *Oeuvres complètes,* IV, 490. "Les Guèbres ou la tolérance," Preface.

[16] Letter to M. Bordes, Ferney, July 14 [1773]: *ibid,* XLVIII, 416–17. Letter to Count Touraille, July 5, 1774: *ibid.,* XLIX, 26.

> ment of your happiness. . . . But what will be the objects of these spectacles? What will one demonstrate there? Anything if one wishes. Plant a stake crowned with flowers in the middle of a market place, assemble the people there, and you will have a fête.[17]

The author of the *Social Contract* invoked the republican festivals of antiquity, particularly those of Sparta, as models for uplifting public and private morals. He advocated similar celebrations aimed at "the preservation of the peace and the prosperity of the Republic." They were necessary, he believed, to make the people love the state and to assure the maintenance of order and the public peace.[18]

In his *Considération sur le gouvernement de Pologne et sa réformation* (1772), Rousseau developed even further his ideas on the essential role of festivals and public games in which "all the people take part equally as with the ancients." National festivals were to make the Poles love their motherland and revive its ancient greatness.[19]

Diderot's predilection for propaganda art is well known. The true role of the artist in society, declared the Encyclopedist, was to inculcate morality. It was the duty of the artist, he insisted, " . . . to celebrate, to eternalize, great and noble actions, to honor virtue, . . . to stigmatize vice, to terrify tyrants; [to become] the preceptors of the human race . . . the avengers of crime, the rewarders of virtue," in a word, "to make us love virtue and hate vice." [20] To satisfy Diderot's requirements, an artist must depict the superb as well as the sentimental. He must study nature and antiquity and become a portraitist and painter of history capable of profoundly moving his audience.[21] So, though he admired the sentimental, moralizing canvases of Greuze, Diderot recognized the weaknesses of this artist, and reserved his praise for David when the latter exhibited at the Salon of 1781.[22] In truth, the young master seemed to be the answer to the philosopher's prayers, for David

[17] *Oeuvres complètes*, ed. Musset-Pathay (Paris: Dupont, 1824), II, 175–76. During the Revolution this passage was quoted with enthusiasm: e.g., J. A. Borrelly in *Journal de l'instruction publique*, VII, no. 34 [n.d.], pp. 58–59.

[18] *Oeuvres complètes*, II, 186–89, 183–84, 176–77.

[19] *Oeuvres complètes*, V, 263, 264.

[20] "Essai sur la peinture" (1765), (in) *Oeuvres complètes*, ed. Assézat (Paris: Garnier, 1876), X, 502–04. Cf. "De la poésie dramatique" (1758), *ibid.*, VII, 313.

[21] "Essai sur la peinture," *ibid.*, X, 152–53, 484, 504–07; "Salon de 1765," *ibid.*, p. 418.

[22] "Salon de 1761," *ibid.*, X, 141, 151–56. *Ibid.*, p. 101; "Salon de 1769," *ibid.*, XI, 438–45. "Salon de 1781," *ibid.*, XII; 63–64.

was a painter of history who studied nature as well as the antique and was one of the greatest of portrait painters. Above all, he had an unshakeable belief in the propaganda mission of the artist. He agreed with Diderot that his talents must be used to mold public opinion.

With such ideas of the philosophers before them, and with three-quarters of the French population illiterate, the revolutionists could not fail to make use of propaganda art and particularly of that "most living art of the Revolution,"[23] the civic festival, as a means of social control. It was characteristic that Mirabeau should recommend that David's *Oath of the Tennis Court* be executed at national expense and should insist that "it is the duty of the fatherland to encourage the arts, especially when they consecrate themselves to the fatherland." "Man," he declared on another occasion, "obeys his impressions rather than his reason. It is not enough to show him the truth; the important point is to rouse his passion for it." More specifically he believed this could be done through a system of public festivals.[24] Mirabeau's demand for national festivals had been anticipated by proposals in the *cahiers de doléance* of 1789 and the ideas of Sieyès. A provision for *fêtes nationales* for the purpose of unification of public opinion was written into the Constitution of 1791 by unanimous vote and was eventually incorporated in the educational plans of Talleyrand, Lakanal, Lequinio, M.-J. Chénier, and others.[25]

Like most of their fellow "patriots," Danton and Robespierre believed that the arts were essential weapons of the new regime. Danton, who had supported the festival in honor of the Swiss of Châteauvieux,

[23] J. Renouvier, *Histoire de l'art pendant la révolution* (Paris: Renouard, 1863), p. 416.

[24] *See*, p. 37. *Courrier de Provence*, XVII, no. 367 [n.d.], p. 224. *A.P.*, XXX, 526–33. *Travail sur l'éducation publique*, ed. Cabanis (Paris: Imp. nat., 1791), pp. 74–107. Cf. H. Monin, "Le discours de Mirabeau sur les fêtes nationales," *R.F.*, XXV (July, 1893), 214–31.

[25] B. F. Hyslop, *French nationalism in 1789 according to the general cahiers* (New York: Columbia University Press, 1934), pp. 178–83; *A.P.*, V, 273. *A.P.*, VIII, 426–27; cf. A. C. Duquesnoy, *Journal* (Paris: Picard, 1894), II, 495; E. Dumont, *Souvenirs* (Paris: Gosselin, 1832), p. 199. *A.P.*, XXX, 153; *Col. Baud.*, XVIII, 10. C. M. Talleyrand-Périgord, *Rapport sur l'instruction publique* [Paris: Imp. nat., 1791], pp. 109–10; *P.V. Nat.*, LXX, 11, 15, 106 ff. *Moniteur*, no. 180 (June 29, 1793), p. 506; *Journal des débats et de la correspondance de la Société des Jacobins*, no. 443 (July 31, 1793), pp. 1–2. *P.V. Conv.*, XV, 68; *C.I.P.*, 541–49, 556. M.-J. Chénier, *Oeuvres*, ed. Robert (Paris: Guillaume, 1826), V, 120–21, 130; *P.V. Conv.*, XXIV, 331; *Journal de l'instruction publique*, IV, no. 22 [n.d.], pp. 309, 317.

insisted that "in order to inspire the love of liberty and the fatherland, the entire people ought to celebrate . . . the great deeds of the Revolution . . . national games . . . [and] festivals of the . . . Supreme Being . . . Give arms to those who can bear them, education to the young, and *fêtes nationales* to the people." [26] As has already been pointed out, Robespierre attacked the use of festivals by the opposition and insisted that they must be employed "to mold the souls of citizens in the ways of virtue, that is to say, in the love of the fatherland and of liberty." [27] "The Incorruptible" finally came to the conclusion that it was essential that the government not only control but also create public opinion by the use of all available propaganda techniques.[28] When Robespierre and his colleagues actually attempted to establish their ideal "Republic of Virtue" during the Terror, it was announced by the Committee of Public Safety that "with a people who are regenerating themselves" the fine arts as well as other agencies must be used for "purifying hearts [and] propagating republican sentiments."[29] The culmination of this policy was the Festival of the Supreme Being, organized, designed, and directed by the painter of *Brutus* and the *Horatii*.[30]

Thus the political leaders turned to David. This patriotic artist had already demonstrated his proficiency in the use of art as propa-

[26] November 26, 1793: *Moniteur,* no. 68 (8 Frimaire, II), p. 276; *Journal de l'instruction publique,* no. 24 [n.d.], pp. 60–63.

[27] *See* p. 68. *Défenseur de la constitution,* no. 4 [n.d.], p. 180.

[28] M.M.I. de Robespierre, "Carnet," ed. Mathiez, *Annales Révolutionnaires,* (hereafter cited as *A.R.*) X (January, 1918), 13; A. Cobban, "The Political Ideas of Maximilien Robespierre during the Period of the Convention," *English Historical Review,* LXI, (January, 1946), 62–63.

[29] J.N. Billaud-Varenne, *Rapport fait à la Convention, premier floréal l'an II . . . sur la théorie du gouvernement démocratique . . . et sur la nécessité d'inspirer l'amour des vertus civiles par les fêtes publiques et des institutions morales* [Paris: Imp. nat., 1794], p. 19.

[30] *See* pp. 121–23. Robespierre, *Rapport . . . sur les rapports des idées religieuses et morales avec les principes républicaines, et sur les fêtes nationales . . . 18 floréal l'an II . . .* [Paris: Imp. nat., 1794]; J.L. David, *Plan de la fête de l'Etre-suprême qui doit être célébrée le 20 prairial . . .* [Paris: Imp. nat., 1794]. Compare the theories of François Lanthenas (e.g., *Bases fondamentales de l'instruction publique . . .* [Paris: Cercle Social, 1793]; *Déclaration des devoirs de l'homme des principes et de la morale universel* [Paris: Cercle Social, 1793], pp. 1–3) and C.F. Volney (*La Loi naturelle, ou Catéchisme du citroyen français,* ed. Gaston-Martin [Paris: Colin, 1934], pp. 104–05.)

ganda by his painting, mobilization of the artists behind the new regime, and masterly handling of the civic festivals. After the storming of the Tuileries, he had been chosen elector by the *Section du Louvre.*[31] The Jacobins proposed him for a seat in the National Convention as "the most patriotic and talented of artists;" Marat personally recommended him, and Danton favored him as a candidate.[32] On September 17 he was elected by an overwhelming majority as deputy of Paris to the body which was to defend and govern France, draft a new constitution, and mobilize public opinion behind the Republic. [33]

When the National Convention held its first meeting on September 21, 1792, David sat among the *Montagnards* with his friends Marat, Danton, Robespierre, Collot d'Herbois, Dubois-Crancé, and other Jacobins associated with his previous propaganda projects. Because of his earlier career, he entered the legislative body as the leader of his profession, noted for his advanced views, and closely linked with the leaders of the Revolution. As a member of the government, David led a rather stormy career; but, having no political ambitions of his own, he was content to follow the lead of such men as Marat and Robespierre. Except when the arts were in question he rarely took part in the debates in the Convention, but occasionally he indulged his excitable temperament in violent exclamations and melodramatic scenes which gained for him the name of "ferocious terrorist." [34]

[31] E. Charavay, ed., *Assemblée électorale de Paris,* III, 15. The *Section du Louvre* met in the parish church, Saint-Germain-l'Auxerrois, where David had been baptized and married (*see,* pp. 7, 15): E. Mellié, *Les Sections de Paris* (Paris: Société de l'histoire de la révolution, 1898), p. 26.

[32] Charavay, *op. cit.,* III, xli, 607.

[33] He obtained 450 votes out of 583: Charavay, *op. cit.,* III, 160.

[34] Mercier, *Le Nouveau Paris,* VI, 188; *Histoire de la révolution . . . par deux amis de la liberté,* XII, 135n; Baron Frénilly, *Souvenirs* (n. ed.; Paris: Plon-Nourrit, 1909), p. 182; [Baron Coiffier de Moret], *Dictionnaire biographique* (London, 1800), I, 388–89; H. R. Yorke, *France in 1802, Letters,* (London: Heinemann, 1906), pp. 126–27; Sir J. Carr, *The Stranger in France,* p. 110; [Viscount Conny de la Fay], *La France sous le règne de la Convention* (3. ed.; Paris: Dentu, 1824), p. 9; F. X. Pagès, *Histoire secrète de la révolution* (2. ed., Paris: Dentu, 1800), II, 215; [Stewarton], *The Revolutionary Plutarch* (London: Murray, 1804), I, 363–70; [Hughes], *Biographical Sketches* (London: Hughes, 1804), p. 66; Mme M. Tussaud, *Memoirs* (Philadelphia: Lea & Blanchard, 1839), II, 36; M. C. de Pougens, *Mémoires* (Paris: Fournier, 1834), pp. 58–59; Millingen, *Recollections,* pp. 106–07; J.B.M. Robert, *Vie politique de tous les députés à la Convention* (Paris: St. Michel, 1814), pp. 90–91. *See* the Bibliographical Essay, p. 143ff.

At the trial of Louis XVI, the painter of Brutus voted for death without delay or appeal.[35] He appears to have followed the dictates of his conscience, and, though it separated him from his wife and led eventually to ignominy and exile, David never expressed regret for the regicidal act.[36] Much of the odium heaped upon David for his vote stems from the common though mistaken belief that he had painted or intended to paint the King's portrait.[37]

In the struggle with the Girondins, David consistently voted with the Mountain, and the artist showed himself a warm partisan of Marat and Robespierre. On April 12, 1793, when the Friend of the People was attacked by the Girondins, David rushed into the middle of the hall, and, baring his breast, he cried, "Strike here—I demand my own assassination; I, too, am a virtuous man! Liberty will triumph." Next day he led the defense of Marat against his denunciators. Five weeks later David tooks the offensive against the Brissotin group by bitterly assailing Vergniaud on the floor of the Convention. Shortly after, the Jacobin artist is supposed to have been one of the instigators of the insurrection of May 31 which resulted in the fall of the Girondins.[38]

Whenever opposition to the new Jacobin regime appeared, David helped to crush it relentlessly. Despite the unreliable nature of the evidence, the artist is even accused of helping to rush his old friend Danton to the guillotine.[39] Well known as one of Robespierre's most

[35] *Appels nominaux . . . sur . . . Louis Capet* [Paris: Imp. nat., 1793], pp. 23, 51, 60. There is an interesting engraving of 1797 of the King's trial showing David seated in the midst of his Jacobin associates: [J. Adolphus], *Biographical Anecdotes* (London: Phillips, 1797), frontispiece. Monnel says that David cried, "L'appel! l'appel nominal! se soir—à l'heur même—non, l'échafaud:" *Mémoires d'un prêtre régicide,* I, 330.

[36] Delécluze, p. 175; David, p. 113; Letter of Redhead Yorke, Paris, 1802: *France in 1802,* p. 125; Coiffier de Moret, *op. cit.,* p. 388.

[37] *See* pp. 49, 57.

[38] *Le Républicain français,* no. 150 (April 14, 1793), p. 607; *J.D.D.,* no. 207 [n.d.], p. 202; *Moniteur,* no. 104 (April 14), p. 465. April 13: *Journal de Perlet,* no. 205 (April 14), p. 109; *Appel nominal . . . du 13 au 14 avril 1793 . . . sur la question: y-t-il lieu d'accusation contre Marat . . .* [Paris: Imp. nat., 1793], p. 9. May 20: *Moniteur,* no. 142 (May 22), p. 616. Conny de la Fay, *op. cit.,* p. 152; [G.J. Senar], *Révélations pris dans les cartons des comités . . . ou mémoires (inédites) de Sénart* (Paris: Tastu, 1824), p. 64.

[39] The accusation is based on the extremely untrustworthy testimony of "Fabricius" and Dufourny at the trial of Fouquier-Tinville: L. Lecointre, *Les Crimes des sept membres des anciens comités . . .* (Paris: Maret, 1794), p. 111; E. B. Cour-

fervent supporters and closest friends, David finally hopelessly compromised himself by offering to "drink the hemlock" with "the Incorruptible" at the Jacobin Club on 8 Thermidor.[40] The following day the painter did not appear at the Convention and so missed the famous proscription. Baudot reports that Barère had shattered David's faith in his idol by showing him a letter which linked Robespierre with British agents.[41] Nevertheless, there is evidence that David, despite a momentary loss of nerve at the fall of Robespierre and a short-lived enthusiasm for Bonaparte, remained loyal to the principles of the Revolution for the rest of his life.[42]

Because of his loyalty, David was appointed to the Committee of General Security on September 14, 1793, when it was reorganized in such a manner as to give control to the Committee of Public Safety.[43] The artist was commonly regarded as Robespierre's spy on the police committee, and his activities as a member of this dreaded security organization earned him the undying hatred of the enemies of the Republic.[44] David served as Associate Commissioner for Navy and

tois, *Rapport fait . . . sur les événements du 9 thermidor . . .* [Paris: Imp. nat., 1796], p. 36; *Procès de Fouquier-Tinville,* no. 26 [n.d.], pp. 1–2; [J. F. E.] Robinet, *Le Procès des Dantonistes . . . documents* (Paris: Leroux, 1879), pp. 593, 595. On the invalidity of this evidence, *see* J. L. Godfrey, *The Organization, Procedure and Personnel of the French Revolutionary Tribunal* (unpublished Ph.D. thesis, University of Chicago, 1942), p. 129. Courtois later gave quite a different version in his "Notes et souvenirs," *R. F.,* XII (1887), 819–20.

[40] Baudot (*Notes historiques,* pp. 14, 185) says that David first offered to die with Robespierre when the dictatorship he favored was proposed two months before Thermidor.

[41] Baudot, *op. cit.,* p. 14. Cf. B. Barère, *Mémoires* (Paris: Labitte, 1842), II, 226–32.

[42] For David's temporary conversion to Bonapartism, *see* Delécluze (*op. cit.,* p. 234). Baudot (*op. cit.,* pp. 158, 294) insists upon the firmness of the artist's Jacobin convictions. According to many, including the Englishman Yorke (*Paris in 1802,* pp. 126–27), David bitterly regretted the passing of the Republic. The anecdote in *Mémoires d'un prêtre régicide* (I, 224–25), though rendered suspect by the source, perhaps indicates David's real attitude.

[43] *P.V. Conv.,* XX, 364–65; *Moniteur,* no. 259 (September 16, 1793), p. 1100; *A.P.,* LXXIV, 109. G. Belloni, *Le Comité de sûreté générale* (Paris: Arnette, 1924), pp. 51–52.

[44] Senar, *Mémoires,* pp. 139–40, 146; [H. M. Williams], *Letters containing a sketch of the politics of France from 28th of July to the establishment of the Constitution in 1795* (London: Robinson, 1796), III, 155; [Monnel], *Mémoires,* II, 147; L. M. Prudhomme, *Histoire générale et impartiale . . .* [Paris: Rue de Marais, 1797], V, 114.

Colonies, but it was as a dominant member of the Committee of Public Instruction that he played his most active and significant role—that of propagandist of the Revolution.[45] For his achievements in this field his colleagues honored him with the presidency of the Jacobin Club and elected him as secretary and later as president of the Convention.[46]

Nevertheless, it is as an artist rather than as a politician that David deserves to be remembered. His desire to free art from the shackles of the old regime and to revive the republican and artistic splendors of an idealized Greece and Rome encouraged him to mingle in the fray. A large tumor which disfigured his right cheek also produced an impediment in his speech,[47] and the resulting lack of oratorical ability effectively prevented his attaining any considerable parliamentary influence. Moreover, he appears to have had neither the inclination nor the temperament for party leadership. Therefore, he left to others the political measures designed to establish the "Republic of Virtue" and concentrated upon the essential role which the fine arts should play in creating and maintaining this regenerated society. From the tribune of the Convention he expressed in passionate terms his belief that neoclassic art should be employed by the state to glorify the events and principles of the Revolution, thereby indoctrinating the populace with Jacobin virtues, and that it should be encouraged and controlled to this end.

It was primarily on the basis of the political and social utility of the arts as propaganda that David was able to safeguard works of art and to advance the interests of the artists in the midst of war and insurrection. Moreover, though the Revolution menaced art because of

[45] David was appointed to the Executive Commission for Navy and Colonies, April 18, 1794: *P.V. Conv.,* XXXV, 317. He was named as one of the original members of the C.P.I., October 13, 1793: *P.V. Conv.,* I, 384; *C.I.P.,* I, iii–iv.

[46] June 16, 1793: Aulard, *Jacobins,* V, 262. July 25, 1793: *P.V. Conv.,* XVII, 243. January 5, 1794: *P.V. Conv.,* XXVIII, 339; *Moniteur,* no. 108 (16 Messidor), p. 435; *Journal de France,* no. 470 (18 Nivôse), p. 1.

[47] Baron Barante, *Souvenirs* (Paris: Lévy, 1890), I, 131n; [Adolphus], *Biographical anecdotes,* p. 337; *Biographical Sketches,* p. 71; *Biographie moderne,* II, 32; Mercier, *Nouveau Paris,* VI, 188; Tussaud, *Mémoirs,* II, 35–36; Delécluze, p. 29; Miette de Villars, p. 38; [Baron Lamothe-Langon], *Histoire pittoresque de la Convention* (Paris: Ménard, 1833), I, 292–93; Millingen, *Recollections,* p. 106. The best known likeness of David is the self portrait he painted in prison in 1794, now in the Louvre: Catalogue no. 202 (32″ high by 25″ wide) *Peint. Louvre,* I, pt. 1, p. 67. Reproduced as frontispiece of this study.

its traditional royalist and clerical character, David, by his reputation as a "liberal" and his political position, was able to give it "a brevet of civism." Contrary to libelous legends which are still current, he really did champion the cause of his fellow artists. The younger men who espoused his artistic principles and political ideals were the special objects of his protective and helpful solicitude. David induced the Minister of the Interior, Roland, to provide studios for his pupils. As deputy of the Convention he secured the release of the "patriotic" artists, Rater and Chinard, who were held by the Roman Inquisition; obtained indemnities and pensions for the pupils of the French School at Rome when they were driven out by riots; and otherwise aided and protected the interests of artists.[48]

David was accused of using his political power for the vindictive persecution of his fellow craftsmen. Stories were circulated by royalist sympathizers that David had artists condemned to prison and the guillotine because of personal jealousy. While it appears that he may have refused to use his influence to save the relatives of various painters, there is absolutely no evidence that he harried artists for other than purely political reasons.[49] He had already condemned decadent rococo art and doomed the Academy to destruction, but he protected the aged master of the one, Fragonard, and the director of the other, Vien.[50] On the other hand, David demanded the death penalty for artists who produced royalist propaganda and denounced émigré painters who disseminated monarchist ideas.[51] If he actually condemned artists as unpatriotic as the journalist Mercier alleged, he

[48] David to Roland, October 16, 1792: C. Perroud, "Deux Lettres de David," *R.F.*, XXXVIII (1900), 359–60; Roland to David, October 17: *ibid.*, pp. 361–62; David to Roland, October 24: *ibid.*, pp. 364–66. Topino-Le Brun to David, October 31, 1792, read by David to the Convention November 21, 1792: *A.P.*, LIII, 500–1. Decree of February 2, 1793: *P.V. Conv.*, VI, 24; *Col. Baud.*, XXVII, 142. Report of David, February 4: *P.V. Conv.*, VI, 52. Decree of July 1, 1793: *P.V. Conv.*, XV, 24; *Col. Baud.*, XXXII, 7.

[49] Mme. Le Brun, *Souvenirs*, II, 267. She herself indicates the political basis of David's hostility (II, 265–66) and later recalls his artistic justice. Thibaudeau (I, 75) and Meyer (II, 208) flatly deny the accusation.

[50] David got Fragonard a better studio in the Louvre (David to Roland, October 24, 1792: Perroud, p. 364); had him named to the Jury of the Arts, November 15, 1793 (*P.V. Conv.*, XXV, 238, 41; *J.D.D.*, no. 423 [n.d.], p. 343); and to the Conservatory of the Museum, January 16, 1794 (*P.V. Conv.*, XXIX, 278–80).

[51] Decree of March 29, 1793 and motion of David: *A.P.*, LX, 699; *Col. Baud.*, XXVIII, 543.

referred only to the aristocratic brethren of the Academy.[52] While he excoriated the latter for holding to the old regime, he helped the younger artists in every way. Hence arises the confusion as to his attitude toward his fellow painters.

Equally ill-founded is the reputation of the revolutionary leaders for vandalism. Actually David shared with these men the credit for preserving from mutilation and destruction many of the art monuments of France, even those bearing the symbols of feudalism and royalty.[53] As a member of the Commission of Monuments and its successor, the Temporary Commission of the Arts, he assisted in their great work of safeguarding the art treasures of the nation.[54]

Most of the artists of the day followed the lead of David and placed their talents at the disposal of the Revolution. Their task was not the creation of a new style: neoclassicism had already emerged as a revolutionary art.[55] Rather, they had to use their art in the formulation of new patriotic attitudes. Not only did visual expression have to be found for the new concepts of *liberté, égalité, fraternité* and *patrie,* but the artists had to impress these ideas upon their compatriots. Thus they faced an essentially dualistic problem: freedom and utility.[56]

David's destruction of the old academic limitations, restrictions, and inequalities had given the artists freedom of individual artistic expression. Freedom implied emancipation from restraint in order to develop a personal art, but carried with it the obligation of placing their talent at the service of the Republic. As has been shown, the utility of art lay in its capacity as a social weapon, namely, to teach revolutionary morality and to inculcate republican ideology. Though the Revolution threatened their material welfare, the majority of the artists followed David and threw in their lot with the new order. They were ready, like their leader, to sacrifice economic security in the name

[52] *Le Nouveau Paris,* II, 97. He says David cried that they "could shoot down the artists without fear of killing a single patriot."

[53] Eugène Despois' epoch making work *Le vandalisme révolutionnaire . . . ,* (Paris: Baillière, 1868) conclusively destroyed this hoary legend. *P.V. Conv.,* IX, 243, XIII, 104, XV, 115, XXIV, 69, 179.

[54] *Procès-verbaux de la Commission des Monuments,* I, 100, 102, 129, 143, 150, 212. L. Tuetey, ed., *Procès-verbaux de la Commission temporaire des arts* (Paris: Imp. nat., 1912), I, 97, 570.

[55] *See* pp. 20–23.

[56] Cf. P. Trahard, *La Sensibilité révolutionnaire, 1789–1794* (Paris: Boivin, 1932), p. 232; Brown, *Painting of the French Revolution,* p. 69.

of moral idealism, and were prepared to utilize their freedom of artistic expression in the cause of revolutionary propaganda.[57]

David's greatest contribution to the Revolution was as a propagandist. Like most great artists, he seems to have been rather closely in tune with the spirit of the times, and he was acutely conscious of the trend of public opinion. France in 1793 desperately needed a man who could unify public opinion in support of the government, for the country was in the throes of a terrific struggle against enemies within and without. Popular support was essential, since the destiny of France lay ultimately with the people. The Committee of Public Safety intended that public opinion should be molded in the patterns which they established. To this end they embarked upon a policy of subvention and censorship of the newspaper press, the theater, and literature in general. But, above all, they turned their attention to the graphic arts in order to influence the public mind.[58] Since they believed that it was essential to control all means of artistic expression, they called on David to establish a "dictatorship of the arts," similar to that exercised by Le Brun under Louis XIV.[59]

Logically, the first step in the establishment of such a regime was the complete destruction of the old Royal Academy of Painting and Sculpture, and the creation of a new organization for the achievement of its work under the control of a fanatically loyal Jacobin, such as David. Complete reorganization or suppression had been this artist's aim since leading the dissident Academicians,[60] and now, after his election to the Convention, he possessed the political power required to carry out his project. The campaign began on November 11, 1792, with the presentation to the Convention of a petition of "free artists" for the suppression of the Academy of Painting and Sculpture. David thereupon laid on the table his patent as a member of "this aristocratic body" and urged immediate dissolution of the Academy. The proposal

[57] For the artists' own justification, *see* the preface of the *Livret* of the Salon of 1793: *Description des ouvrages . . . exposées au Sallon* [*sic*] *du Louvre . . . 10 août 1793* [Paris: Imp. nat., 1793], pp. i–ii.

[58] F. A. Aulard, "L'art et la politique en l'an II," in his *Etudes et leçons sur la révolution française* (Paris: Alcan, 1893), ser. 1, p. 243 (hereafter cited as *Etudes*); R.R. Palmer, *Twelve Who Ruled* (Princeton: Princeton University Press, 1941), pp. 317–19; J.M. Thompson, *Robespierre* (Oxford: Blackwell, 1935), II, 85–88; Cobban, "Political Ideas of Robespierre," *op. cit.*, pp. 60–73.

[59] *See* p. 80.

[60] *See* pp. 29–33.

was sent to the Committee of Public Instruction. Later that month the royal group elected David's enemy, "that horrible aristocrat" Suvée, as Director of the French School at Rome. On November 25 David scored a personal victory when the Convention abolished the Directorate and suspended nominations to the Academy in preparation for suppression.[61]

For the time being the Academy continued to exist by default. The King's trial, war and revolts, and the struggle for power occupied the stage. Eventually, however, official opposition to the royal corporation, apparent since the establishment of the Republic and kept alive by continuous attacks by independent artists, was renewed after the fall of the Girondins and the establishment of the dictatorship of the Mountain. A request of the Minister of Public Contributions that the Convention clarify the anomolous position of the Academy of Painting and Sculpture precipitated an investigation by the Committee of Public Instruction on July 1, 1793. The Convention gave official sanction to the Commune of the Arts on July 4. Thereupon David's pressure group took over the meeting place of the Academy (July 18) and was put in charge of the annual Salon on August 7. Meanwhile no direct action was taken, for the actual suppression of one Academy involved the existence of them all, and the Committee, while recognizing the principle of suppression, was trying to save the Academy of Science which was employed on the new metric system of weights and measures and other useful projects.[62]

Finally on August 8, Grégoire, in the name of the Committee of Public Instruction, made a blistering attack upon the Academy of Painting and urged that all the patented and endowed societies be suppressed without exception. David then rose to make an impassioned plea, in the name of humanity and justice, the arts and youth, for the liquidation of the blind selfishness, heartless cruelty, and

[61] November 11, 1792: *P.V. Conv.*, III, 142; *Moniteur,* no. 318 (November 13, 1792), p. 1350. November 20: *P.V. Acad.*, X, 189; Wille, pp. 365–66; cf. Letter of David to Topino-Le Brun, December 24: David, pp. 120–21. November 25: *A.P.*, LIII, 357–79; *Moniteur,* no. 331 (November 26), p. 140; *C.I.P.*, I, 81–89; *Col. Baud.*, XXV, 235.

[62] Letter of Minister of Public Contributions to the Convention, June 28, 1793: *C.I.P.*, II, 242–3. *P.V. Conv.*, XV, 23, 114, 116; *P.V. Acad.*, X, 216–19; *C.G.A.*, pp. xxxii, 4–5. August 7: *P.V. Conv.*, XVIII, 197–98; *Col. Baud.*, XXXIII, 49; *Moniteur,* no. 222 (August 10), p. 944. Letters of Lavoisier to Lakanal, July 17–18: E. Grimaux, ed., *Oeuvres de Lavoisier* (Paris: Imp. nat., 1864), IV, 615, 623.

hideous injustice of "the animal which they call academician." The Convention thereupon decreed the suppression of all the monopolistic bodies and the sequestration of their equipment.[63] David's victory over the old regime of the arts was complete; he could now erect a new structure upon the ruins of the artistic Bastille.

The initial construction for this edifice involved the reorganization of the official art commissions. After the dissolution of the Academies the Convention entrusted the sealing of their quarters and the preservation of their equipment to David and three colleagues. Within a few days the powers of these men were extended to embrace the entire artistic and scientific resources of France and experts were appointed to assist them.[64]

This new Commission of the Arts, as it became known, soon clashed with an older and less capable organization, the Commission of Monuments, which exercised identical functions. At first a merger of the two was discussed, but after the earlier body was accused of negligence and ignorance, it was abolished by the Convention on 28 Frimaire (December 18, 1793). At David's insistance a new Temporary Commission of the Arts was chosen from the ranks of artists of revolutionary sentiments. The new organization worked in close cooperation with David and his colleagues and made a valuable contribution by preserving France's artistic heritage from destruction by ignorant or malicious vandals.[65]

Meanwhile Roland's creation, the Commission of the Museum, in charge of the National Museum of the Louvre, was attacked by art experts, and David seized the opportunity to urge that it be destroyed. The Convention accepted his recommendation on January 16, 1794, and with it a hand-picked Conservatory composed of David's adherents. While they were selected for Jacobin sentiments and personal

[63] *P.V. Conv.*, XVIII, 212; B.H. Grégoire, *Rapport et projet de décret, presentés . . . à la séance du 8 août* . . . [Paris: Imp. nat., 1793]. J. L. David, *Discours . . . sur la nécessité de supprimer les Académies* . . . [Paris: Imp. nat., 1793]. *Col. Baud.*, XXXIII, 56. Cf. Grégoire, *Mémoires* (Paris: Dupont, 1837) , I, 350.

[64] **Decrees of August 12, 15, 18, 1793: *P.V. Conv.*, XVIII, 306, 422, XIX, 69;** *Col. Baud.*, XXXIII, 83.

[65] Through a member (*see* above p. 43), David no longer participated in the activities of the monuments commission. *C.I.P.*, II, 489–90, III, 8, 167. *P.V. Conv.*, XXVII, 301, XXXI, 52; *Col. Baud.*, XXXVII, 253; *Moniteur*, no. 90 (30 Frimaire, an II), p. 364. *Procès-verbaux de la Commission temporaire des arts.*

loyalty as much as for ability, the new guardians of the Louvre performed their work exceptionally well.[66]

The next step in the evolution of David's so-called "dictatorship" was to win control of the art contests. Under the old regime the Royal Academy of Painting and Sculpture had monopolized publicity through its Salons and had thereby exercised a dominant influence upon artistic production. If art was to be used as propaganda to advance the cause of the Jacobins, then the art contests must be regulated so as to encourage the representation of "patriotic" subjects. David sympathized with the desire of his fellow artists for artistic exhibitions and competitions for public commissions which now replaced the academic expositions and royal and aristocratic patronage of former days. As quasi-official representative of the artists he strove to obtain publicity and financial aid for them. On the other hand, as a "virtuous Jacobin," David dealt ruthlessly with any attempt on their part to interfere with his control of the art contests.

At first David worked through his partisans in the Commune of the Arts, the pressure group which he had created to fight the Academy, and for which he had secured official recognition. The Salon of 1793 which opened on August 10 under the auspices of the Society, left something to be desired aesthetically, but it was gratifying from the point of view of Revolutionary ideology. Soon afterwards the Commune of the Arts not only snubbed its founder but also began to show symptoms of academic pretensions and finally made the fatal error of attempting to usurp actual control over all the art contests. On October 29, David had the Convention suppress the Commune and create a "Jury of the Arts."[67]

The fifty members of this jury were named by David and were accepted unanimously by the legislature on November 15, 1793. When the Salon was judged the recorded opinions of the jury indicated that the prize was awarded to Herriot, a seventeen-year-old pupil of David,

[66] *P.V. Conv.*, XXIX, 278–80, XXXI, 52; *Moniteur,* no. 79 (19 Frimaire), p. 360, no. 90 (30 Frimaire), p. 367; *Col. Baud.*, XXXVIII, 266. *C.I.P.*, III, 9, 167, 190. A. Tuetey and J. Guiffrey, eds., *La Commission du museum et la création du Musée du Louvre (1792–1793*); *Documents* . . . (Paris: Capiomont, 1910).

[67] *C.G.A.*, pp. xl, 4–5, 18–19, 174. H. Lapauze, "Une Académie des beaux-arts révolutionnaire," *Revue des deux mondes,* ser. 5, XVIII (December 15, 1903), 890. *C.I.P.*, II, 364–71, 569, 635, 648–49. *P.V. Conv.*, XXIV, 193; *J.D.D.*, no. 409 [n.d.], pp. 118, 120.

less for the plastic qualities of his painting than for its classical personification of political "virtue." Artistic ability was then somewhat rare in any case because so many artists were in the army, but there was no dearth of national sentiment.[68]

Its task completed, the national jury transformed itself into a revolutionary club and fraternized with the members of the Popular and Republican Society of the Arts. The latter association was established by the more radical members of the dissolved organization on October 30, 1793, the day after the suppression of the Comune of the Arts. This revolutionary art society actively solicited encouragement of artists, but David was now its master. Its purges, delegations and other manifestations of civism were due to his influence and he was constantly consulted in all matters. Wicar, his pupil and spokesman, denounced his émigré rivals of the old regime and presented the leader's ideas to the club.[69]

Thus by the end of 1793, David stood supreme and unchallenged as a kind of "dictator of the arts." He had suppressed the Academy, captured the art commissions, organized the artistic contests, and brought the artists' societies to heel. The way now lay open for him to put into practice his propaganda program for the fine arts, which would, he believed, reform all Frenchmen and create a "Republic of Virtue." This program fitted perfectly into that of the Committee of Public Safety, which, as has been noticed, emphasized the arts. Obviously, David's theories of the social utility of the arts, his popularization of classical symbols, and his position as so-called "dictator of the arts" could be of real service to the *Montagnard* regime. Thus it was that David was called upon by Robespierre and his colleagues to become in effect an official propagandist of the Revolution.

Among the artistic forces pressed into the service of the Republic by the new "dictator" was one which through the centuries had cap-

[68] *P.V. Conv.*, XXV, 238, 241; *J.D.D.*, no. 423 [n.d.], p. 343; *Moniteur*, no. 57 (27 Brumaire), p. 231. *Procès-verbal . . . du Jury des art* [with] *opinions motivés* [Paris: Imp. nat., 1793], p. 90. Cf. Courtois, "Notes et souvenirs," *R.F.*, XII (1887), 939. David's studio had sent so many volunteers to the army that it was almost empty. Letter of David to Topino-Le Brun, December 24, 1792: David, pp. 120–21. Cf. Letter of Guyton to Gillet, Brussels, July 15, 1794, and General Order of July 16, 1794: *N.A.A.F.*, ser. 3, VI (1890), 358–59.

[69] *C.I.P.*, II, 828–29, III, lxxxix, 546n. Lapauze, *op. cit.*, pp. 891–92, 897. *C.G.A.*, pp. li, 181–422 *passim* (e.g., 196, 199, 201–4, 260, 278, 308, 316–17, 321, 324).

riciously determined taste in costume, furniture, and painting, namely, fashion. The influence of David's neoclassical paintings upon clothing, furniture, and coiffure was apparent even before the outbreak of the Revolution.[70] In 1792 he is supposed to have tried a new republican attire. His pupils wore it, but only such features as long trousers and short jackets became popular.[71] The Deputies-on-mission and later all members of the Convention distinguished themselves with the tricolored sash and plumes proposed by David.[72] Later he designed the uniforms for the students of that famous republican military school, the *École de Mars*.[73] Meanwhile, through his pressure group, the Popular and Republican Society of the Arts, he continued to urge a new form of civilian dress.[74] Apparently convinced of the importance of reform of the national costume, the Committee of Public Safety invited David to propose improvements "appropriate to republican manners and the character of the Revolution."[75] His picturesque designs were engraved in color and distributed in an attempt to revolutionize the clothing of Frenchmen.[76] Only David's followers

[70] *See*, p. 18 note 111.

[71] John Moore, *A Journal During a Residence in France From the Beginning of August to the Middle of December, 1792* (London: Robinson, 1793), II, 433–34; A. C. Thibaudeau, *Mémoires*, ed., Berville and Barrière (Paris: Baudouin, 1824), I, 56–57, 75.

[72] Decree of April 4, 1793: *P.V. Conv.*, IX, 68; F.A. Aulard, *Recueil des actes du Comité de salut public*, (Paris: Imp. nat., 1890), III, 63 (hereafter cited *C.S.P.*); *Moniteur*, no. 97 (April 7), p. 433. Decree of 17 Prairial [June 5]: *Col. Baud.*, XLIII, 77; *P.V. Conv.*, XXXIX, 61; *Moniteur*, no. 259 (19 Prairial), p. 1056; *Journal de Perlet*, no. 622 (18 Prairial), pp. 43–44.

[73] 13 Prairial [June 1]: B. Barère, *Rapport . . . sur la formation de l'École de Mars* [Paris: Imp. nat., 1794], pp. 11–12; *Journal de l'instruction publique*, VII, no. 34 [n.d.], p. 20. For reproduction and description of David's design *see* A. Chuquet, *L'École de Mars* (Paris: Plon-Nourrit, 1899), frontispiece, pp. 76–79.

[74] *C.G.A.*, pp. 260–308; *Considérations sur les avantages de changer le costume français* [Paris: Fantelin, 1794]; *Décade philosophique*, I, no. 1 (10 Floréal), pp. 60–62.

[75] Decree of 25 Floréal, an II [May 14, 1794]: Aulard, *Etudes*, I, 260; *C.S.P.*, XIII, 509; *Moniteur*, no. 263 (23 Prairial), p. 1070; *Mercure français*, no. 25 (25 Prairial), p. 332; *Journal de la Montagne*, III, no. 54 (2 Messidor), p. 443.

[76] Decrees of 5 Floréal an II [April 14, 1794], 5 Prairial [May 24], and 14 Prairial [June 2]: Aulard, *Etudes*, I, 261; H. Dupre, "Some French Revolutionary Propaganda Techniques," *The Historian*, II (Spring, 1940), 158–59. The engraving was done by Vivant Denon, an ex-noble protected by David, and later Napoleon's Minister of Fine Arts. Some of the original drawings by David are preserved in the Louvre: *Inv. dess.*, IV, 80. Repr.: *ibid.*, p. 81, and Jules David, II, unnumbered plate.

donned the tunic, buskins, and ample cloak called for by this project. Under the Directory, somewhat to the master's disgust, some of his more harebrained pupils wandered about in classical flowing robes.[77] Republican furniture and bric-a-brac under Davidian inspiration were more successfully based on Roman models and decorated with appropriate slogans and symbols.[78]

The origins of revolutionary symbolism have already been mentioned, and David's part in the development of the various emblematic representations has been discussed.[79] Now, as an "official" propagandist, David tried to popularize the cause of his party by identifying the policies of the Jacobins with the principles of the Revolution and associating them with the classical and other older forms already familiar and revered.

David's varied activities as propagandist during the Terror included national fêtes, comprising public funerals of Jacobin heroes, triumphal celebrations in honor of republican achievements, and religious festivals such as the Fête of the Supreme Being; public works, involving monuments, statues and city planning; and graphic representations such as paintings, engravings, and caricatures. These phases of artistic endeavor will be considered as methods of social control in the chapters which follow. As will appear, David's propaganda works proved to be an effective means of arousing the passions and directing the opinions of the restless masses of Paris, thereby influencing their actions. Pictorial and spectacular methods were found to be especially potent in controlling the attitudes of a largely illiterate population during this period of revolutionary crisis.

[77] Barante, *op. cit.*, I, 132n; Delécluze, p. 212; Jules David, p. 335.

[78] Under subsequent regimes this severely classical style became known as "Directoire" and "Empire."

[79] *See* pp. 1, 41, 45, 49–50, 54, 60, 65–66, 78.

CHAPTER V

The Blood of The Martyr

One of the most effective of all propaganda techniques is the festival or pageant. Roman emperors, French "Terrorists," and twentieth-century Bolsheviks, Nazis, and Fascists alike have found it an excellent means of maintaining their regimes by channeling mass emotions and directing the current of public opinion. During the French Revolution the fête perhaps achieved the highest development heretofore of its political, social, and aesthetic functions as the consummate assertion of solidarity, the highest mode of collective enjoyment, and the supreme expression of contemporary culture.

The effectiveness of the Revolutionary festivals as political demonstrations of national and party unity may have been dependent upon the arousal of a feeling of universality. Their social appeal was due, perhaps, to the spectacular features of colorful floats, the irresistible psychological attraction of martial music, the emotional exaltation of solemn ceremonials, the overpowering impressiveness of colossal monuments, and the hypnotic fascination of marching processions. Finally, the aesthetic appeal of the finest in painting and sculpture, song and poetry, rhetoric and oratory, made them the highest embodiment of French culture of the day.

Someone has described the Revolution itself as "a lyrical drama, verse by Chénier, music by Gossec, setting by David," and the simile is an apt one. The fêtes of the period were indeed embellished by the greatest artists of the time, but they were much more than mere popular spectacles—the French equivalent of "circuses" to satisfy the mob. Besides their important political, social, religious, and aesthetic functions, they helped greatly in unifying public opinion in support of the government at a time of serious crisis. The people, at once active participants and interested spectators, were flattered by being given a feeling of importance, and their interests were identified with those of the regime. Skillful employment of republican symbols, exploitation of the sensational as well as the aesthetic, and emphasis upon lavish display and mass participation, enabled artists such as David to rouse considerable zeal for the Mountain, its leaders, and their principles.

These festivals may be classified under three general types: funeral fêtes of Jacobin heroes, triumphal fêtes in celebration of republican accomplishments, and religious fêtes, of which the Fête of the Supreme Being is the leading example.

As has been indicated, David's endeavors began with the processional translation of the remains of Voltaire to the Panthéon in a funeral car designed by the artist.[1] The classical pagan character of this festival served as the keynote for those which followed. David's Festival of Liberty added the all-important factors of republican symbolism and mass participation. The artist also showed that he realized that the "blood of the martyr" was indeed the "seed" of the revolutionary faith. He knew that the "sacred enthusiasm" of the crowd, so necessary to the continuance of the Revolution, was more easily moved by cults of martyrs of liberty than by the worship of such vague abstractions as Reason and Law. During the Terror, David applied on a grander scale the techniques he had developed during 1791 and 1792. As official propagandist, he was highly successful in the canonization of the Jacobin saints—Le Peletier, Lazowski, and Marat.

On January 21, 1793, Louis XVI died upon the guillotine—and a life and death struggle between the revolutionists and their enemies began. The King's tragic end redeemed his mistakes and weaknesses; indeed, it hallowed his memory. But the Jacobins could face the future with a clear conscience—they, too, had a martyr. On the night before Louis' execution the distinguished deputy, Michel Le Peletier de Saint-Fargeau,[2] innocent of fanaticism or violence, had been assassinated by a former royal bodyguard for having voted for the death of the monarch. While they remained calm at the death of their King, many Frenchmen were indignant at the murder of a deputy in the performance of his duties.[3] The propaganda possibilities of the situation were

[1] *See*, pp. 48–50.

[2] Contemporaries spelled his name Lepelletier, Lepeletier, Le Pelletier, and Le Peletier, but modern scholars generally prefer the last form.

[3] Besides the unanimous chorus echoed in the Paris press, the feeling of indignation extended to Jacobins abroad: *Journal de la Société des amis de la liberté et de l'égalité à Bruxelles,* no. 63 (January 31, 1793), pp. 497–99. Cf. Letter of Mme. Jullien, January 26: Lockroy, *Journal,* p. 339; *Oeuvres de Michel Lepelletier de Saint-Fargeau* (Brussels: Lacrosse, 1826), pp. 406–08; *The Despatches of Earl Gower,* p. 281; Duval, *Souvenirs de la Terreur,* III, 53–61; Touchard-Lafosse, *Souvenirs d'un demi-siècle,* IV, 1–2.

not lost upon the members of the Jacobin Club.[4] Believing themselves threatened with similar violence, Le Peletier's colleagues took measures to protect themselves and to arouse public opinion against the royalists by exalting their fellow regicide as a "Martyr of Liberty."

In an "Address to the French People" the Convention announced:

> Citizens, it is not one man alone who has been struck, it is you; it is not Michel Lepelletier [sic] who has been basely assassinated, it is you; it is not against the life of a deputy that the blow has been dealt but against the life of the nation, against public liberty, against popular sovereignty.[5]

David was called upon to organize a state funeral which should drive this point home. In the naked corpse exposed in the Place Vendôme and escorted to its last meeting place in the Panthéon, the people saw themselves and were inspired by mingled fury and determination. The death of a king was forgotten in the horror produced by the threat to their own safety and that of the nation. According to all the press accounts[6] this classically inspired and majestically executed ceremony produced a profoundly moving impression upon the huge crowds which witnessed it. The lucid symbolism of bloody sword and colossal fasces was not lost: Frenchmen must unite against the foe or meet the fate of Le Peletier.[7]

[4] *Journal des Jacobins,* debates, no. 342 (January 22, 1793), p. 3, no. 343 (January 23), pp. 1–2; *Courier français,* no. 24 (January 24), p. 4; *Premier journal de la Convention nationale,* no. 22 (January 22), pp. 87–88; cf. Mme. Roland, *Appel à l'impartiale posterité* (Paris: Lauret, 1793), II, 71; [Lamothe-Langon], *Histoire pittoresque,* II, 89–93; G.V. Vasselin, *Mémorial révolutionnaire de la Convention . . .* (Paris: Baillo & Colas, [1797]), I, 303 and others.

[5] *Col. Baud.,* XXVII, 86, 89. The text appeared in almost all of the newspapers: e.g. *Auditeur national,* no. 128 (January 27, 1793), pp. 7–8.

[6] It must be remembered that all but four of the royalist papers had disappeared after August 10. As a result it is extremely difficult to find hostile contemporary accounts of the revolutionary festivals. Memoirs and other works written much later have had to be used for the counter-revolutionary viewpoint.

[7] *Procès-verbal de la Convention nationale,* V, 348; *Défenseur de la vérité,* no. 4 (January 26), pp. 61–66; *Auditeur national,* no. 123 (January 22), pp. 6–7, no. 126 (January 25), pp. 5–6, no. 127 (January 26), pp. 6–7; cf. *Mercure universel, Journal de Perlet, Thermomètre, Premier journal de la Convention, Le Républicain français, Chronique de Paris, Annales patriotiques, Journal de Paris, Révolutions de Paris, Annales de la République française, La Chronique du mois, Journal des amis* (Fauchet), *Journal de France, Journal historique et politique, Je suis le véritable Père Duchêne,* (Hébert), *Journal du soir sans réflexions, Bulletin des Amis de la

The day after the funeral, when Le Peletier's daughter was adopted by the Convention, David precipitated a violent debate on the subject of civic equality and honors by demanding a marble monument in addition to pantheonization of "our virtuous colleague." A commission for a statue of Le Peletier in the position in which he had been shown to the people at the Place Vendôme was to be awarded by public contest. David wanted to leave permanent memorials of his propaganda celebrations in accordance with classical precedents, and at the same time to reward artistic genius and to encourage it to glorify the Fatherland. A month later, his motion that Fleuriot's bust of Le Peletier be placed next to that of Brutus in the meeting place of the Convention was adopted.[8]

In the meantime, David was busy with a canvas which realistically and movingly depicted the martyr's corpse as it had been exposed at the funeral. The position of Le Peletier was the same as that of Hector in David's earlier painting of the *Grief of Andromache* and strikingly like Christ in a *Pietà*. Suspended by a thread above the naked body was a bloody sword, thrust through a paper inscribed with the words, "I vote the death of the tyrant." [9] On March 29, 1793, the artist presented his famous *Le Peletier assassinated* to the National Conven-

vérité, Courier français, Courier de l'égalité, Bulletin national, ou papier-nouvelles, Feuille villageoise, Moniteur, Courier universel, ou l'écho de Paris, Chronique de Paris, and other journals; *Ordre de la marche et des cérémonies qui seront observée aux funérailles de Michel le Pelletier* [*sic*] [Paris: Imp. nat., 1793]; *Oeuvres de Lepelletier,* pp. 419–25, 439–40; Dispatch of J. Lama to Count Ventura, Paris, August 19, 1793: Grouchy, *Correspondance . . . de Virieu,* pp. 426–28; Touchard-Lafosse, IV, 10–12; Duval, I, 293–94, III, 97–102; Wille, *Mémoires,* II, 370–71; *Mercier, Le Nouveau Paris,* I, 176–77. For contemporary engravings, see *Révolutions de Paris,* no. 185 (January 26), p. 226; *Tableaux historiques,* II, 307; no. 5026, Col. Vinck, III, 239, pl. VIII.

[8] January 25: *P.V. Conv.,* V, 403; *Col. Baud.,* XXVII, 99; *A.P.,* LVII, 654; *Auditeur national,* no. 127 (January 27, 1793), p. 4; cf. *Journal des amis* (Fauchet), *Journal de Paris, Journal de France, Courier de l'égalité, Bulletin des Amis de la vérité, Le Défenseur de la vérité; C.I.P.,* I, 321, 329–30; *Oeuvres de Lepelletier,* pp. 442–47. February 21: *P.V. Conv.,* VI, 359–60; *A.P.,* LIX, 69; *Col. Baud.,* XXVII, 261; *Oeuvres de Lepelletier,* pp. 466–68; *Annales patriotiques,* no. 54 (February 23), p. 247; *Journal de France,* no. 154 (February 23), p. 1. This bust was produced in smaller copies by the Sèvres factory.

[9] Contemporary descriptions: Delécluze, *Louis David,* p. 150; Lenoir, "David, Souvenirs historiques," p. 6; Coupin, "Notice," pp. 46–48; Déy, "Histoire de . . . Saint-Fargeau," Société des sciences de l'Yonne, *Bulletin,* XII (1858), 600.

tion. It was on this occasion that David expressed his concept of the propaganda role of the patriotic artist as quoted above.[10] His painting was gratefully accepted, and it was decreed that it should be engraved and distributed to the departments and to the deputies of the "liberated countries" which were to be annexed by France. David was voted a civic crown and, in spite of his protests, the sum of 11,000 livres. He asked that the money be given to the widows and orphans of those who had died for the Republic.[11] The painting itself was hung in the chamber of the Convention. After various vicissitudes, its ultimate fate was to become one of the great unsolved mysteries of art history. Today it is known only through a few contemporary descriptions, a single mutilated proof of the engraving in the Bibliothèque Nationale, and an obscure drawing discovered eighteen years ago in the Museum of Dijon.[12]

Three days after the funeral of Le Peletier, another celebration was held which showed how revolutionary festivals could be used to crush enemies as well as to win friends. On January 7, 1793, the Place du Carrousel had been the scene of a patriotic mass oath to defend the liberty, equality, and indivisibility of the Republic and to exterminate all tyrants. It was taken by *fédérés* of the departments, deputations from the Paris sections, the Commune, and the revolutionary societies. It was decided to commemorate this demonstration of solidarity be-

[10] *See* p. 79.

[11] *P.V. Conv.*, VIII, 344, 346; *Col. Baud.*, XXVIII, 541; *Révolutions de Paris*, no. 90 (March 31), p. 400; *Annales patriotiques*, no. 89 (March 30), p. 412; *Moniteur*, no. 90 (March 31), p. 400.

[12] *Oeuvres de Lepelletier*, pp. 447–48; Baron Choillou des Barres, *Les châteaux . . . de Saint-Fargeau . . .* (Paris: Vaton, 1845), pp. 90–113; L. Réau, "Musée de Dijon, un dessin inédit du Lepeletier de Saint-Fargeau de David," *Bulletin des musées de France*, II (January, 1930), 17–18; J. Vallery-Radot, "Un tableau disparu depuis cent ans: Le 'Lepeletier de Saint-Fargeau'," *Revue de l'art ancien et moderne*, XLIV (January, 1926), 54–60, "Lepeletier de Saint-Fargeau, gravure de P. A. Tardieu d'après David," *Les Trésors des bibliothèques de France*, II, fasc. 7 (1928), 110–14; M. Tourneux, *N.A.A.F.*, ser. 3, V (1889), 52–59; Déy, *op. cit.*, pp. 596–602; *Gazette des tribunaux*, XII, no. 3706 (July 26, 1837), p. 943; M. G. T. Villenave, "Mon livre, ou moi et d'autres," *Revue rétrospective*, XX (February, 1894), 120; *Intermédiare des chercheurs et curieux*, XIII (1880), 633, 685, 697–99; XXIII (1890), 319; XLI (1900), 725, 773–76; LV (1907), 666–67, 734, 172–93, 850, 901–02; LXVII (1913), 633–34; LXIX (1914), 163; LXXXV (1922), 859, 967; LXXXVI (1923), 10–12. A. Fontainas, "David et ses tableaux inconnus," *L'Art et les artistes*, n.s., XII (January, 1926), 135–37. *See* plate XIII, opposite p. 102.

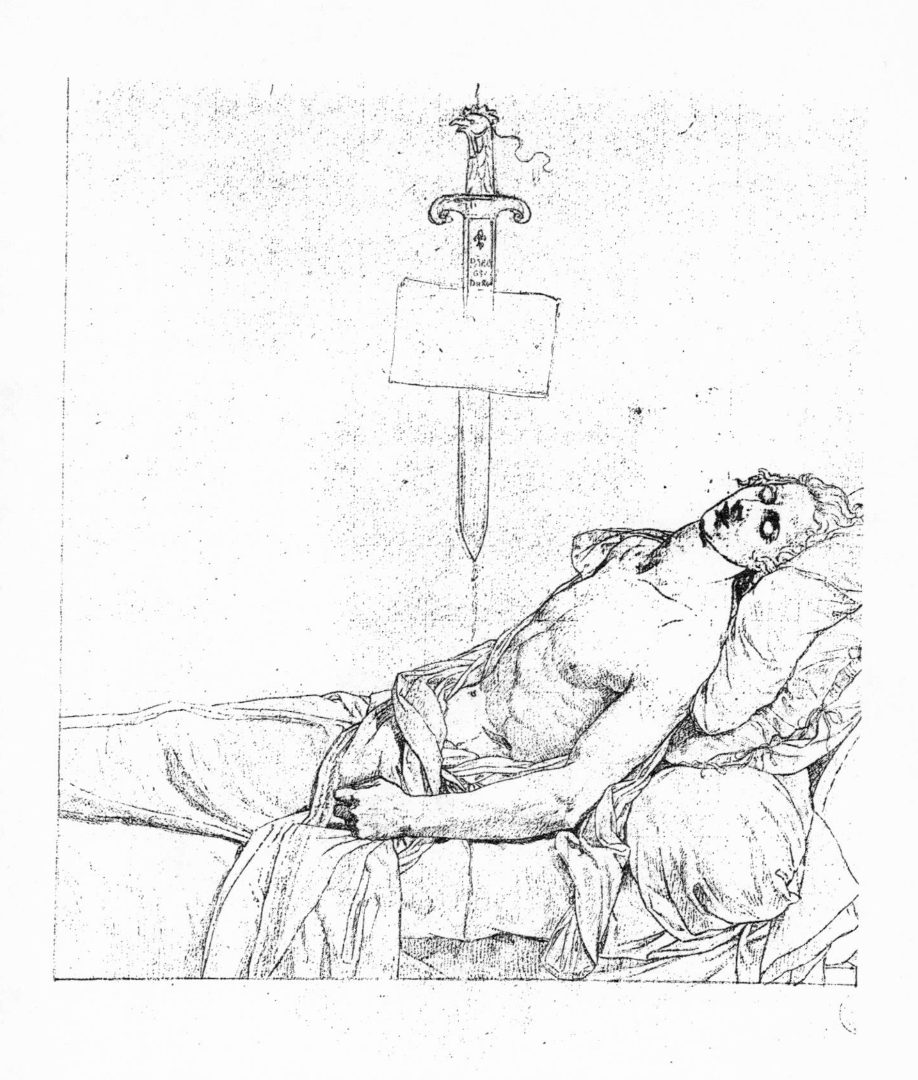

XIII LE PELETIER DE SAINT FARGEAU ASSASSINATED

Contemporary Drawing after David *Musée de Dijon*

tween Paris and the provinces by planting a Tree of Fraternity on the site. On Sunday, January 27, the departmental *fédérés,* citizens of Paris, and municipal officials joyously danced and sang around their oak tree while Santerre's National Guards entertained with military evolutions. Suddenly the troops, *fédérés,* peace officers, magistrates, and police moved off in perfect order, and within four minutes had thrown a tight cordon of infantry, cavalry, and artillery around the neighboring Palais de l'Égalité (former Palais-Royal). Émigrés, spies, royalist agents, and deserters were known to haunt the gambling dens and brothels of this notorious edifice where the accomplices of Le Peletier's assassin might be hiding. The raid was a success, and hundreds of suspects who could not produce a *"carte civique"* were arrested, and numerous "public enemies" were caught in the dragnet.[13]

Lazowski, member of the Paris Commune and son of a wealthy Pole, was canonized as the second *Montagnard* saint. He had distinguished himself on June 20 and August 10, and had been recently denounced by Vergniaud for his part in the anti-Girondin riots of March 8–10, 1793. When he died suddenly (there were whispers of poison), the Jacobins determined to turn his obsequies into a demonstration against the Gironde. Robespierre pronounced a eulogy, the members swore to avenge his death, and David took charge of the public funeral which the Commune voted in Lazowski's honor. The celebration was a marvelous opportunity for the Jacobins to assemble their forces and to rally the masses to their cause; they used it to the utmost. Girondin editors such as Gorsas fulminated in vain against David's propaganda demonstration.[14]

Nevertheless, on April 28, 1793, the popular societies and the Paris sections turned out in imposing strength, Gossec provided heart-rending music, and David created a splendid funeral cortège "worthy of an ardent friend of the Revolution." The procession with its red flag, tocsin bell, pikes, and cannon breathed the spirit of insurrection while other symbols were calculated to rouse popular fury against Lazowski's enemies—the Girondins. The hero's remains were solemnly

[13] *Lettres de Robespierre à ses commettans,* 2e trim., no. 3 [n.d.], pp. 100–02; *Journal de Paris,* no. 21 (January 21, 1793), p. 83, no. 25 (January 25), p. 98, no. 26 (January 26), p. 104; cf. *Journal historique et politique, Feuille villageoise, Annales patriotiques, Annales de la République française, Journal du soir sans réflexions, Journal de Perlet,* and others.

[14] *Courrier de Gorsas,* ser. 3, VII, no. 28 (April 28, 1793), pp. 436–38.

borne in triumph through the streets to the Hôtel de Ville on a tricolored bier. Finally they were laid to rest at the foot of the Tree of Fraternity on the Place du Carrousel—where he had given the signal for the storming of the Tuileries on August 10. As far as can be determined from contemporary accounts, this festival was as successful as that of Le Peletier.[15] Just one month later the Girondins were destroyed in the insurrection of May 31–June 2, by the people who had mourned Lazowski.

When the Girondins instituted their offensive against the *Montagnard* leaders in the fall of 1792, Lazowski had been only one of the men they had attacked. Marat, along with Danton and Robespierre, had borne the brunt of their fire. Almost reluctantly the Jacobins had undertaken the defense of the violent and inflammatory "Friend of the People." One fanatical supporter Marat did have: the artist Louis David.[16] When the ugly little journalist had been indicted by the Convention on April 12 for issuing an anti-Girondin petition, David, almost alone, had rushed to his defense.[17] Twelve days later Marat was acquitted by the new Revolutionary Tribunal and brought back in triumph to the Convention. The fall of the Girondins followed (June 2).

Some of the Girondin leaders escaped to organize the so-called Federalist Revolt in the departments. Just as the essential weakness of this insurrection was appearing, a decisive weapon was placed in the hands of the Jacobins by the Girondins themselves: Marat was assassinated. The knife of Charlotte Corday precipitated not a Girondin victory, but a Jacobin triumph. One of the most violent critics of the Convention was gone. The announcement of the murder of the

[15] For motives and descriptions, see *Journal des Jacobins,* debates, no. 401 (April 26, 1793), p. 1, no. 402 (April 27), p. 4; *Premier journal de la Convention,* no. 27 (April 27), pp. 107–08, no. 28 (April 28), p. 111, cf. *Je suis le véritable Père Duchêne* (Hébert), *Le Républicain, journal des hommes libres, Révolutions de Paris, Courrier universel, Journal de Paris, Gazette de France, Journal de France, Bulletin des Amis de la vérité, Thermomètre, Courier français, Courrier de Gorsas, Chronique de Paris, Bulletin national, Courier de l'égalité, Moniteur, Journal de Perlet, Annales de la République française,* and other journals. Duval, III, 223–31.

[16] Barante, *Souvenirs,* I, 131n; *Le Publiciste de la République française* (Marat), no. 178 (April 25, 1793), p. 7; A. Chénier, *Oeuvres complètes,* III, 263–65; Deseine, *Notices,* pp. 183; Lacretelle, *Histoire,* V, 57; Duval, III, 360; Conny de la Fay, *France sous la Convention,* pp. 176–77.

[17] *See* p. 86.

"Friend of the People" roused to fever pitch the emotions of the masses who loved him. Parisian workingmen cried out for vengeance upon Marat's enemies. Unlike the case of Le Peletier's state funeral, it appears to have been the spontaneous demand of the people themselves which instituted a fête in honor of Marat. The Jacobins lost no time in exploiting the proposed demonstration in the interests of their party.[18] In response to popular mandate, the Convention decreed a national funeral for the third martyr of the Mountain; naturally enough, his devoted friend David was asked to take charge.

The day before Marat's death, the Jacobin Club under David's presidency had sent a deputation to visit him. They found the great man "in his bathtub with a board before him on which he was writing his last thoughts for the people's salvation." It was in this attitude that David urged that he be shown to the populace. The following day, while giving the actual details for the organization of the funeral, the artist declared that putrefaction of the corpse made it impossible to expose it in the bath. Instead it would be swathed in wet cloths and sprinkled from time to time and interred that very night in a simple sepulchre under the trees where Marat had taught the people. "Plato, Aristotle, Socrates. . . . I have never lived with you, but I have known Marat, and I have admired him as I do you. Posterity will render him justice." [19]

Before the funeral, the victim's body with its gaping wound, together with his bathtub and inkstand, was exhibited to a packed crowd

[18] *P.V. Conv.*, XVI, 148–49; *Annales de la République française*, no. 198 (July 15, 1793), pp. 996–97, no. 199 (July 16), pp. 999, 1001, no. 200 (July 17), p. 1003; cf. *Mercure universel, Je suis le véritable Père Duchêne* (Hébert), *Courrier universel ou l'écho de Paris, Journal de Paris, Journal des Jacobins, Gazette de France, Journal de la Montagne, Le Républicain français, Thermomètre, Journal de Perlet, Annales patriotiques* (Salaville), *Correspondance politique de Paris et des départements, Courier de l'égalité, Mercure universel,* and other journals. Dispatch of Lama to Ventura, Paris, July 13, 1793: Grouchy, *op. cit.*, pp. 457–58. Cardenal, *Province*, pp. 319–21.

[19] Jacobin delegation, July 12, 1793: *Journal des Jacobins*, debates, no. 449 (July 16), pp. 1. 3; *Le Républicain français*, no 224 (July 17), pp. 990–91; *Journal de la Montagne*, no. 44 (July 15), p. 243. Report of July 15, 1793; *P.V. Conv.*, XVI, 183; *Col. Baud.*, XXXII, 104; *Courrier universel*, (July 17), p. 1; cf. *Moniteur, Journal de Paris, Gazette de France, Journal du soir sans réflexions, Mercure universel, Correspondance politique,* and other journals. Report of July 16: *P.V. Conv.*, XVI, 206; *Mercure universel*, no. 867 (July 17), p. 270; cf. *Journal du soir sans réflexions, Courrier universel, Chronique de Paris, Journal de la Montagne, Thermomètre, Gazette de France,* and other journals.

in the Church of the Cordeliers in the same bed of state used for Lazowski. The obsequies, held that night, were attended by the Convention, by the sections, by the popular societies, and by enormous crowds. Following the bier, a procession wound through the streets of Paris to the accompaniment of music, roll of muffled drums, cannon, and the pale light of torches. Silently and respectfully the sorrowing throngs accompanied the cortège back to the garden of the Cordeliers, where Marat was buried at midnight under the trees.

Here was no crude incitement to mass vengeance. At this moment of uncertainty, a popular insurrection would have been highly dangerous for the government. Even those who execrated the man remarked on the grandeur and solemnity of his "simple and patriotic funeral" and the calm dignity of the people who mourned him. No less impressive than that of Le Peletier, Marat's funeral excited a more profound emotion, for there was no need to stimulate a grief which was spontaneous and apparently sincere.[20]

Internal peace in Paris was essential if the newly reconstituted Committee of Public Safety was to organize France against her external and internal enemies. That summer the foreign war, the revolt in the Vendée, the financial disorder, the food shortage, and the violent demands of the *Enragés* for a social revolution created a serious crisis. Marat's funeral festival, therefore, was not an attempt to stir up mob violence as has been alleged, but was clever direction of popular emotion into channels useful to the government. It was agreed that Marat must be avenged, but in the words of Hébert:

> The day of vengeance has not yet come. The country must be shown that Paris is not a habitation of cannibals; let us weep on the tomb of Marat, but let us be calm and peaceable. That is the way to exterminate our enemies.[21]

[20] *Courier français,* no. 198 (July 17), pp. 3, 6; *Journal de la Montagne,* no. 48 (July 19), p. 278; cf. *Défenseur de la vérité, Journal de Perlet, Courier de l'égalité, Thermomètre, Révolutions de Paris, Annales patriotiques, Annales de la République française, Correspondance politique, Courrier universel, Journal de Paris, Mercure français, Chronique de Paris, Gazette de France,* and other journals; C. Nodier, *Souvenirs,* I, 100–02; Duval, III, 360–64; Robinet, *Le Mouvement religieuse à Paris,* II, 519–37; [Adolphus], *Biographical Memoirs,* II, 56.

[21] July 13, 1793: *Mercure universel,* no. 866 (July 16), p. 248; cf. *Journal de Paris, Annales de la République française, Courrier universel, Le Républicain français,* and other journals.

Paris remained calm, and the confidence of the departments, shaken by June 2, was restored. It was noticeable that within a few weeks after Marat's funeral, active measures against the federalist insurrection were instituted. Suspects and rebels were rounded up, the reorganized Revolutionary Tribunal became more active, disciplinary decrees were passed, the army high command was purged, and police controls in the provinces were tightened.

While the Jacobin politicians exploited the effects of Marat's gruesome lying-in-state and public burial, David set to work to dramatize his idol's martyrdom in his most effective revolutionary canvas. When the news of Marat's death had been announced in the Convention, a spokesman from a Paris section had cried: "Where are you, David? You have given posterity the image of Le Peletier; there still remains a picture to be done." And the artist had replied, "I will not forget."[22] Under the impulse of popular passion as well as his own profound grief, David painted his famous *Marat Assassinated*[23] from a sketch he had made just after the fatal thrust.

On November 14, 1793, the artist presented to the Convention one of the world's most skillfully executed propaganda pictures, which he himself considered to be one of his finest works and which many critics regard as his greatest painting.

> Citizens, [he said] the people were again calling for their friend; their desolate voice was heard: 'David! take up your brushes . . . avenge Marat.' . . . I heard the voice of the people, I obeyed . . . . It is to you, my colleagues, that I offer the homage of my brush; your glances, running over the livid and blood-stained features of Marat will recall to you his virtues, which must never cease to be your own . . . . I vote for Marat, the honors of the Panthéon.[24]

The Convention decreed that the painting, together with that of Le Peletier, should, after being engraved for propaganda purposes, be

[22] July 14, 1793: The *P.V. Conv.*, does not report this episode but details may be found in: *Journal du soir sans réflexions*, no. 308 (July 14), p. 3; cf. *Courier de l'égalité, Courrier universel, Thermomètre, Le Républicain français, Annales de la République française, Mercure universel, Gazette de France, Journal de Paris,* and other journals.

[23] Museum of Fine Arts, Brussels, Catalogue no. 169 (canvas, 6′ high by 5′5″ wide), signed and dated "A Marat David, l'an II." *See* plate XIV, opposite p. 108.

[24] *P.V. Conv.*, XXV, 221–22; *J.D.D.*, no. 422 [n.d.], pp. 325–27; *Col. Baud.*, XXXVI, 188; *Journal de l'instruction publique*, IV, no. 20 [n.d], pp. 153–55; cf. *Moniteur, Journal de Paris, Gazette de France.*

preserved for all time in their meeting place. The engravings were not completed, and a single proof of each has alone survived.[25] After being publicly exhibited in the courtyard of the Louvre, the two paintings were hung on each side of the president's chair in the hall of the Convention, where they remained until February 10, 1795.[26] David's work became the icon of the Jacobins and aided in the development of the cult of Marat into a religious movement of some importance.

The funeral of Marat was the last great fête given in honor of an individual, for the celebration which was to extol the virtues of young Barra and Viala was never held. On 8 Nivôse, Robespierre asked the honors of the Panthéon for Joseph Barra, the youthful hero of the Vendée and symbol of patriotic virtue. A "prompt and pompous ceremonial" to be embellished by that "Genius of the Arts," David, was to inspire the youth of France and rally them to the regime. David was at work on a picture depicting the death of the young soldier which connoisseurs consider to be one of his best works.[27] Barère demanded that engravings of the young martyr, after David's painting, be placed in every primary school to inculcate republican ideals. The Convention had applauded and decreed both measures.[28] Evidently these arrangements took considerable time, and the celebration was twice postponed.[29]

[25] Imperfect proofs are preserved in the Bibliothèque Nationale, Cabinet des Estampes: F. Courbouin, ed., *Catalogue . . . des gravures . . . Réserve* (Paris: Rapilly, 1901), nos. 8462 and 10701, II, 177, 326; Repr.: J. Guibert, *Le Cabinet des estampes* (Paris: Le Garrec, 1926), p. 160; Cantinelli, pl. XXIV.

[26] P. Fassy, *Marat . . . documents* (Paris: Dormand, 1867), p. 11; Villenave, "Mon livre ou moi et d'autres, *op. cit.*, p. 120; Lenoir, p. 6n; Delécluze, p. 174; Miette de Villars, pp. 148–49. For the subsequent history of the painting and its copies, *see* F. Chèvremont, *Marat* (Paris: Chez l'auteur, 1876), pp. 351–53; E. Durand-Greville, "'La Mort de Marat' de David," *L'Artiste,* LII (August, 1889), 79–93; C. Saunier, "Le 'Marat expirant' de Louis David et ses copies," *G.B.A.*, ser. 4, X (June, 1913), 24–31; G. Brière and L. Rosenthal, "Additions et rectifications," S.H.A.F., *Bulletin,* 1913, pp. 123–24.

[27] It remained unfinished. Today it is in the Musée Calvet, Avignon. Repr.: Cantinelli, pl. XLI; Holma, pl. XXV.

[28] December 28, 1793: *Col. Baud.*, XXXVIII, 60; *J.D.D.*, no. 465 [n.d.], pp. 124–25; *P.V. Conv.*, XXVIII, 148; *Moniteur,* no. 100 (10 Nivôse, an II), p. 403; cf. *Feuille villageoise, Journal de Perlet, Journal de l'instruction publique, Journal du soir, de politique et de littérature, Gazette de France, Journal de Paris,* and other journals.

[29] David was not only engaged in painting the two infant heroes, but he was overseeing the work of embellishing the Tuileries Gardens. Decrees of 18 Floréal

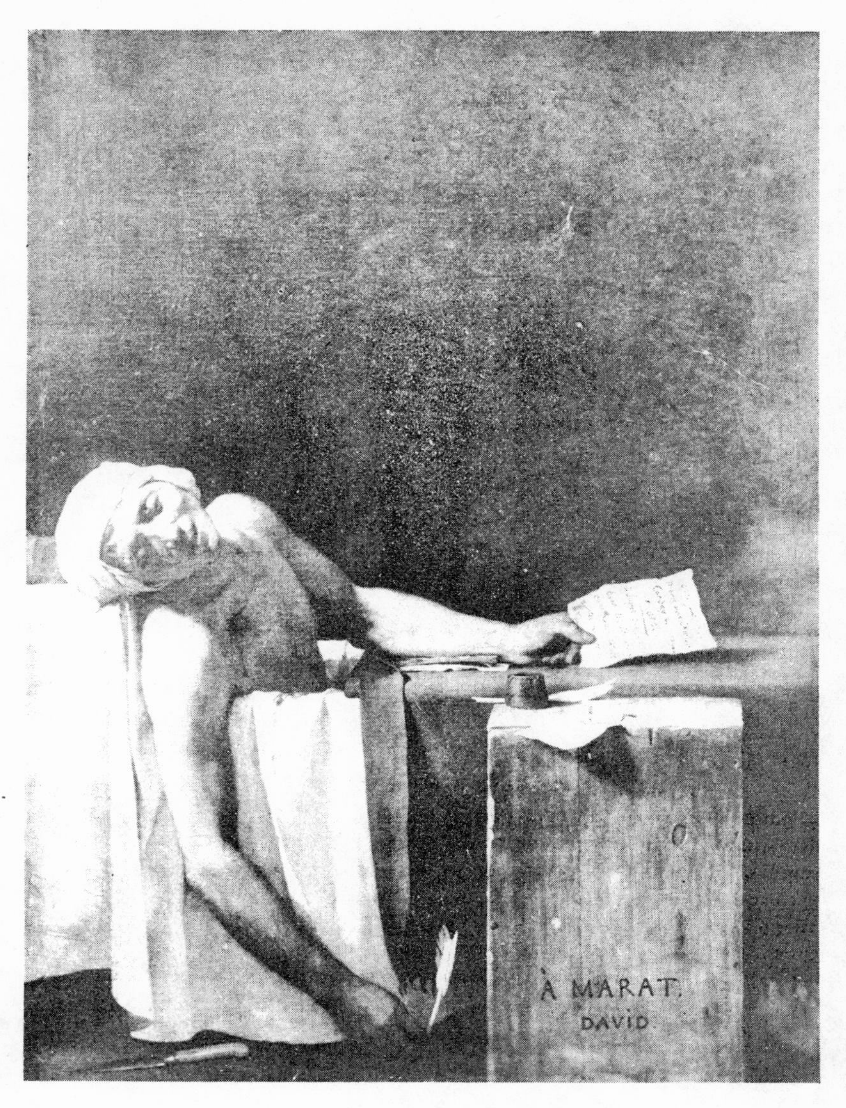

XIV. MARAT ASSASSINATED

Painting by David — *Musée des Beaux Arts, Brussels*

It was not until July 11, 1794, that David reported on the "*Fête héroique*" for the honors of the Panthéon for both Barra and Agricola Viala, the child martyr of the Midi. This celebration, designed by those in power to whip up hatred against royalists and other enemies of the government, was to begin at three o'clock on 10 Thermidor. It was to include a review of the cadets of the Jacobin military academy, the *École de Mars,* as well as dancers, singers, musicians, and poets. The day before the scheduled event, the famous political *coup* precipitated the planners of the festival into prison and onto the scaffold, and the fête did not take place. It was rumored that Robespierre had planned to use this festival as the occasion for a *coup d'état* to be carried out by the young fanatics of the *École de Mars* who were to have massacred his opponents and proclaimed him dictator.[30]

After the death of Marat the federalist insurrection did not long survive. The Jacobins won over the followers of their opponents by launching a moral offensive. One of the most potent factors in the defeat of Federalism was the hastily written Constitution of 1793 which decentralized France under a democratic government. Shrewdly the *Montagnards* removed suspicion of radicalism and domination from Paris, not only by maintaining order there when Marat was killed, but by submitting their constitution to a popular referendum. The plebiscite in July was virtually a call for a vote of confidence by the authors of the insurrection of May 31. The result was an overwhelming acceptance of the new Constitution by a vote of 1,801,918 to 11,610. At the same time the Convention tried to win popular support by such measures as the sale of confiscated estates of the émigrés and the abolition of the last remnants of feudalism.

The situation was critical during that midsummer crisis of 1793. The revolt in the Vendée remained formidable; the war was going

[May 7, 1794]: *J.D.D.,* no. 595 [n.d.], p. 229; *Col. Baud.,* XLIII, 77; *Auditeur national,* no. 592 (19 Floréal), p. 6; and 17 Prairial [June 5]: *Journal de Perlet,* no. 622 (18 Prairial), p. 44; cf. *Nouvelles politiques.*

[30] 23 Messidor, an II: David, pp. 208–16; *Nouvelles politiques,* no. 249 (9 Thermidor), pp. 994–96; *Le Messager du soir,* no. 707 (July 28), pp. 1–3; *Moniteur,* no. 305 (5 Thermidor), pp. 1247–48; J. L. David, *Rapport sur la fête héroique pour les honneurs du Panthéon à décerner aux jeunes Barra et Viala* [Paris: Imp. nat., 1794]. Music: Pierre, *Musique des fêtes,* pp. 387–89; *Esprit des journaux,* XXIII, t. 9 (September, 1794), pp. 220–21. *Histoire de la révolution par deux amis de la liberté,* II, 357–58; Lacretelle, *Histoire de la révolution,* VI, 87–88; Courtois, *Rapport sur les événements du 9 thermidor,* pp. 33–34, 37; Fantin-Desodoards, *Histoire philosophique,* V, 306; Courtois, "Notes et souvenirs," *R.F.,* XII (1887), 931.

badly on the northern and eastern fronts; the financial crisis and food shortage were unabated; and the left-wing radicals (*Enragés*) continued to attack the Convention. In the face of these dangers it was necessary to affirm in the most positive manner possible the union of Frenchmen and their resolution to defend the principles of the Revolution. A demonstration of party strength and national solidarity which should restore unity and confidence in the Jacobins, in Paris, and in the Republic was in order. The approaching anniversary of the overthrow of monarchy, August 10, and the acceptance of the new Constitution might be combined in a grand protest against Girondin federalism.

On May 30 one of the demands made of the Convention by the insurrectional sections had been a national festival on August 10 "to restore the ties of unity and indivisibility." The next day this measure had been decreed along with the arrest of the Girondin deputies. A month later the Convention decided that at the civic reunion planned for August 10 the delegates of the primary assemblies should cast their votes for the new Constitution, David, the "pageant-master of the Republic," was asked to organize the festival. His report, presented to the legislative body on July 11, 1793, gave a long and elaborate description of the organization, order of march, and composition of this "Fête of Reunion." This lyrical masterpiece was greeted with applause, adopted, and ordered printed and distributed for propaganda purposes.[31]

David gave a further account of the celebration on July 20, and asked for an appropriation of 1,200,000 livres for expenses. The festival was considered so important that the sum was voted without question. The day before the celebration the artist presented his final instruc-

[31] Decree of May 31, 1793: *P.V. Conv.*, XII, 297; *Col. Baud.*, XXX, 265; *Journal de Paris*, no. 152 (June 1), p. 607, no. 153 (June 2), p. 611. Decree of June 27: *Col. Baud.*, XXXI, 247; *Annales patriotiques*, no. 179 (June 29), p. 826. Report and decree of July 11: *P.V. Conv.*, XVI, 52; *Col. Baud.*, XXXII, 79; *Moniteur*, no. 196 (July 15), pp. 840–41; *Journal de la Montagne*, no. 42 (July 13), p. 233, no. 51 (July 22), p. 307, no. 52 (July 23), pp. 311–313; cf. *Journal de France, Journal de l'instruction publique, Thermomètre, Annales patriotiques, Journal de Paris, Gazette de France, Journal des hommes libres, Mercure universel, Chronique de Paris*, and others. A facsimile of David's autograph report is reproduced by C. Normand, "David et la Fête de la Réunion," *L'Art*, LVII (1894), 60–73. The official *Rapport et dècret sur la fête de la réunion républicaine du 10 août . . .* [Paris: Imp. nat., 1793] was reprinted in many variant forms.

tions for the order, the march, and the ceremonial. These were adopted by the Convention and appeared in almost all the newspapers and in pamphlet form. Those journals which did not print the *Instruction* presented the official program in its full or abbreviated form.[32]

Since bread riots and even insurrection threatened, elaborate precautions were taken by the authorities to insure that violence should not mar the peace of the tenth of August. Extra guards were called up in the sections; weapons, clubs, and even canes were forbidden. Food shops and bakeries were ordered to remain open, and extra provisions were placed on the market.[33]

According to David's plan:

> All Frenchmen who wish[ed] to celebrate the Festival of Unity and of Indivisibility [were to] rise before the dawn, so that the touching scene of their gathering [might] be illumined by the sun's first rays . . . . [which were to] be for them the symbol of Truth to which they would address their songs of praise.

Except for the fact that the ceremony began at seven instead of at four in the morning, everything went off as scheduled.[34] The delegates of the Convention, the departments, the primary assemblies and the enor-

[32] July 20: *P.V. Conv.*, XVII, 27; *Col. Baud.*, XXXII, 162; *Moniteur*, no. 204 (July 23, 1793), p. 874; *Mercure universel*, no. 871 (July 21), p. 330; *Journal de l'instruction publique*, I, no. 1 [n.d.], p. 64. August 9: *P.V. Conv.*, XVIII, 241–42; *Col. Baud.*, XXXIII, 68; *Moniteur*, no. 222 (August 10), p. 946; *Journal de Perlet*, no. 323 (August 10), p. 77; cf. *Journal de la Montagne, Courrier français, Journal de Paris, Chronique de Paris, Gazette de France, Gazette générale de l'Europe; Instruction pour l'ordre à observer le jour de la Fête de la Réunion* [Paris: Imp. nat., 1793].

[33] *Courrier universel*, (August 10, 1793), p. 3; *Journal des Jacobins*, debates, no. 470 (August 13), p. 1; cf. *Courier de l'égalité, Gazette de France, Thermomètre, Journal de Perlet*, and others.

[34] For contemporary descriptions: *Annales patriotiques*, no. 223 (August 12, 1793), pp. 1025–26, 1029–30; *Feuille villageoise*, III, pt. 6, no. 46 (August 15), pp. 475–78; cf. *Journal de l'instruction publique, Annales de la République française, Le Républicain français, Nouvelles politiques, Courier de l'égalité, Gazette de France, Courier français, Journal des hommes libres, Journal du soir sans réflexions, Journal de Paris, Gazette générale de l'Europe; Journal de France;* Dispatch of Lama to Ventura, Paris, August 12, 1792: Grouchy, *op. cit.*, pp. 465–68. Cf. Touchard-Lafosse, IV, 193–200; Conny, *op. cit.*, pp. 189–92; C. F. Beaulieu, *Essais historiques sur la révolution* (Paris: Maradan, 1803), V, 466–68; Dulaure, *Esquisses*, III, 63–64; *Tableaux historiques*, II, 346–48. For music, *see* Pierre, *Musique*, pp. 52–70; J. Tiersot, *Les fêtes et les chants de la révolution française* (Paris: Hachette, 1908), pp. 94–96.

mous crowds assembled on the site of the Bastille where a colossal goddess of Nature "jetted from her breasts the waters of regeneration." In turn each of the fête's five monuments was the scene of an imposing ceremony punctuated by a multitude of "harangues," "fraternal kisses," "salvoes of artillery," and "joyous songs." [35] After the symbolic ritual of fraternal regeneration the great procession moved off along the boulevards.

In the first group marched the popular societies in force carrying a banner with the all-seeing eye of surveillance. Next came the members of the Convention as a group, escorted by the envoys of the primary assemblies, bearing in their midst the ark which enclosed the official copy of the Constitution. The third group consisted of "all the sovereign people" mingled without distinction of class, color, or office. A chariot of liberty; floats, and groups honoring the aged, the blind, the foundling, the worker with his tools, the soldier who died for his country; and military units were featured. The whole symbolic procession, which underlined the principles of unity, liberty, equality, and fraternity, was decked with garlands and sheaves, liberty caps, tricolored ribbons, fasces, and olive branches; enlivened by drums, trumpets, and choruses; and embellished with inscriptions. David kept this enormous parade moving on schedule by an ingenious system of signals.

The second station was a triumphal arch on the Boulevard Poissonière where the participants were greeted by the heroines of October 6. On the pedestal of Louis XV's statue in the Place de la Révolution was erected a colossal statue of Liberty before which royal symbols were burned and thousands of birds were liberated. At the Place des Invalides a gigantic figure of the French people annihilating federalism dominated the scene. The Constitution was proclaimed at the fifth station, the Altar of the Fatherland on the Champ de Mars, and

[35] For descriptions of the monuments, *see* in addition to those cited above: *Procès-verbal des monumens . . . de la fête . . .* [Paris: Imp. nat., 1793]; *P.V. Conv.*, XVIII, 253–68; *Moniteur*, no. 224 (August 12, 1793), p. 954; Wille, *op. cit.*, II, 387–92; R. Farge, "Les Derniers pierres de la Bastille," *A.R.*, VII (January, 1914), 27–28. Contemporary prints: "Monuments nationaux élevés pour la Fête de la Fraternité" by Blanchard (medallions of the 5 stations); repr.: Normand, *op. cit.*, p. 77; cf. six sketches possibly by David: repr.: E. F. Henderson, *Symbol and Satire in the French Revolution* (New York: Putnam, 1912), pp. 356–57. "La Fontaine de la régénération sur les débris de la Bastille," by Monnet, engr. by Helman. (*See* plate XV, opposite p. 112); "Acceptation de la Constitution républicaine," by S. Desfontaines, engr. by Bertault: no. 86, *Tableaux historiques*, II, 348.

XV. FESTIVAL OF UNITY AND INDIVISIBILITY, AUGUST 10, 1793

"La Fontaine de la Régénération"

Engraving by Helman after Monnet

the people swore to defend it to the death, to the sound of artillery salvoes and loud cries of *"vive la République!"* Finally, the precious document enclosed in its cedar "ark," and the fasces, symbols of national unity, were solemnly deposited at the Convention. The ceremonies closed with songs, dances, embracing, fraternal banquets, and a military pantomine of the siege of Lille. The last was extremely effective in firing the emotions of the spectators.

Though the Constitution of 1793 remained a dead letter (the nation had first to be saved before it could be decentralized), the sensation created by David's splendid fête was very great. A crowd of more than 200,000 enthusiastically applauded this panorama of the Revolution. Though the celebration lasted at least sixteen hours, there was no disorder, but only "joyous tranquillity." With extra food in the shops the day passed without bread riots. Despite sinister rumors of trouble and the "efforts of evil intentioned persons," there were no untoward incidents.[36]

The festival was hailed by the press as signifying a "fraternal accord between the deputies of the departments and the Parisians," foretelling the speedy destruction of "federalism, royalism, and of all the aristocracies which wish to destroy the liberty and indivisibility of the Republic." [37] These remarks were typical of those made by the journals still being published. It was only later that the opponents of the Jacobins could publish their scathing denunciations of "this hideous and disgusting ceremony," "this saturnalia of regicides and atheists." They were particularly enraged by such gruesome details as the severed heads painted on the Arch of October 6. Only one Jacobin appears to have publicly criticized the fête. He did so on the grounds that the time would have been better spent in military training.[38] As a matter of fact, the festival turned out to be a means of preparing public

[36] *Annales de la République française,* no. 225 (August 12), pp. 1109; *Courier français,* no. 223 (August 11), p. 3. *See* descriptions cited above, and in addition: *Courier de l'égalité,* no. 359 (August 12), p. 342; *Thermomètre,* no. 589 (August 12), p. 346; *Je suis le véritable Père Duchêne* (Hébert), no. 271 [n.d.], p. 3; *Courrier universel* (August 10), p. 3; and others.

[37] *Gazette de France,* no. 225 (August 13), p. 971. *Gazette générale de l'Europe,* no. 359 (August 11), p. 4; *Le Républicain français,* no. 268 (August 10), p. 1090.

[38] Vasselin, *Mémorial,* (1797), II, 219. Lacretelle, *Histoire* (1825), XI, 65. Conny, *op. cit.,* pp. 189–90; Beaulieu, *op. cit.,* V, 468; André Chénier, "Odes français," 6: "Un vulgaire assassin . . . ," *Oeuvres complètes,* III, 250. Jacobin meeting, August 11, 1793: *Journal des Jacobins,* debates, no. 471 (August 14), p. 1.

opinion for the *levée en masse* and the law of suspects demanded by the deputies from the departments.

The Convention, by appropriating a million livres for the festival, indicated how much importance it attached to the symbolism of David's pageant. The constitutional ark and the fasces of unity which had figured so prominently in it were enshrined in their meeting hall next day. The deputies decreed that a medal designed by David in commemoration of the festival should be struck and distributed. It was even suggested that it be given monetary value. On October 10 the Convention decreed that the national seal and the new coins should bear the emblems of the festival—the ark, fasces, and goddess of Nature. The other fragile plaster monuments of the fête made such a striking impression upon the people that the Committee of Public Safety later voted that they should be executed in bronze and marble. Durable materials were lacking, however, so the statues remained standing for many years in a dilapidated condition.[39]

Then, too, dramatic representations of the symbolic ceremonies of the festival were given in the Paris theaters for many months to come. The five acts of the topical drama, *La Réunion du dix-août, ou l'inauguration de la République française; sans culottide dramatique . . . au peuple souverain* by Gabriel Bouquier and Pierre Louis Moline, reproduced the scenery of the five stations of David's festival, and its action merely re-enacted the ceremonial of the program. This play's popularity seems to indicate that the public did not soon grow tired of the Fête of August 10. Such coordinated theatrical presentations became characteristic features of the revolutionary festivals.[40]

The confidence of the Convention was not misplaced. By composing an immense living fresco of the Revolution, David had depicted the ideology of the times and synthesized and rendered concrete and

[39] Decrees of August 11, 20 and October 10, 1793: *P.V. Conv.*, XVIII, 290–91, XIX, 112–13, XXII, 206; *Col. Baud.*, XXXIII, 193, XXV, 171; *Journal de l'instruction publique,* I, no. 3 [n.d.], pp. 187–88, no. 4 [n.d.], pp. 191–92, III, no. 14 [n.d.], p. 69. C.P.S. decree of 5 Floréal, an II [April 24, 1794]: *C.S.P.*, XIII, 23–24. Dulaure, *op. cit.*, III, 64; Beaulieu, *op. cit.*, V, 468; Farge, *op. cit.*, pp. 27–28; Letter of November 24, 1796: A. Babeau, ed., *La France et Paris sous le directoire* (Paris: Firmin-Didot, 1888), p. 97.

[40] *La Réunion du dix-août* . . . (Paris: Vatar, an II [1793]). B. F. Hyslop, "The Parisian Theater During the Reign of Terror," *Journal of Modern History,* XVII (December, 1945), 344–45; *Journal de la Montagne,* no. 124 (March 19, 1794), p. 1002.

intelligible the essential aims of the Government. Through the living symbolism of his procession, David painted for the illiterate masses of Paris a magnificent illustration of the principles of the Revolution. The painter had once more proved himself a master of the art of manipulating significant symbols—the festival was virtually a catalogue of revolutionary figures and emblems.

Like its predecessors, the Festival of Unity and Indivisibility was purely secular in spirit as well as in symbolism. Aulard's statement that this celebration was "the first of the national fêtes which had a purely civic, or, as we should say, secular character," is somewhat misleading.[41] Nevertheless, though it was by no means the first lay festival, the Fête of August 10 contributed powerfully to the still growing dechristianization movement. It may be concluded that the festival was a brilliant success and a propitious symbol of the reunion of the French people after the event of June 2. France demonstrated to the world "her strength, her moral credit, and her faith in the future." [42] Confidence replaced the tragic feeling of despair which had prevailed earlier in the summer.

This victory of the Jacobins was based on their conviction that war had made unity a necessity and federalism a crime. August 10 propagated this idea and symbolized the confidence of the country in Paris and the Convention. The festival helped to identify Jacobinism with the Revolution and the anti-Jacobinism of the Royalist or Girondin variety with counter-revolution.

The Convention had now to make good and justify the confidence of the country by exercising its powers in the national interest. Once public opinion had been prepared, one energetic decree followed another. The delegates for the primary assemblies had brought with them demands that all suspects be arrested and that a *levée en masse* be carried out. On August 23 universal military service and the mobilization of all resources of the nation, human and material, was decreed. If France was to be saved from disintegration and annihilation, nothing short of Herculean efforts would suffice.

By the end of the summer of 1793 the federalist revolt had virtually collapsed, but the foreign invasion still hung like a cloud on the hori-

[41] *Le Christianisme et la révolution française* (Paris: Rieder, 1925), pp. 102–03. *See* p. 50.

[42] J. L. Jaurès, *La Convention* [*Histoire socialiste,* IV] (Paris: Rouff, [1905]) , II, 1634.

zon. The surrender of Toulon to the English (August 28) was the culmination of a series of military disasters. The immediate effect of this alarming news was to intensify the policy of Terror which had already begun. Reorganization of the Revolutionary Tribunal, adoption of the Law of Suspects (September 17), reform of the Committee of General Security, and many other drastic measures followed. Under the powerful and vigorous Committee of Public Safety the nation was transformed into a vast military machine with but one object, namely, to save France. On October 10, the Convention suspended the Constitution of 1793 for the duration of the war and the government became "revolutionary until the peace." According to the contemporary phrase Terror was "the order of the day."

The first military objective was of course the recapture of Toulon. During the long siege that ensued, the tide gradually turned in favor of the Republic. Restored confidence of the French and disunity of their enemies resulted in the victories of Hondschoote, Wattignies, Wörth and Weissenburg which cleared the way to the Rhine during the closing months of 1793. The unity symbolized and inspired by the Fête of August 10 was manifested in the complete success of the Revolutionary armies by the end of the year. When Toulon was retaken from the English on December 18, a wave of enthusiasm swept the country.[43]

David, always sensitive to the ebb and flow of public opinion, seized the opportunity to propose a new propaganda demonstration which should clearly associate in men's minds the policies of his party and the military successes of the Republic. On December 24, 1793, at the moment the good news was announced by Barère, the Convention decreed a celebration in honor of the victory at Toulon which should also be "a triumph of the Mountain party" observed in all parts of France.[44] Next day David presented a plan of the national fête which

[43] *See* the reports of the secret police printed in P. Caron, ed., *Paris pendant la Terreur* (Paris: Société de l'histoire contemporaine, 1910), I, 371–79, and contemporary newspaper accounts such as *Feuille villageoise, Journal de Paris, Mercure français, Gazette de France, Journal de la Montagne, Journal de Perlet, Journal du soir, de politique et de littérature, Mercure universel,* and others. Cf. Cardenal, *Province,* p. 312; Fantin-Desodoards, *Histoire philosophique,* V, 189; Gallois, *Histoire de la Convention,* VI, 1.

[44] Decree of 4 Nivôse, an II: *P.V. Conv.,* XXVIII, 84–85; *Col. Baud.,* XXXVIII, 36; *Mercure universel,* no. 1019 (December 25, 1793), pp. 78–79; cf. *Courrier universel, Gazette de France, Moniteur,* and others.

was to honor the successes of *all* the armies of the Republic. Wounded veterans of the campaigns were to ride in chariots in the place of honor in the procession.[45] The following day the artist's program was adopted and received wide publicity in the press, in the Commune, and in the Jacobin Club where his talents were praised by Robespierre's brother.[46]

Accordingly, at seven o'clock on the "cold but serenely beautiful" morning of December 30, a salvo of artillery signaled the beginning of the victory celebration.[47] In marked contrast to the triumphal processions of the old order, civilians as well as the military participated in this republican "march past" which honored not generals but the common soldiers and the workers.[48] The armed delegates of the forty-eight sections and of the fourteen armies; the triumphal cars full of wounded, draped with captured battle flags and escorted by young girls in white; deputations of the popular societies with their respective banners; the members of the National Convention *en masse* with other officials; and a military escort—all these marched through the streets of Paris to the rolling thunder of massed drums, the martial music of brass bands, and the sonorous strains of triumphal hymns. The national fasces, statues of Victory, *bonnets rouges,* tricolor ban-

[45] December 25: *P.V. Conv.,* XXVIII, 100–01; *J.D.D.,* no. 463 [n.d.], p. 28; *Journal de la Montagne,* II, no. 44 (7 Nivôse), p. 352; cf. *Moniteur, Gazette de France, Mercure universel;* David, *Rapport fait . . . en mémoire des victoires des armées françaises et notament à l'occasion de la prise de Toulon* [Paris: Imp. nat., 1793].

[46] December 26, 1793: *P.V. Conv.,* XXXII, 288; *J.D.D.,* no. 464 [n.d.], p. 9; *Journal du soir, de politique et de littérature,* no. 459 (December 27), p. 3, no. 463 (December 30), p. 4; cf. *Journal de Paris, Moniteur, Gazette de France, Journal de l'instruction publique, Courrier universal, Courier républicain, Mercure universel, Courier de l'égalité, Nouvelles politiques, Journal de la Montagne,* and others.

[47] For descriptions, see *Journal de l'instruction publique,* V, no. 28 [n.d.], pp. 383–84; *Journal de France,* no. 466 (14 Nivôse), p. 4; *Feuille villageoise,* IV, pt. 7, no. 15 (January 9), p. 353; *Nouvelles politiques,* no. 41 (December 31), p. 163; *Courier républicain,* no. 62 (December 31), pp. 4–6; *Le Républicain français,* no. 410 (12 Nivôse), pp. 1659–60; *Journal de Perlet,* VIII, no. 465 (December 31), pp. 246–48; *Mercure universel,* no. 1025 (December 31), pp. 165–66; *Je suis le véritable Père Duchêne* (Hébert), no. 329 [n.d.], pp. 1–8; *Révolutions de Paris,* XVII, no. 220 (14 Nivôse), pp. 377–79; *Courrier universel* (December 31), p. 4. *Ordre de la marche de la fête . . . 10 nivôse an II en mémoire des victoires des armées françaises, et notament à l'occasion de la prise de Toulon* [Paris: Imp. nat., 1793].

[48] Several papers commented on this contrast; e.g., *Mercure universel,* XXXV, no. 1025 (December 31, 1793), p. 165; *Feuille villageoise,* IV, pt. 7, no. 15 (January 9, 1794), p. 356.

ners, a ship,[49] and other symbols figured prominently. Leaving the Tuileries Gardens the triumphal procession wound its way through the city and across the Seine to the Hôtel des Invalides, and was finally brought to a close with a hymn by M.-J. Chénier and a banquet for the wounded heroes on the Champ de Mars.

This great victory demonstration, the first of a series in honor of the defenders of the Fatherland and their successes, was enthusiastically acclaimed by patriotic Frenchmen. Since the opposition press had been virtually driven from the field, the newspapers of the day agreed with the *Journal de Perlet* and the *Nouvelles politiques nationales et étrangères,* who claimed that the ceremony was "a really magnificent spectacle" which had been "celebrated with the pomp and majesty which recalled to mind the festivals of the republics of Greece and Rome." Such comments were typical of the periodical press.[50]

A writer for the *Révolutions de Paris,* (perhaps Momoro) who had criticized the classical allusions of the symbolism, insisted that the parade "created a great sensation." "The people," he continued, "were a show in themselves, so vast was the procession. There was no ostentation; gold did not dazzle the eyes; but harmony and gaiety reigned supreme." The enormous crowds which witnessed the ceremonies were said to have expressed great joy and high spirits and to have wildly expressed their hatred of the enemy, their enthusiasm for the armed forces, and their gratitude to the Convention.[51]

The reports of the special observers of the Ministry of the Interior corroborated the enthusiastic press accounts. According to one of these secret agents the festival "was very brilliant, very gay and very patriotic . . . . Everyone showed the greatest spirit of fraternity." "The design of the festival was," according to another special agent, "superb, noble, great, in a word, worthy of him who conceived it, David." It

[49] This ship model labeled "Naval Army" was hastily included by David at the last moment to represent the French Navy: *Moniteur,* no. 100 (10 Nivôse), p. 403; *Journal du soir, de politique et de littérature,* no. 463 (10 Nivôse), p. 2; *Nouvelles politiques,* no. 41 (December 31), p. 163.

[50] *Journal de Perlet,* no. 465 (December 31, 1793), p. 246. *Nouvelles politiques,* no. 41 (December 31), p. 163. Cf. *Le Républicain français,* no. 410 (12 Nivôse), p. 1659, and *Journal de France,* no. 466 (January 31, 1794), p. 4 and others.

[51] *Révolutions de Paris,* no. 220 (14 Nivôse), pp. 377–79. *Je suis le véritable Père Duchêne* (Hébert), no. 329 [n.d.], pp. 4–6; cf. *Le Républicain français, Journal de France, Courier de l'égalité, Courier républicain, Nouvelles politiques, Courrier universel,* and others.

is true that two of the ubiquitous police agents overheard cynical murmurings of "bread and circuses" and observed an occasional "suspect" who failed to share in the public joy. Nevertheless, most accounts agree that "patriotic enthusiasm was the order of the day" and that the sight of the wounded veterans profoundly excited the emotions of the great majority of the crowd.[52]

Nor was the victory celebration limited to Paris alone. In accordance with the decree of December 24, civic rejoicings in honor of the surrender of Toulon were also celebrated by Jacobin clubs and local officials in the various provincial centers with "much lustre." The demonstration in the capital was such a distinct success that, to express its satisfaction, the Convention honored David with the president's chair within the week (January 5). All the Parisian theaters presented plays on the Toulon victory theme to reinforce the fête's message.[53]

The last and most brilliant of the great festivals, the Fête of the Supreme Being, was celebrated not long before the fall of Robespierre and the end of the regime of "Virtue." It was therefore significant as the culmination of David's propaganda pageants and marks the height of Robespierre's power. More than this it represented the triumph of the dechristianizing deism of the Enlightenment and the fruition of the educational program of the Committee of Public Instruction. Last of all the scheme has been commonly regarded as a personal project of Robespierre to acquire pontifical and dictatorial powers.

Since the Feast of the Supreme Being is the best known of the revolutionary festivals, and various aspects of the problem have already been discussed by such scholars as Aulard and Mathiez,[54] the present

[52] Reports of Bucon, Charmont, Le Harivel, Mercier, and Rolin: Caron, *op. cit.*, II, 79, 80, 88–89, 90, 93, 94. *Révolutions de Paris,* no. 220 (14 Nivôse), pp. 377–78; *Feuille villageoise,* no. 14 (January 7), p. 328; *Mercure universel,* no. 1025 (December 31), p. 165, and others.

[53] H. Labroue, ed., *La Société populaire de Bergerac pendant la révolution* (Paris: S.H.R.F., 1915), p. 344; F. Martin, ed., *Jacobins au village* (Clermont-Ferrand: Juliot, 1902), pp. 102–19; B. Bois, *Les Fêtes révolutionnaires à Anger* (Paris: Alcan, [1929]), pp. 26–31; G. Laurent, *Les Fêtes révolutionnaires dans le département de la Marne* (Reims: 1899), pp. 13–14; Cardenal, *op. cit.*, p. 299; *C.I.P.*, IV, 243. *See* p. 88 note 46. *P.V. Conv.*, XXVIII, 339. Hyslop, "The Theater during the Terror," p. 344.

[54] Aulard, *Le Culte de la Raison et le culte de l'Etre-suprême* (Paris: Alcan, 1892); *Le Christianisme et la révolution.* Mathiez, "Robespierre et le culte de l'Etre-suprême," *A.R.*, III (1910), 209–38; "Robespierre et la déchristianization," *A.R.*, II (1909), 321–55, 513–40.

treatment is confined to a brief summary with some elaboration of its less known aspects.

The *philosophes* and the early leaders of the Revolution had emphasized the vital role that festivals should play in government; and in all of the educational plans of the Committee of Public Instruction they were regarded as a fundamental method of social control. Marie-Joseph Chénier merely expressed their thought when he declared on 15 Brumaire that the purpose of instruction was "to form republicans" and that the fêtes were fundamental for this purpose.[55]

The Convention agreed and ordered the Committee to make a report on a system of national festivals. David was named as one of the commissioners who drew up a system of five annual and thirty-six *fêtes décadaires.* When ready, their report was read by Mathieu to the Committee, which discussed it and had it printed. On March 31 the Committee of Public Safety was consulted.[56]

Robespierre and his colleagues immediately realized the part that the project could play in their policy so they took the matter into their own hands. They had just struck down Danton and Hébert, and many patriots were confused and divided. Furthermore, the Jacobin social and economic policy, though not unsympathetic to the interests of the masses, had failed to win over the workers and peasants completely, and the grave economic situation threatened famine and inflation. Robespierre had come to the conclusion that fêtes should be used to create as well as to control public opinion. This plan for a system of festivals provided the basis for a state religion identified with patriotism which might well be used by the government for this very purpose.

Robespierre, and probably most of the Convention, conceived the ideal state as the reign of justice and virtue. The establishment and maintenance of the purity of these great ideals, they believed, required a great moral force, such as religion. Since they had discarded the Roman Catholic faith, a new cult must be found. The new revolutionary religion must satisfy the people's spiritual longing for God and

[55] November 5, 1793: *Discours prononcé à la Convention . . . de l'instruction publique* [Paris: Imp. nat., 1793], pp. 2, 8; *Journal de l'instruction publique,* IV, no. 22 [n.d.], pp. 309, 317.

[56] *P.V. Conv.,* XXIV, 331. C.P.I. meetings, November 19 and 23, 1793, January 2, 10, 22, February 27, March 31, 1794: *C.I.P.,* II, 867, III, 2, 232, 267, 505, IV, 55. J. B. C. Mathieu-Mirampal, *Projet de fêtes nationales* [Paris: Imp. nat., 1794]. Cf. *P.V. Conv.,* XXVI, 141, XXVII, 335.

immortality, and at the same time must inculcate patriotism and democracy by means of regular ceremonies. Their aim was a social and political one: to provide a rallying point for the divided patriots around a doctrine and around the Government.

As early as April 6, 1794, Couthon announced a project of *fêtes décadaires* as a means of purifying public morals and creating a regenerated people.[57] During the next month government spokesmen prepared public opinion,[58] and Robespierre carefully elaborated a report on the harmony of religious and moral ideas with patriotic and republican principles, and their inculcation by means of national fêtes.

This famous speech, perhaps the greatest of Robespierre's career, was delivered to the Convention on 18 Floréal. In it "The Incorruptible" adapted Rousseau's worship of the Supreme Being to existing political conditions and had it accepted as the official faith, with David to furnish an appropriate inauguration. The artist himself then read a carefully worked out plan for the cult's first great festival. His plan was unanimously adopted by the Convention and the Committee of Public Instruction was charged with its execution.[59]

Public opinion was carefully prepared for the establishment of the new cult. The decree of 18 Floréal was ordered translated into all languages and was publicly read each *décadi* in the former churches for a month. Jacobin spokesmen rhapsodized over the coming fête,

[57] Convention meeting, 17 Germinal, an II: *J.D.D.*, no. 564 [n.d.], p. 289; *Mercure français,* VIII, no. 15 (23 Germinal), p. 332; *Journal de Paris,* no. 462 (18 Germinal), p. 1867.

[58] Speeches of Payan, national agent of the Commune of Paris (April 19, 1794): *Moniteur,* no. 228 (18 Floréal), p. 924; *Décade philosophique,* I, no. 1 (10 Floréal), pp. 59–60; of Amar, president of the Convention (April 20): *J.D.D.*, no. 578 [n.d.], pp. 2–3; and of Billaud-Varenne, spokesman of the Committee of Public Safety (April 20): *Rapport . . . sur la théorie du gouvernement démocratique . . . et sur la nécessité . . . des . . . fêtes publiques . . .* [Paris: Imp. nat., 1794].

[59] May 7, 1794: *P.V. Conv.*, XXXVII, 45, 49; *J.D.D.*, no. 595 [n.d.], p. 229, no. 596 [n.d.], pp. 239–59, no. 597 [n.d.], pp. 27–74; *Col. Baud.*, XLII, 113; *Moniteur,* no. 229 (19 Floréal), pp. 928–32; M. M. I. de Robespierre, *Rapport . . . sur les rapports des idées religieuses et morales avec les principes républicains, et sur les fêtes nationales suivi du Plan de la Fête à l'Etre-suprême qui doit être célébrée le 20 prairial, proposé par David* [Paris: Imp. nat., 1794]. The speech was also published in most of the newspapers, e.g., *Auditeur national,* VII, no. 592 (19 Floréal), p. 2 through no. 603 (30 Floréal), p. 7. Cf. *Feuille villageoise, Journal de Paris, Journal de Perlet, Décade philosophique, Journal de la Montagne,* and others.

the commissioners in charge were carefully instructed, and the program was published in detail.[60] Under David's direction, temporary stands, vast monuments, and even an artificial mountain were erected, and streets and houses were elaborately decorated for the event. The pains taken to insure the success of the fête were great, and they served to indicate the high importance attached to it by the government.

The appointed day, 20 Prairial, dawned clear and beautiful.[61] At

[60] *P.V. Conv.*, XXXVII, 49; *J.D.D.*, no. 595 [n.d.], p. 229; *C.S.P.*, XIII, 526. Speeches of Payan, Collot d'Herbois, Julien, and Couthon (May 14–16, 1794): *Moniteur*, no. 243 (3 Prairial), p. 988, no. 238 (28 Floréal), p. 968; *Adresse lue au nom des Jacobins par Julien . . . à la barre de la Convention 27 floréal . . . ; discours par . . . Couthon* [Paris: Imp. nat., 1794]; *Journal de Paris*, no. 502 (28 Floréal), p. 2026. *Instruction particulière pour les commissaires chargés des détails de la fête de l'Etre-suprême* [Paris: Imp. nat., 1794]. *Détail des cérémonies et de l'ordre à observer dans la fête à l'Etre-suprême* [Paris: Imp. nat., 1794]. Reprinted in most of the newspapers, e.g., *Le Messager du soir*, no. 657 (June 5), pp. 2–3.

[61] The best known account of the féte is in the *Moniteur* (no. 265 [25 Prairial], p. 1077). Even the hostile critic Charles Nodier when he wrote years later based his imaginative description upon it instead of drawing solely upon his own fancy as he has been accused of doing. Other newspapers give equally vivid narratives, however: e.g., *Le Républicain français*, no. 567 (25 Prairial), pp. 2329–30; cf. *Journal universel, Courier républicain, Journal de Perlet, Journal de la Montagne, Journal du Soir* (Feuillant), *Le Messager du soir, Gazette générale de l'Europe, Nouvelles politiques, Mercure universel, Journal de France, Courier de l'égalité, Décade philosophique, Gazette française, Journal de Paris*. Unfortunately, most of the other press accounts seem to be copied or paraphrased from the official program: *Détail des cérémonies et de l'ordre à observer dans la fête à l'Etre-suprême* [Paris: Imp. nat., 1794]. Other eyewitness accounts used were: Baudot, *op. cit.*, pp. 171–73; P.N. Berryer, *Souvenirs* (Paris: Dupont, 1839), I, 222–24; P.T. Durand de Maillane, *Histoire de la Convention . . .* (Paris: Baudouin, 1825), pp. 185–89; Millingen, *Recollections*, pp. 276–79; J. Vilate, *Causes secrètes de la révolution du 9 au 10 Thermidor* (Paris, [1794]), pp. 35–37; [H.M. Williams], *A Residence in France* (Elizabethtown [N.J.]: Kollock, 1798), p. 329, *Letters from France*, II, 86; P.C. Lecomte, *Mémorial ou journal historique . . .* (Paris: Duponcet, 1801), I, 282 ff.; C.F. Ruggieri, *Précis historique sur les fêtes . . .* (Paris: l'auteur, 1830), pp. 327–30; P.F. Tissot, *Histoire complète de la révolution* (Paris: Baudouin, 1835), V, 219–26. The following memoirs and recollections though of uneven value provided additional information: Beaulieu, V, 488–89; Conny de la Fay, pp. 292–94; Duval, IV, 344–62; Delécluze, pp. 7–8; Dulaure, III, 265; Lenoir, p. 7; [Lamothe-Langon] *Histoire*, IV, 24–31; Mercier, *Nouveau Paris*, IV, 146–50; [Monnel], II, 184–86; Pougens, pp. 174–76; Senar, pp. 188–89; Touchard-Lafosse, V, 27–29; Vasselin, III, 322–23. C.A. Dauban, ed., *Paris en 1794* (Paris: Plon, 1869), and F.A. Aulard, *Le Culte de la Raison et le culte de l'Etre-suprême*, pp. 307–21, quote extensively from archival documents.

sunrise, to the strains of martial music the eager populace poured into the streets, formed by sections, and marched to the Tuileries Gardens. The members of the Convention, clad in new uniforms, carrying bouquets, and headed by Robespierre, their president, soon took their places on the platform. To the assembled throng the "Incorruptible" preached a sermon, and then, after a hymn, he descended and with a torch presented by David, ignited a cardboard statue of Atheism, which went up in flames, revealing underneath a somewhat smoke-stained image of Wisdom. Following a second speech by Robespierre and a "simple song," the procession formed up and moved off in perfect order toward the Champ de Mars. This procession, in which classicism and emotionalism were balanced and patriotic and humanitarian symbols were combined, was David's masterpiece in this art. At its destination the painter had constructed a huge symbolic mountain. Robespierre led the Convention to its lofty summit while the delegates of the sections occupied the slopes, and the enormous crowds sang appropriate verses and fraternized below. Then the youths and old men re-enacted the symbolic rite depicted in David's *Oath of the Horatii.*[62] The celebration ended with salvoes of artillery, fraternal embraces, and prolonged cries of *"Vive la République!"*

This great festival marks the apex of the Jacobin regime. The apotheosis of Robespierre and the whispers against his rumored personal theocracy hastened his fall. During the procession there were ominous mutterings against dictatorship, and the sarcasms of some of Robespierre's colleagues indicated the approach of Thermidor.[63] Nevertheless, contemporary and later accounts are generally agreed that 20 Prairial was the most brilliant and popular of all of the fêtes of the Revolution.[64] This was true in the departments, too, for it

[62] *See* p. 1 and reproduction opposite p. 2.

[63] [Baron Lamothe-Langon], *Mémoires et souvenirs d'un Pair de France* (Paris: Tenon, 1829), II, 349; J. Vilate, *Les Mystères de la Mère de Dieu dévoilés* (Paris: Baudouin, 1825), p. 313; and memoirs of Baudot, pp. 4–5, 80; Conny, pp. 294–95; Duval, IV, 356–57; Dulaure, III, 284–85; [Monnel], II, 184–86; Sergent, p. 315; Thibaudeau, I, 64; Courtois, *Rapport,* pp. 35n, 48; Lacretelle, *Histoire,* VI, 15–18.

[64] *See* references in note 61. On this point even Aulard (*Le Culte,* pp. 323–68) and Mathiez ("Robespierre et le culte de l'Etre-suprême," p. 228) for once come close to agreement. Dissenting voices are few: A.C. Merlin (de Thionville), *Opinion . . . sur les fêtes nationales* [Paris: Imp. nat., 1794], pp. 2 ff.; [Williams], *Residence,* p. 330; Mercier, *Nouveau Paris,* IV, 149.

[65] There is a wealth of material on this and other festivals in the provinces, e.g.: *Journal de la Montagne,* no. 43 (20 Prairial), p. 341; V. Forot, ed., *Le Club des*

realized a common dream.[65] Even abroad, "it was really believed that Robespierre was about to close the abyss of the Revolution."[66] Though for Robespierre it might be the beginning of the end, for the people it had been a triumphant success.

For one brief day the Republic of Virtue was a reality. On the morrow the Law of 22 Prairial was to shift the machinery of the Terror into high gear only to be checked by the Thermidorian reaction against both blood and virtue. But for the moment the aim of Robespierre, of the Committee of Public Safety, and of the Convention had been attained: patriots rallied round a common doctrine and round the Government. The French revolutionaries felt the thrill of a religious glorification of liberty, equality, and fraternity, and a tremendous patriotic self-confidence in the face of their enemies.

Jacobins de Tulle. Procès-verbaux . . . (Tulle: Corrézien Républicain, 1912), pp. 393, 607; Martin, ed., *Jacobins au village,* pp. 167, 169; *Fête à l'Etre suprême . . . à Chaumont* (n.p., n.d.); Cardenal, *op. cit.,* pp. 331–33; Déy, *op. cit.,*p. 566, Laurent, *op. cit.,* p. 15; Bois, *op. cit.,* p. 19; Dommanget, "Le déchristianisation à Beauvais," *A.R.,* XIII (1921), 274; R. Fagé, "Les fêtes . . . à Toul," Société de Corrèze, *Bulletin,* XXVII (1905), 364–67; E. Lemaire, *Les Fêtes publiques à Saint-Quentin pendant la révolution* . . . (Saint-Quentin: Moureau, 1884), pp. 73–75.

[66] J. Mallet du Pan, *Mémoires et correspondance,* ed., Sayous (Paris: Amyot, 1851), II, 99n.

CHAPTER VI

Propaganda and the Republic of Virtue

The Festival of the Supreme Being was the last one organized and directed by David, and it was at the same time the last important fête fulfilling his requirement of popular participation. After only occasional experiments during the following century and a quarter, David's technique was again employed on an extensive scale by another generation of self-styled revolutionists in Moscow, Rome, and Berlin. There seems to have been little doubt as to the effectiveness of the pageant technique in the hands of the followers of Lenin, Mussolini, and Hitler. The problem here is to evaluate the potency, significance, and results of the *fêtes nationales* of the French Revolution as a propaganda weapon.

It is clear that the festival is a social control technique of fundamental importance. It can exert a powerful influence upon the opinions, or more correctly, the sentiments of large popular groups. Through its use new collective attitudes can be created by exposure to the dramatic appeal of pageantry and symbolism, and potential loyalties can be expressed and reinforced through mass participation in common ceremonies. Political authorities and other groups have frequently availed themselves of these social advantages. During the French Revolution the festival reached its highest development up to that time. When the emotional and dramatic appeal of colorful pageantry and ceremonial, parades, music, slogans, symbols, and oratory were combined by revolutionary artists with official processions, theatrical programs, and, above all, with mass participation, then the ancient institution of the festival was found to be one of the most potent methods of controlling public opinion employed during the period.

Originating in 1790 in the spontaneous federation celebrations in provincial centers,[1] festivals continued to flourish in the departments as well as in the capital. As has already been noted, each important fête in Paris came to have its counterpart in the provinces.[2] Festivals

[1] *See*, pp. 45–46.

[2] *See* for example, p. 99 note 3, pp. 119, 123.

of Liberty, Reason, Victory, the Supreme Being, and other revolutionary abstractions were organized all over France and were patterned after those held in Paris. More and more they became mere reflections of the festivities in the capital until centralized control was established, and the programs of the fêtes of Paris were repeated in provincial centers with greater or less success. One shortcoming of these local celebrations was the small scale on which most of them had to be conducted. Ceremonies which were impressive on the vast boulevards and squares of Paris became insignificant or even ludicrous in the narrow streets and tiny market places of country towns and villages. Nevertheless, the local Jacobin societies, municipal officials, and deputies-on-mission enthusiastically promoted the new cult of patriotism with the propaganda technique which was so successful in Paris.[3]

Nor was this method of social control used only in France. Examples of festivals are to be found in French colonies such as Saint Domingue, and even in the United States. There was a *fête civique* in Petit-Goave, Saint-Domingue, as early as May 21, 1790, which reflected similar flag blessings and constitutional proclamations in the mother country. In February, 1793, a rather crude imitation of David's Fête of Liberty was produced in Boston. A somewhat more sophisticated festival in honor of the destruction of despotism and the inauguration of the worship of the Supreme Being was celebrated in Philadelphia on August 10, 1794, under the auspices of the French minister. In its details it aped the great Davidian celebration of Paris but fell short in execution. Next year on the anniversary of the King's execution (January 21) the French colony conducted a festival to show its "hatred for tyranny." A *fête civique* observed on April 17, 1795, by French, Dutch, and American "patriots" to celebrate the "emancipation" of Holland called forth a letter from the embarrassed French Commissioners in America to the Committee of Public Safety. They said that few Americans attended the festivals, and continued, "For to tell the truth, these methods, excellent in France where the mass

[3] C. Brinton, *The Jacobins* (New York: Macmillan, 1930), pp. 185–202; Cardenal, *op. cit.*, pp. 310–13; Pariset, *op. cit.*, I, 215; W. M. True, *The De-Christianizing Movement, 1793–94* (unpublished Ph.D. thesis, Harvard University, 1939), p. 425. Good descriptions of typical local fêtes are reported in the *Feuille villageoise* (e.g., II, pt. 3, no. 5 [October 6, 1791], pp. 112–14; pt. 4, no. 46 [August 26, 1792], pp. 460–61, 468; III, pt. 5, no. 15 [January 10, 1793], pp. 343–350) and in the *Journal de la Montagne* (e.g., II, no. 45 [8 Nivôse, an II], p. 355; III, no. 43 [20 Prairial], p. 341).

of the people take part, have here only a shabby (*mesquin*) air." [4]

Thus the attempts of the French in America to celebrate the festivals of the new cult decreed by the Convention on 18 Floréal[5] were extremely embarrassing to their harassed envoys who were trying to keep on good terms with the somewhat pious and sedate Republic to which they were accredited. It can be concluded that when transplanted to America this technique was not very successful, largely because of the lack of popular participation.[6]

The popular reaction to individual Parisian fêtes, as recorded in newspapers, private letters, journals, diaries, memoirs, police reports, and official accounts, and presented in the preceding chapters, indicates that these celebrations were in the main highly successful. It remains to present some of the contemporary evaluations of the festivals as a whole. Mirabeau, Danton, Hébert, Robespierre, and others were convinced that *fêtes nationales* were an essential technique of government propaganda. Even after 9 Thermidor had liquidated Robespierre and imprisoned David, many leaders remained convinced that the festivals must be continued. A typical comment was as follows:

> We are brought then to the conclusion that there is nothing more important than national festivals. For they furnish us with the best means to confer social virtues upon a whole people, and to preserve these for them; to establish and purify the national customs; to give birth to and to reinforce for them that powerful, active and fruitful enthusiasm for the laws of the Fatherland, liberty, equality and for all the principles which lay the foundation for the common honor and for the happiness of all.[7]

[4] *Fête civique au Petit-Guave* [Port-au-Prince: Bourdon, 1790]. *Gazette de France*, no. 120 (April 30, 1793), pp. 551–52; *Chronique de Paris*, no. 121 (May 1), pp. 2–3. *Procès-verbal de célébration de la fête du 23 thermidor . . . (10 Août [1794] v. style)* [Philadelphia: Parent, 1794]; *Courrier Français* (Philadelphia), I, no. 103 (August 13, 1794), pp. 509–12. *Procès-verbal de la fête . . . 2 Pluviôse (21 Janvier v. st. [1795])* [Philadelphia: Parent, 1795]. *Fête civique, célébrée par les patriotes Français, Américains et Hollandais* [Philadelphia: Parent, 1795]; *Courrier français* (Philadelphia), II, no. 3 (April 18, 1795), pp. 9–11. 30 Germinal, l'an III [April 19, 1795]: F. J. Turner, ed., *Correspondence of the French Ministers to the United States, 1791–97* (Washington: Gov. print. off., 1904), pp. 646–47.

[5] *See* p. 121.

[6] Cf. Frances Childs, *French Refugee Life in the United States, 1790–1800* (Baltimore: Johns Hopkins Press, 1940), *passim*.

[7] D. Thiébault, "Mémoire sur les fêtes nationales," *Journal de l'instruction publique*, VII, no. 37 [n.d.], pp. 298–99.

Even such an ardent Thermidorian as Merlin of Thionville, who attacked Robespierre and the Festival of the Supreme Being, was enthusiastic for the technique itself. On 1 Nivôse, year III, M.-J. Chénier's report on the *fêtes décadaires* precipitated a debate in the course of which all members of the Convention were invited to present their views on the subject. Many of them did; most were favorable, and only a very few were actually opposed to the use of festivals as a means of social control.[8] The festival technique was coordinated into a system of periodic national festivals centralized in the hands of the state.

Under the Directory these public ceremonies, aimed at generating sentiments of patriotism and fraternity, played an important role in the republican and revolutionary education of the people. Through them the Government tried to revivify the rites and ceremonies of the civic religion, and to infuse the patriotic cult with an emotional vitality which could counteract the growing revival of Catholicism. However, the "pageant-master of the Republic" had retired to his studio to paint an ultra-classical canvas of *The Sabine Women,* leaving art propaganda in less skilled hands; and the financial difficulties of the Directory deprived it of the material resources required to carry on David's festival program. With the advent of Bonaparte the *fêtes civiques* were replaced by military parades in which the people had no part except as spectators.[9]

Since a sufficiently large number of festivals has been examined in the foregoing chapters, it is now possible to analyze their essential characteristics. These included the physical "properties;" the processions; the ceremonies, music, oratory, theatricals; and popular participation.

First of all was the physical equipment: the stationary but temporary monuments, such as colossal statues, arches of triumph, columns, temples, altars, and even mountains which punctuated the line of march; then there were the warehouses full of moveable items, such as

[8] Merlin (de Thionville), *Opinion . . . sur les fêtes nationales,* pp. 2–20. M.-J. Chénier, *Rapport fait au nom du Comité d'instruction publique . . .* [Paris: Imp. nat., 1794]; *P.V. Conv.,* LII, 26–28. E.g., J. B. C. Mathieu-Mirampal, *Projet de fêtes nationales* [Paris: Imp. nat., 1795], and similar proposals of J. F. Barailon, J. M. de Lequinio, J. Remeau, etc.; D. B[oissieu], *Réflexions sur la festomanie . .* [Paris: Boulard, 1795?].

[9] For festivals after 1794 *see*: S. B. Dunn, *The National Festival in the French Revolution, 1794–1797* (unpublished Ph.D. thesis, Cornell University, 1939); A. Mathiez, *La Théophilanthropie et le culte décadaire 1796–1801* (Paris: Alcan, 1904).

the *chars,* floats, and litters used to transport the various emblematic devices as well as the costumes, standards, and banners which figured in the procession; finally there were the inscriptions, paintings, bas-reliefs, and other symbolic *décor,* inspired largely by classical antiquity, which adorned these physical objects. A small army of dressmakers, carpenters, painters, and other artisans was required to fabricate and maintain this equipment, at a cost of 100,000 livres per month in the spring of 1794.[10]

Second was the official procession or *cortège* itself, which consisted of high civil functionaries; delegates from, or the entire membership of, certain legislative, administrative, judicial, municipal, and semi-official bodies, such as the Convention, the Paris Commune and Sections, the electors and judges, and the popular societies. These worthies might be escorted formally by regular troops or National Guards in full dress uniform, or accompanied by children, old men, young girls, or even by members of certain special groups such as the market porters, or the workers who tore down the Bastille. The procession was accompanied and directed by marshals under the *ordonnateur* (usually David), who saw that all went smoothly.

Next was the dramatic, colorful pageantry of the ceremonies themselves which marked the principal stages of the festival. These symbolic rites and observances included civic oaths, invocations, and official orations or sermons, as well as music and occasionally dancing. The instrumental and vocal accompaniment included stirring marches, solemn hymns, triumphal choruses, and sad or joyous songs. Theatrical productions were sometimes included on the program and frequently were coordinated with the festival to reinforce its message. Finally, and probably most potent of all, was the element of mass participation. The importance and significance of this characteristic has been sufficiently emphasized. It probably represents David's greatest contribution to the perfection of the festival technique.

Thus almost all the arts—architecture, painting, sculpture, poetry, oratory, music, drama, and the dance—were combined to form a flexible propaganda weapon, a skillful technique of social control, and a

[10] Committee of Public Safety orders of 24 Germinal, an II [April 13, 1794] (H. Dupre, "Some French Revolutionary Propaganda Techniques," *The Historian* [Spring, 1940], 158), and 27 Floréal [May 16] (*C.S.P.,* XIII, 547). Cf. A. Mathiez, "Le Coût des fêtes publiques à Paris en 1794," *Annales Historiques de la Révolution Française,* VI (September, 1929), 503.

truly "revolutionary" art. Nor were the individual arts neglected by the republican leaders in their program to mold and direct public opinion in favor of the new government.

Eagerly they availed themselves of the propaganda values of architectural and plastic media. Psychological control can be exerted through the impression of irresistible might and timeless solidity that are connected with pyramids, triumphal arches, obelisks, columns, and colossal sculptured figures. The specific political symbolism embodied in such monuments (e.g., those in conjunction with the various festivals already described) can likewise exert a profound influence upon public opinion. Therefore, the men who had organized victory tried also to organize the plastic arts, and, by decree, to create a regenerate and moral art which would be the auxiliary of their political designs. It was David, the so-called "dictator of the arts," who provided them with a virtuous, energetic, and idealized neoclassic style, perfectly suited to their aims. He drew up for them an extensive project of public works designed to advance their propaganda schemes, as well as to encourage his fellow artists.

David's maiden speech in the Convention (October 26, 1792) was a proposal for the erection of monuments in the cities of Lille and Thionville in memory of their heroic defense against the foreign invaders. The address he made at that time clearly demonstrated the keynotes of his policy: love of antiquity, fervent revolutionary patriotism, and solicitude for the arts. These monuments were to be pyramids or obelisks of enduring French granite, after the Egyptian example, which would "convey to posterity the glorious memory of the inhabitants" whose names were to be inscribed thereon. Likewise, "in the manner of the Greeks and Romans," there was to be distributed to the inhabitants of the two cities a bronze medal, cast from the bronze of royal statues. Last of all the artist suggested that the reconstruction of the towns be according to a general plan—an anticipation of his later project for Paris itself.[11]

The temporary statue of the French people crushing Federalism, erected on the Place des Invalides for the Fête of August 10, 1793, had made a powerful impression on the Parisian populace. Therefore, when David proposed to erect a similar colossus in bronze at the most

[11] October 26, 1792: *P.V. Conv.*, II, 223. Text: *Archives Parlementaires*, LII, 686–87; *Moniteur*, no. 302 (October 28, 1792), p. 1276; David, *Le Peintre Louis David*, I, 111–13.

frequented place in Paris, the idea was hailed in the press. He made a report to the Convention on the subject on 17 Brumaire, but it was not until ten days later (November 18, 1793), after consulting his fellow artists and getting the project approved by the Committee of Public Instruction, that he fully described the fifty-foot Hercules. Holding figures of Liberty and Equality in one hand and supporting itself with the other on its massive club, it was to be engraved with appropriate inscriptions. This monstrous "symbol of unity" was to be erected upon the broken fragements of royal statues at the site of the Pont-Neuf statue of Henry IV which the mob had overthrown after August 10.[12]

The proposal, which included two art contests for the design, was greeted with great applause and adopted.[13] It was also decreed that the figure should appear on the seal of state and the new coins.[14] The date of the contests for the statue itself was delayed, however, and complaints of negligence were made.[15] David, exerting pressure through the Minister of the Interior, had the Temporary Commission of the Arts name a committee on January 9 to choose the débris for the foundation of the colossus.[16] Later in the same month he complained that the contest was not sufficiently known.[17] Nevertheless, publicity was not the only essential, and victories were insufficient, for the necessary bronze was not forthcoming. The Convention on January 5 had already called for an investigation of means of executing such monuments in bronze, and now (January 25) a second decree

[12] *See,* pp. 78–79. *Révolutions de Paris,* XVII, no. 217 (18 Frimaire, an II), p. 289. Speech of 17 Brumaire: *see* p. 78 n. 2. Committee of Public Instruction meetings of 19 and 21 Brumaire [November 9–11]: *C.I.P.*, II, 785, 794, 808. Report of 27 Brumaire [November 17]: *P.V. Conv.*, XXV, 286–89; *Rapport fait à la Convention nationale* . . . [Paris: Imp. nat., 1793]; Mercier, *Nouveau Paris,* II, 85–86, 96–97, IV, 85–87; Wille, *Mémoires,* II, 356.

[13] *P.V. Conv.,* XXV, 286–89; *Auditeur national,* no. 422 (November 18), p. 4; *Journal de l'instruction publique,* IV, no. 11 [n.d.], pp. 238–40; *Révolutions de Paris,* no. 216 (9 Frimaire), pp. 278–79; *Col. Baud.* XXXVI, 221.

[14] 27 and 28 Brumaire, an II [November 17–18, 1793]: *Moniteur,* no. 59 (29 Brumaire), p. 240; *P.V. Conv.,* XXV, 310; *Journal de l'instruction publique,* IV, no. 22 [n.d.], pp. 301–02; *Col. Baud.,* XXXVI, 219.

[15] C.P.I. meeting, 7 Nivôse, [December 27]: *C.I.P.,* III, 215.

[16] 20 Nivôse, an II [January 9, 1794]: *Procès-verbaux de la Commission temporaire des arts,* I, 45.

[17] C.P.I. meeting, 5 Pluviôse [January 24]: *C.I.P.,* III, 324

reiterated the invitation.[18] The acute shortage of bronze was caused by the war, and this critical material had to be devoted exclusively to national defense and coinage. Though the Committee of Public Safety later ordered the prompt execution in bronze of the Pont-Neuf statue, the plaster Hercules was never replaced by a more durable counterpart.[19]

David, however, had in mind an extensive scheme of construction for the fine arts. His pressure group, the Popular and Republican Society of the Arts, after consulting his wishes, read a petition embodying his suggestions to the Convention on January 17. Since David himself occupied the president's chair at the time, this proposal was favorably received and it was sent to the Committee of Public Instruction for further consideration. On 3 Floréal, the education committee instructed David and Fourcroy, the chemist, "to consult together for the most immediate establishment of the monuments consecrated to liberty." These two conferred with Barère, the member of the great committee charged with such matters, and presented a plan of construction. Barère claimed that he thereupon drew up that remarkable series of decrees of the Committee of Public Safety relative to the fine arts, letters, and science which marked the month of Floréal.[20]

The purpose of these decrees was threefold: to encourage the arts and aid the artists, to embellish and improve the capital of the Republic, and finally to immortalize the Revolutionary epoch and popularize *Montagnard* aims. Thirty orders were issued between 5 and 30 Floréal and a few more in Messidor. Some of them merely reiterated earlier decrees while others inaugurated entirely new contests. All the plans and reforms therein embodied had been conceived and drawn up with the collaboration of David, and it is quite probable that he had personally inspired the greater number of them. They expressed his neoclassic ideals as to the form, the content, and the social purpose

[18] Decrees of 16 Nivôse and 5 Pluviôse [January 5, 24]: *P.V. Conv.*, XXVIII, 314, XXX, 110; *J.D.D.*, no. 473, [n.d.], p. 232; *Col. Baud.*, XXXVIII, 115, XXXIX, 42.

[19] Decree of 5 Floréal [April 24]: *C.S.P.*, XIII, 24–25; *Décade philosophique*, I, no. 5 (20 Prairial), pp. 318–19; *Journal de Paris*, no. 507 (3 Prairial), p. 2048.

[20] Meetings of 19 and 23 Nivôse [January 8, 12]: *C.G.A.*, pp. 196, 198. Convention meeting, 28 Nivôse [January 17]: *P.V. Conv.*, XXIX, 309; *Moniteur*, no. 119 (29 Nivôse), p. 480. Text of Petition: David, pp. 163–65. C.P.I. meetings of 5 Pluviôse and 3 Floréal [January 24, April 22]: *C.I.P.*, III, 326, IV, 242. Barère, *Mémoires*, II, 139, 142, IV, 234.

of the arts, and the government intended especially to translate his temporary festival monuments into lasting memorials. Furthermore, David and his brother-in-law, Hubert, the Inspector of National Buildings, were put in charge of overseeing the execution of these projects.

David had complained three months earlier of lack of publicity for his contests; now he handled this matter himself. On 6 Floréal, the master announced the first nine decrees of his great art project at the meeting of the Republican Society of the Arts. This organization was now completely dominated by him. He received a tremendous ovation and was hugged and kissed by his ecstatic followers. He had indeed used his supreme powers for the benefit of his fellow artists. Official publication of the program, including the rest of the decrees of Floréal, was made later in the *Moniteur* and other contemporary newspapers. The published announcements called upon "republican artists" to submit their entries in the public competitions which were thereby opened, for the design and execution of these extensive projects for the beautification of Paris and the glorification of the Revolution.

The decrees of 5 Floréal ordered that the plaster monuments of the "Reunion" of August 10—the figures of Nature, Liberty, and the People, and the Arch of October 6—be duplicated in bronze and marble, and that David's pet project, the Pont-Neuf statue, be similarly executed. Likewise, the Panthéon Column and the Place des Victoires Monument, both dedicated to the victims of August 10, were to be completed. Construction of a covered arena for festivals during inclement weather was also decreed. David was empowered to select statues for the Pont de la Révolution (the present Pont de la Concorde). The Champs-Elysées was to be adorned with a statue of Rousseau, ordered long before by the Constituent Assembly; a temple of Equality; and two magnificent sculptured horses by Coustou which David had transported from the abandoned gardens of Marly to their present location at the entrance to the avenue on the Place de la Concorde.[22]

[21] April 25, 1794: *C.G.A.*, p. 289; David, p. 182. *Moniteur,* no. 261 (21 Prairial, an II), pp. 1063–64, no. 263 (23 Prairial), p. 1070; *Auditeur national,* no. 582 (9 Floréal), pp. 4–6, no. 600 (27 Floréal), pp. 5–6; *Journal de Paris,* no. 482 (8 Floréal), pp. 1947–48, no. 499 (25 Floréal), p. 2016, no. 507 (2 Prairial), p. 2048, no. 515 (11 Prairial), p. 2082; *Arrêtés du Comité de salut public relatifs aux monuments publics, aux arts et aux lettres* [Paris: Imp. nat., 1794]; *C.S.P.*, XIII, 23–28, 69–70, 110, 177–79, 203–04, 509–12, 545–46, 572, 588.

According to other decrees, the National (Tuileries) Palace and Gardens and their surrounding *places,* terraces, and bridges, together with the Place de la Révolution and the Place du Carrousel, were to be beautified in accordance with classical republican tastes. David was authorized to select and carry off orange trees, statuary, and antiquities from former royal palaces for this purpose. A public gymnasium and plunge, porticoes and colonnades, exedras, and two triumphal arches were to be constructed without delay. Though the work was never completed, a year later travelers "recognized the genius of David" in the extensive improvements.[23] The Louvre Museum was to be enlarged under his direction and was eventually to be connected with the Tuileries. Here again the changes he wrought were noted with approbation by foreign observers.[24]

French architecture, both civil and rural, was to be reformed along more functional and beautiful lines, and rendered more convenient and healthful. The Committee of Public Safety, in fact, was inspired by David to envision a complete reconstruction of Paris and other cities according to a general plan for sanitation and embellishment.[25]

[22] The Panthéon column decree, originally authorized on 28 Germinal, an II [April 17, 1794], is dated by Aulard 3 Floréal at one place (*Etudes,* I, 243) and 5 Floréal in another, (*C.S.P.,* XIII, 26). The Place des Victoires monument and the Temple of Equality were both decreed 12 Floréal [May 1]: *C.S.P.,* XIII, 177–79. All the others were promulgated on 5 Floréal: *C.S.P.,* XIII, 23–29. On the horses of Marly, see *Journal de Paris,* no. 551 (7 Prairial), p. 2068; *Journal de l'instruction publique,* VI, no. 31 [n.d.], pp. 221–22; [Williams], *Letters,* III, 10; Letter of H. Swinburne, February 12, 1797: Babeau, ed., *France et Paris sous le directoire,* p. 263.

[23] Decrees of 25 Floréal, an II [May 14, 1794]: *C.S.P.,* XIII, 509–12; *Journal de Paris,* no. 551 (7 Prairial), p. 2064, no. 552 (8 Prairial), pp. 253–56; cf. Sergent, *Reminiscences,* pp. 279–80; *Annales patriotiques,* IV, no. 115 (April 15, 1793), p. 529. J. H. Meister, *Souvenirs . . . (1795)* (Paris: Picard, 1910), p. 100.

[24] Decree of 13 Floréal [May 2]: *C.S.P.,* XII, 203; *Mercure français,* no. 25 (25 Prairial), p. 332; *Lettre bougrement patriotique de la Mère Duchêne,* no. 11 [n.d.], pp. 7–8. Cf. *P.V. Conv.,* XIV, 444, XVII, 287–88; *C.I.P.,* IV, 480–85; *Décade philosophique,* II, no. 10 (10 Thermidor), pp. 22–24, IV, no. 28 (10 Pluviôse, an III), pp. 211–17; Sergent, *op. cit.,* p. 275. Letter of an English woman, November 25, 1796: Babeau, *op. cit.,* p. 101.

[25] Decree of 13 and 28 Floréal, an II [May 2 and 17, 1794]: *C.S.P.,* XII, 203–04. Decree of 10 Messidor [June 28]: *Moniteur,* no. 296 (26 Messidor), p. 1209; David, p. 191; *C.I.P.,* IV, 1016–17; *C.S.P.,* XIV, 554–56. Cf. *P.V. Conv.,* XI, 75–76, XIV, 441–47; *Esprit des journaux,* XXIII, t. 10 (October, 1794), pp. 267–70; *Journal de Paris,* no. 200 (July 19, 1793), p. 806.

Thus was born the famous *Plan des Artistes,* honored by one of the leading British experts in the field as "one of the most remarkable pieces of town planning in existence." [26] Though the importance and even the historical reality of this plan have been challenged, it really did exist.[27] Moreover, it formed the basis of many subsequent civic improvements in Paris, including those of Baron Haussmann during the reign of Napoleon III. Such broad thoroughfares as the Rue de Rivoli, the Avenue de l'Observatoire, the Boulevard Saint-Michel, and many others are prefigured in this project. David later described and explained these proposals to Napoleon I, who brought a number of them to fruition. By 1854 a great many more and by 1871 almost all of these projects had been practically completed.[28] In the meantime, the Revolutionary Government, while stressing the utilitarian and aesthetic value of these plans, underlined their propaganda function in the establishment of the Republic of Virtue:

> Republican artists, while our heroes assure the triumph of liberty and prepare for peace by victory, it is you who will make it loved; it is for you to embellish it . . . . with the genius of the arts and with that of the Revolution. . . .[29]

Artists, writers, and musicians were called upon to glorify the Revolution and its heroic events. David's fellow painters were the object of special solicitude, but sculptors were similarly aided.[30] In fact, Barère had the Government buy Houdon's statue of Saint Eustace, and, rechristening it "Philosophy," had it placed in the lobby of the Convention.[31] According to the "Anacreon of the guillotine," even

[26] P. Abercrombie, "Paris: some influences that have shaped its growth," *Town Planning Review,* II (November, 1911), 309.

[27] J. W. Simpson, "Town-planning in the French Revolution," in his *Essays and Memorials* (London: Architectural Press, 1923), pp. 69–125. A. Bruel, "Note sur le . . . 'Plan des Artistes'," Société de l'histoire de Paris, *Mémoires,* IV (1877), 115–24; "Recherches . . . sur le . . . 'Plan des Artistes'," *ibid.,* VIII (1882), 293–310; A. Bonnardot, *Etudes archéologiques sur les anciens plans de Paris* (Paris: Deflorenne, 1851), p. 245; A. Alphand and others, *Les travaux de Paris 1789–1889* (Paris: Imp. nat., 1889), pl. X; *Report of the Royal Commission on London Traffic* . . . (London: H.M.S.O., 1905), VIII, pl. 2.

[28] This statement is based upon a careful comparison of the *Plan des Artistes* with detailed maps of later dates.

[29] "La Commission des travaux publics aux artistes, 23 Floréal, an II [May 12, 1794]," *Auditeur national,* VIII, no. 600 (27 Floréal), p. 6; David, p. 184.

[30] Decrees of 5, 27, 28 Floréal, an II [April 24, May 16, 17, 1794]: *C.S.P.,* XIII, 25, 545–46, 572.

Ledoux's *barrières* of Paris were to proclaim the revolutionary victories.[32] Finally, the works of the old masters, regarded by David as fit "models for young republicans," were to be carefully preserved and restored by the so-called iconoclasts of the Terror.[33] The members of the Committee of Public Safety, especially Robespierre, seem to have attached great importance to these art projects designed to enshrine the Revolution and its leaders in the hearts of all Frenchmen.[34]

This vast program was not completed by those who conceived it. The contests, open until 30 Messidor, were to be judged on 10 Thermidor. David reported on the organization of a jury of the arts on the fifth,[35] but 9 Thermidor swept him and his plans into political oblivion. On Thibaudeau's motion of 9 Frimaire[36] the contests were finally judged, and almost half a million livres in prizes were awarded. Gérard, David's pupil, won first place.[37]

David's dilapidated plaster monuments, like so many other ambitious revolutionary projects, failed to achieve permanent form in their own time, but the artist's grand concepts for an improved and beautified Paris were eventually carried out by Napoleon and his successors during the next century.

In addition to managing festivals and planning monuments, David and his fellow artists were called upon to provide graphic representations for the Revolution. The Committee of Public Safety did not neglect the cruder aspects of art propaganda. They "invited" David to execute paintings, and caricatures "suitable to awaken the public spirit, and to expose how atrocious and ridiculous the enemies of

[31] Decree of 12 Floréal [May 1]: *C.S.P.*, XIII, 179. Barère took sole credit in his *Mémoires*, II, 143. An independent account attributes the idea to Mme. Houdon: Meyer, *Fragments*, II, 225–27.

[32] Decree of 13 Messidor [July 1]: *P.V. Conv.*, XL, 328–29; Barère, *Rapport au nom du Comité de salut public sur . . . les monumens nationaux environans Paris* . . . [Paris: Imp. nat., 1794], pp. 3–4. *Col. Baud.*, XLIV, 108.

[33] Decree of 6 Messidor [June 24]: *P.V. Conv.*, XL, 134–35; *Moniteur*, no. 277 (7 Messidor), pp. 1131–32; David, pp. 193–96; *Col. Baud.*, XLIV, 44. Decree of C.P.S., 7 Messidor: *C.I.P.*, IV, 690–91; *C.S.P.*, XIV, 511–12.

[34] E. Hamel, *Histoire de Robespierre* (Paris: Lacroix, 1867), III, 507; Aulard, *Etudes*, I, 241–42; Barère, *Mémoires, loc. cit.;* A. Cochin, *Précis des principales opérations du gouvernement révolutionnaire* (Paris: Champion, 1936), pp. 128–30.

[35] C.P.I. meeting July 23, 1794: *C.I.P.*, IV, 846.

[36] Convention meeting November 29, 1794: *P.V. Conv.*, L, 181–83

[37] *C.I.P.*, IV, 254–62; Renouvier, *Histoire de l'art pendant la révolution*, p. 22.

liberty and the Republic are."[38] He appears to have designed a number of such patriotic cartoons, some of them in colors, and was paid from the special propaganda fund of 50 million livres.[39] Though now extremely rare, a few of these caricatures have been preserved in the Archives Nationales and offer an interesting field of study. For example, one entitled *"L'Armée royale-cruche"* represents an English army of jugs (a play on the word *cruche,* which also means fool) commanded by George III, who is led by the nose by Pitt in the guise of a turkey. Fox, in the form of a goose, brings up the rear, mounted on the back of John Bull.[40] In another, *"Le Gouvernement Anglais,"* is personified as a horrible chimerical devil clothed in the royal ornaments, who monopolizes commerce and vomits a host of taxes upon the luckless people.[41] Though lacking in humor, these satirical designs are interesting for their sincere conviction and for their masterly execution of line and composition. They are, even with their scatological crudeness, infinitely superior in craftsmanship to most caricatures of the period.

As has already been shown, David's paintings of classic and revolutionary subjects were engraved and widely distributed. These reproductions became extremely popular and, along with similar works by other revolutionary artists, appeared in homes, schools, and meeting places all over the country. Popular engravings of David's *Horatii, Brutus, Jeu de Paume,* and *Marat* had an honored place on the walls of patriots and played their role in kindling the hearts of Frenchmen. Even after the downfall of Robespierre had carried David into political oblivion, his painting of *The Death of Socrates* was considered to be so valuable as propaganda that it was ordered engraved by the Committee of Public Instruction.[42]

[38] This order which exists in the Archives Nationales is quoted by H. Dupre ("Some French Revolutionary propaganda techniques," p. 157) who dates it December 12; by A. Copin ("Le peintre Louis David, caricaturiste par ordre du grand Carnot," *Intermédiaire,* XXI [1888], 224) who indicates September 17; and by J. Lortel ("David caricaturiste," *L'Art et les artistes,* XVIII [March, 1914], 274), and A. Blum (*La Caricature révolutionnaire* [Paris: Jouvre, 1916], p. 195), who specify September 12.

[39] Order of 29 Floréal, an II [May 18, 1794]: *C.S.P.,* XIII, 587; Dupre, *op. cit.,* p. 158; Lortel, *op. cit.,* p. 274; Copin, *op. cit.,* p. 224; Blum, *loc. cit.*

[40] No. 604 in Blum, *op. cit.,* p. 195; repr.: Lortel, *op. cit.,* p. 275.

[41] No. 605 in Blum, *op. cit.,* pp. 195–96; repr.: Lortel, *op. cit.,* p. 273.

[42] *See* pp. 1–3, 16–20, 39–40, 107–08. While the official reproduction of David's celebrated painting of *Marat assassiné* was never finished, an engraving of

Needless to say art had other functions besides that of social control during the French Revolution. An artist is also a recorder of history, and David's propaganda efforts had an influence which was felt long after his actual political career had ended. Not only did his caricatures, paintings, and sketches of contemporary persons and events have a profound effect upon public opinion in their own time and upon succeeding generations of various shades of "liberals," but they remain today authentic documents of the period. Present-day historians may turn with confidence to David's portraits of his colleagues and to his surviving sketches of revolutionary events.

Rarely has there been a case comparable to David—a great artist who played an active part in a revolution, who was able to record the scenes and characters of the great historical drama in which he lived. A fervent enthusiast of the Revolution, he is its painter and historiographer. Among his studies for the *Jeu de Paume* he has left us vivid pencil drawings of Bailly, Barère, Père Gérard, the Abbé Grégoire, Prieur de la Marne, Rabaut Saint-Etienne, and other notable figures.[43] Magnificent are his oil on canvas portraits of the affable and slippery Barère; the handsome erstwhile Baron Jean de Bry, nicknamed "Tyrannicide;" that solid peasant Père Gérard, shown surrounded by his numerous progeny; competent and hardworking Jeanbon Saint-André; youthful and haughty Saint Just; J.-B. Milhaud, earnest and military looking in his picturesque uniform as Representative of the People to the Army; and that aloof doctrinaire Sieyès, somewhat mellowed with age as he gazes down benignly from the walls of Harvard's Fogg Museum of Art.[44] These portraits by David are the most lifelike

Tête de Marat by Copia after David's sketch of the dead man was extremely popular (announced in the *Courrier universel,* [December 31, 1793], p. 4; cf. *Col. Vinck,* III, 333). There is a copy of it in the White Collection at Cornell University. David's original pen sketch is in the Museum of Versailles (*Inv. dess.,* no. 3200). The *Socrates* was considered at a meeting of the Temporary Commission of the Arts, 25 Pluviôse, an III [February 13, 1795] (*Procès-verbaux de la Commission temporaire des arts,* II, 113) and the Committee of Public Instruction meeting of 24 Pluviôse authorized the T.C.A. to have the work done (*C.I.P.,* XV, 487).

[43] *See* p. 40 note 67.

[44] The *Barère in the Tribune* (Coll. Baron Lambert), usually attributed to David, may be by Laneuville (Jules David, *Quelques observations . . .* [Paris: Havard, 1883], pp. 14–16; P. Dorbec, "Le Portrait pendant la révolution," *Revue de l'art,* XXI [January, 1907], 49–50), but some still feel it may actually be by the master. The *De Bry* is owned by Wildenstein & Co., New York; *Gérard* by Mans

XVI. BAYLE AND BEAUVAIS, MARTYRS OF THE REVOLUTION

Preliminary drawing by David for *Le Triomphe du Peuple Français*

Courtesy of the Fogg Museum of Art

and accurate images we have of these men, for they were painted by a great master who knew his subjects intimately. Even more valuable for the historian are the spontaneous and rapid sketches of his associates, friends, and enemies which David drew during interminable debates in the Convention, whiling away dull reports at committee meetings, or even watching the tumbrils pass from some sidewalk cafe. His fine little drawing of his idol Robespierre in the tribune, and his celebrated sketches of Danton and Marie Antoinette on their way to the guillotine provide unique flashes of insight into historic moments in the lives of tragic figures of the period.[45]

It has been alleged by critics of David that he painted or planned to paint a portrait of Louis XVI sometime between September 1791 and March, 1792, when the artist was already an active propagandist for the Jacobins. The point at issue would perhaps be one of relatively minor importance were it not for its implications. If true, the charge would lend color to the artist's reputation among his opponents of disloyalty; but, more important from the propaganda point of view, it would raise the question of whether David's efforts were conscious and intentional, or otherwise. If the artist used his propaganda talents in behalf of the monarchy and simultaneously in direct opposition to it, then either he did not know what he was doing or else he was attempting to work for both sides.

Museum (repr.: J. Romero-Brest, *Jacques Louis David* [Buenos Aires: Poseidón, 1943], frontispiece); *Saint-André* by Bichon (repr.: Cantinelli, pl. XLIV); and *Saint Just* by A. Duruy, Paris (repr.: P. Sagnac, *La revolution de 1789* [Paris: Editions Nationales, 1934], II, 362). Milhaud later was one of Napoleon's crack cavalry generals and led a charge at Waterloo. His fine portrait in the Louvre may not be entirely from the hand of David (Holma, p. 120 n. 8). The *Sieyès,* painted in 1817 when artist and sitter were in exile in Brussels is part of the Winthrop Bequest.

[45] The *Robespierre* is in the Hadengue Coll. (repr.: Sagnac, *op. cit.,* II, 346). Robinet ("Les portraits de Danton," *R.F.,* XIV [1888], 710) describes five David portraits of Danton. Of these the following are the best known: The sketch from memory in the Saint-Albin Coll. (C. Blanc, *Histoire des peintres; Ecole française* [Paris: Renouard, 1865], II, 10–11; repr.: H. Wendel, *Danton* [New Haven: Yale University Press, 1935], p. 332); the drawing from life in the Lille Museum (repr.: *G.B.A.,* LIV [1884], 221); and the death cart caricature made from the Regency cafe in the Lyon Museum (Courtois, *Rapport sur 9 thermidor,* p. 135n). The *Marie Antoinette* is in the Baron Edmond de Rothschild Coll. (no. 540, Blum, *op. cit.,* p. 179; "Marie Antoinette conduite à l'échafaud, dessin de David," *Les Trésors des Bibliothèques de France,* II, fasc. 7 [1928], 114–16) *see* plate XVII, opposite p. 140.

However, on the basis of the evidence now available, it is clear that David never painted the King, nor does it appear that he intended to execute a royal portrait at that time.[46] The *Louis XVI entrant dans le lieu des séances de l'Assemblée nationale, le 4 février 1790,* and its variant (the caption alone being changed), *Louis XVI à l'Assemblée nationale accepte solennellement la Constitution, le 14 septembre 1791,* so often attributed to Jacques-Louis David have been proved beyond the shadow of a doubt to be the work of François-Anne David (1741–1824).[47] Richard Cantinelli insists that David had a commission for a painting of the King prior to March 9, 1792, but the validity of the evidence he offers is sharply challenged by the Danish art scholar, Ernst Goldschmidt.[48] Rumors regarding such a portrait of Louis were circulated at just that time either because of confusion with F.-A. David's engraving which had been announced shortly before, or, perhaps, as has been suggested in this study, as part of an organized attempt to discredit the Jacobin artist.[49] Both factors were combined in the posthumous mendacious memoirs of Count Paroy. This ultraroyalist declares that David importuned the King to allow him to paint the monarch accepting the constitution! An article at the time in the *Journal de la cour et de la ville,* close to court circles, suggests that, though no such commission was accepted by David, it was quite possible that it may have been offered to him.[50] Finally, the famous draw-

[46] *See* p. 57.

[47] *Col. Vinck,* no. 4252, II, 777; repr.: pl. XXII. Thomé, pp. 47–48 Robert, *Vie politique,* p. 90; *Biographie moderne,* II, 32; [Coiffier de Moret], *Dictionnaire biographique,* I, 388; *Revolutionary Plutarch,* I, 363; G. Grappe, "La psychologie de David," *L'Art vivant,* I, (December 15, 1925), 29; J. F. van Deene, "David," *Elsevier's geillustrierd maandschrift,* XXIX (February, 1930), 88. *Biographie universelle,* ed. Michaud, LXII, 123–4; *Biographie nouvelle des contemporains,* V, 233; C. Saunier, *La Chronique des Arts,* no. 10 (March 5, 1904), pp. 80–82.

[48] Cantinelli, *David,* p. 19, "Autour d'une signature du peintre David," *Trésor des Bibliothèques,* III, fasc. 11 (1930), 122–23. The discovery of the alleged signature appears to have been made four years earlier by J. Guibert, (*Le Cabinet des Estampes,* p. 114). Goldschmidt, *Frankrigs Malerkunst* (Copenhagen: Glydendalske, 1934), V, 171–72. Cf. Humbert, *Louis David,* p. 81n.

[49] *Folies d'un mois,* 5e mois, no. 7 [n.d.], p. 4; *Journal de Paris,* no. 78 (March 18, 1792), sup. no. 31, p. 1; *Révolutions de Paris,* XI, no. 141 (March 24), pp. 548–49. *Mercure de France,* no. 41 (October 8, 1791), p. 83; *Annales patriotiques,* no. 733 (October 5), p. 2034. *See* p. 57.

[50] Paroy, *Mémoires,* p. 261. *Journal de la cour et de la ville,* no. 47 (April 16, 1792), p. 374.

XVII. MARIE ANTOINETTE

Drawing from life by David *Collection Baron Edmond de Rothschild*

ing in the Louvre of *Le Roi refugié auprès de l'Assemblée législative le 10 août 1792,* is unquestionably the work of his pupil François Gérard.[51] So far as is known, no other portraits of Louis XVI have ever been attributed to the revolutionary artist, so there appears to be no foundation to the legend that David executed one.

Long after the artist's death his painting of *Marat assassiné* was regarded with veneration by the spiritual heirs of the Jacobins. The reputation of David and his propaganda pictures languished under the restored Bourbons,[52] but with the July Revolution his ardent partisans appeared once more.[53] When the *Marat* was publicly shown in 1846 for the first time since the Terror, it created a sensation, and the "men of '48" gathered to praise David and his masterpiece—the *pietà* of the Jacobins and a symbol of insurrection.[54] Thus it is not strange that in the wake of the Revolution of 1848 came David's warmest apologist—Miette de Villars.[55] Later, Jean Jaurès and the French socialists took up the cause of the revolutionary artist, and even the Russian Social Democrats such as Plekhanov,[56] urged their followers to "make their obeisance" before David's work. Judging from their recent publications,[57] twentieth-century Marxists have a greater enthusiasm than ever for the painter of Marat.

How are we to explain this predilection of the revolutionary radicals for David's art? Perhaps it was because of an impulsive sympathy

[51] Pen and wash 26.22" by 36.07" signed "F.G.," Louvre no. 26725: *Inv. dess.,* no. 4139, V, 119. Repr.: *ibid.,* p. 118; Sagnac, *La Révolution de 1789,* II, 56–57. Cf. Blondel, *L'Art pendant la révolution,* p. 48. Saul K. Padover, *The Life and Death of Louis XVI* (New York: Appleton, 1939), pp. 280–81 claims that it is an unknown David.

[52] *See* pp. 24, 85 note 34 and Bibliographical Essay, pp. 148–50.

[53] E.g., B. Hauréau, *La Montagne* (1834), pp. 65–76. *See* pp. 151–52.

[54] The great art critic T. Thoré ("Les Peintres du XIXe siècle. Louis David," *Trésor national,* ser. 2, III [1843], 77; *Le Salon de 1846* [Paris: Alliance des Arts, 1846], p. 9) who praised David so highly at this time was later exiled for his activities during the Revolution of 1848. *See also,* L. Gallois' famous *Histoire de la Convention* (1834–48), IV, 176, and other appreciations of the Jacobin artist and his work by the men of 1848. *See* Bibliographical Essay, p. 153.

[55] *Mémoires de David* (1850).

[56] Jaurès, *Histoire Socialiste* (Paris, [1905]), III–IV, *passim.* Plekhanov, *Sochineniia,* XIV, 112. *See* Bibliographical Essay, p. 157.

[57] Milton Brown, *The Painting of the French Revolution* (1938) and Agnes Humbert, *Louis David, peintre et conventionnel; essai de critique marxiste* (1936), *passim.* *See* Bibliographical Essay, pp. 161–62.

for a fellow revolutionist who nourished somewhat similar aims. Perhaps it was because of the clear-cut propaganda motive apparent in his art. In the hands of this artist, neoclassicism received an infusion of a vigorous content capable of moving the illiterate masses to revolutionary activity. From the *Horatii* to the *Marat* his works had a conscious propaganda message. They were the manifestoes of a new order. The neoclassic style was combined with a dynamic realism to form a comprehensible vehicle whereby the abstract ideas of the eighteenth-century philosophers could be conveyed to all Frenchmen. As has been seen, David's characteristic combination of classicism and naturalism had an appeal for all classes. Workers, peasants, and bourgeoisie could comprehend its lucid symbolism.[58] For them the Horatii, Socrates, and Brutus became the precursors of Le Peletier, Marat, and Robespierre. In the opinion of contemporaries, David's paintings had prepared the people for the Revolution. For this "philosopher painter" appealed to the minds, to the consciences, and to the emotions of his countrymen.

It has been shown that the artistic revolution led by David had triumphed before the political revolution. Neoclassicism was born before David, but to the cold and bloodless beauty of this aristocratic and intellectual art David added the morality and philosophy of the middle classes and a powerful and vital realism comprehensible to the masses. The use of art as propaganda was also not a Jacobin innovation but was a legacy of the monarchy and was advocated by the *philosophes* as a means of establishing their own ideas. However, it was David's forceful mind, virile talent, and revolutionary spirit which forged neoclassic art into a potent propaganda weapon—the "Sword of the Revolution."

[58] *See* pp. 1–3.

BIBLIOGRAPHICAL ESSAY

There are no works dealing directly or exclusively with David's use of art as propaganda during the French Revolution. Nevertheless, a large number of printed books has been used in the preparation of this study and a brief discussion of some of them is included here. The purpose of this essay is (1) to call attention to the various books on David, the Revolution and French art which are of special significance for the study of the artist's career as a propagandist of the Revolution; and (2) to characterize these works and, where necessary, to indicate the authors' attitude towards David as politician or artist. They are mentioned in approximately chronological order so as to show whatever general trends there may have been in the fluctuations of David's reputation.

Historical opinion of David underwent a series of changes in accordance with the personal predilections, social views, and political passions of various individuals; the relative strength of the revolutionary spirit in various periods; and finally, an aesthetic factor—the transformations of taste and style during various art epochs. When the Neoclassical School of David was supplanted around 1824 by Romanticism and the latter was followed in turn by Realism (ca. 1848–1870), Impressionism (ca. 1870–1900) and finally the various Post-Impressionist Schools of the twentieth century, popular and, to some extent, critical appraisal of David's artistic qualities exhibited fluctuations roughly approximating the changing tastes in painting.

I

Before 1789 David had emerged as the recognized leader and regenerator of French art. For the most part his work received an increasingly enthusiastic reception from his artistic *début* at the Salon of 1781 onward. The catalogues of these exhibitions were reprinted by J. J. Guiffrey, ed., *Collection des livrets des anciennes expositions,* 42 nos. (1869–72).* The early successes of David's works at the Salons of painting were recorded in contemporary memoirs, periodicals, pamphlets, *nouvelles à la main* and gossip of the salons of the intellectuals. Of the last two sources the most useful were the *Mémoires*

* All works referred to were published in Paris unless otherwise indicated.

secrètes pour servir à l'histoire de la république des lettres en France, 36 vols. (London, 1784–87), begun by L. P. de Bachaumont and continued by Pidanzat de Mairobert, and for the period here used by Moufle d'Angerville; the literary bulletins by the Abbé Raynal, Grimm, Diderot and others, *Correspondance littéraire, philosophique et critique,* ed. M. Tourneux, 16 vols. (1877–82); F. Métra, Imbert de Bourdeaux, Grimod de la Reynière and others, *Correspondance secrète politique et littéraire,* 18 vols. (London, 1787–90), a reprint of the *Correspondance littéraire secrète* (Neuwied, 1774–93) as far as 1785; and the gossipy newsletters of M. F. Pidanzat de Mairobert, *L'Espion anglais ou Correspondance secrète entre Milord All'Eye et Milord All'Ear,* 10 vols., new ed. (London, 1784–85), sent from Paris to London between December 1775 and February 1779. Other interesting commentaries on David's painting are to be found in such odd places as N. E. Restif de la Bretonne's *Les Nuits de Paris, ou le spectateur nocturne,* 7 vols. (London and Paris, 1788–89) where Count Potocki's remarks on the Salon of 1787 were reprinted.

The beginning of the Revolution interjected a political note into art criticism and David was generally lauded as a "precursor of liberty" (*see* p. 20). Despite the attacks of the hostile and conservative Academy and its sympathizers, the favorable estimate of David's work expressed by J. J. Sue, "Rapport sur les tableaux de David, lu à la séance publique du 5 mai [1793 du Lycée des arts]" (in) *Esprit des journaux,* 22 an., t. VIII (August, 1793), 275–80, appears to have been held by most contemporaries. The first published work of the greatest poet of the period, André Chénier, was an ode, *Le Jeu de Paume à Louis David* (1791), reprinted in his *Oeuvres complètes,* ed. P. Dimoff, 3 vols. (1908–20), III, 230–43.

II

When David entered political life by becoming a fervent Jacobin and placing at the Society's disposal his talents as an artist and *ordonnateur* of revolutionary festivals, and especially after he became a delegate to the Convention and a member of the Committee of General Security, Girondins, Constitutional Monarchists, royalists and reactionaries of all complexions attacked him in the press and on the floor of the Assembly. After the fall of his friend Robespierre (July 26, 1794), David was denounced as a terrorist, deprived of membership on the Committee of General Security and imprisoned. Laurent Lecointre's first attack upon David and the other members of the Great Committees, (*A la Convention nationale* . . . [August 8, 1794]), was declared calumnious by the Convention. The formal denunciation of the artist by Lecointre, *Les Crimes des septs membres des anciens Comités* . . . (20 Brumaire, an II [November 10, 1794]), was largely based on hearsay and some highly questionable testimony at the Fouquier-Tinville trial (*see* p. 86 n 39). Lecointre's tirades and the mendacious diatribe of E. B. Courtois, *Rapport* . . . *sur les événements du 9 thermidor* (Floréal, an IV [April, 1796]) (Cf. his later "Notes et souvenirs," *R.F.*, XII (1887), 813, 819–20) provided an arsenal for anti-Jacobin propagandists. Courtois, a disgruntled Dantonist who lost his job when David suppressed the Commission of Monuments, was the source of some bloodcurdling legends linking the artist with the September massacres and the execution of Danton. During David's imprisonment and even after his release for lack of evidence, these stories were widely repeated and embellished during the reaction after Thermidor. For instance, the sensational and unreliable six-volume counter-revolutionary pamphlet of the journalist L. M. Prudhomme, *Histoire générale des crimes commis pendant la révolution française* (1796–97) popularized Courtois' lurid and apparently apocryphal tale of David sketching the dying victims of the September massacres.

The artist's pro-Jacobin propaganda activities also came in for a great deal of criticism. In 1796 the narrowly prejudiced royalist A. E. N. Fantin Desodoard's *Histoire philosophique de la révolution* and next year G. V. Vasselin's bombastic indictment of the Jacobins, *Mémorial révolutionnaire,* 4 vols. (1797) castigated "the hideous and disgusting" revolutionary festivals of David. In his vivid but biased picture of revolutionary Paris the journalist L. S. Mercier, *Le Nouveau Paris,* 6 vols. (1798), expressed his contempt for artists in general and David in particular in bitter invective. Like Prudhomme's account of revolutionary atrocities, it has been extensively quoted ever since.

David's royalist colleagues in the Louvre also did their best to spread these and other calumnies as we learn from F. J. L. Meyer's *Fragmente aus Paris* (*see* p. 174). When Meyer and other impartial observers attempted to verify the stories of David's cruelties, no evidence beyond hearsay could be found. Though these legends were attributed to professional jealousy by the more critical, they were widely circulated in contemporary publications designed to enrich their authors and to stimulate counter-revolutionary sentiments. The "fantastic and mediocre" compilation of the romance writer and recanting ex-Jacobin F. X. Pagès, *Histoire secrète de la révolution fran-*

çaise, 7 vols. (1797–1802) and Vol. XII (1798) of the influential and much quoted *Histoire de la révolution par deux amis de la liberté,* 19 vols. (1792–1803), simply reiterated and perpetuated Courtois' libels.

How these stories grew in the telling and were adapted for propaganda purposes in England is illustrated by the anti-Jacobin *Biographical Anecdotes of the Founders of the French Republic* (London, 1797). Moreover, royalist pamphleteers from the émigré stronghold in the North repeated and embellished the tales in the *Dictionnaire des Jacobins vivans* (Hamburg, 1799), attributed to L. Calinau of Metz; and the *Dictionnaire biographique et historique des hommes marquans de la fin du 18e siècle,* 3 vols. (London [i.e. Hamburg], 1800) of Baron Coiffier de Moret (or Verseux). The article on David in the better known second edition of the last work, issued under the title *Biographie moderne,* 4 vols., 2. ed. (Leipzig [i.e. Hamburg], 1806–07), was somewhat toned down by the new editors.

III

In 1800, David was named official painter by Bonaparte, but attacks continued under the Consulate and Empire. Royalists could publish bitter indictments such as C. F. Beaulieu's *Essais historiques sur les causes et les effets de la révolution française,* 6 vols. (1801–03) which, while it did not mention David by name, ridiculed his work. Though the sober and impartial Vicomte de Toulongeon, *Histoire de la France depuis la révolution de 1789,* 7 vols. (1801–10), treated David as favorably as he dared, the Napoleonic censorship prevented the rehabilitation of the reputations of republicans such as David. On the other hand, the imperial police were unable to prevent the circulation of Maton de la Varenne's unscrupulous forgery, *Histoire particulière des événements . . . de juin à septembre 1792* (1806), the *Biographie moderne* (*see* above) and other works damaging to the artist's political reputation.

Nevertheless, the accounts paid more or less grudging tribute to David's artistic pre-eminence. Unquestionably he was still regarded as the "Chief of the French School" and as the greatest of all contemporary painters. The extent of David's European reputation became particularly apparent when the lull in the war brought hordes of foreigners, including many English tourists, flocking to David's studio in the Louvre in 1802. These visitors recorded their impressions of the great man as well as the terrorist legends which still circulated in the corridors of the Louvre and the salons of the aristocracy.

With the resumption of the war English propagandists used these tales to rouse their countrymen against the expected invasion by the French. Examples are the *Biographical sketches and characteristic traits of the French generals who are appointed by Buonaparte to invade England; also anecdotes of the republican painter David . . .* (London, [1804]), published by Hughes, which reprints a fantastic libel from a British newspaper; and the scurrilous sketch in *The Revolutionary Plutarch,* 3 vols. (London, 1804), attributed to Stewarton.

Some were still willing to raise a voice in David's defense, primarily on artistic grounds. His pupil "Publicola" Chaussard included a laudatory "Notice historique et inédite sur Louis David" in his *Pausanius français. Etat des arts du dessin en France à l'ouverture du XIXe siècle. Salon de 1806* (1806). This account was considered so valuable a source that it was reprinted by Paul Lacroix (Bibliothile Jacob) in his *Revue universelle des arts,* XVIII (November, 1863), 114–28. Its lasting value lay in its preservation of oral tradition then current among those who knew David well. Though inaccurate in certain details and silent on his political career, it provides a picture of David at the height of his reputation. A similar notice was included by the distinguished C. P. Landon in his monumental *Annales du musée et de l'école moderne des beaux-arts,* 40 vols. (1800–24).

On the other hand, the personal hostility of the new academicians of the Fine Arts Section of the Institute to David, First Painter of H. M. The Emperor, was openly expressed by their secretary, the bureaucrat J. Le Breton, in the *Rapport sur les beaux-arts* (1808) to Napoleon; and by their exclusion of David from the award he coveted among the *prix décennaux* in 1810. Alexandre Lenoir, the curator of the Museum of French Monuments, undertook to refute their criticisms of David in his *Examen du tableau des "Sabines" et de l'école de M. David . . .* (August, 1810). The year 1810 marked the apogee of the School of David and the beginning of the decline of neoclassicism. The academic artists were more rigorously neoclassical than David, but art critics and amateurs were just beginning to feel the vague stirrings of a new artistic movement. Young Guizot in his contemporary article on the "Salon de 1810" (reprinted in his *Etudes sur les beaux-arts en général* [1852]) praised David for the "happy revolution" by which he "restored" French art but calls upon him to forsake the imitation of Greek sculpture for colorful medieval subjects. Other amateurs made similar suggestions at this time, for example Countess Potocka, *Memoirs,* ed. C. Stryienski (London, 1901), p. 152.

IV

After the fall of Napoleon David went into exile at Brussels, rejecting both the amnesty of the Bourbons and the Ministry of Fine Arts of the Hohenzollerns. During the First Restoration and for a long time after David had left Paris, a deluge of vituperation was directed against him. The reactionary opponents of reform and of suppression of the former Academy, such as the sculptor L. P. Deseine, *Notices historiques sur les anciennes Académies royales de peinture* [*etc.*] (1814), and the amateur painter Marquis de Paroy, *Précis historique de l'origine de l'Académie royale de peinture* [*etc.*] (1816), not only demanded restoration of the old corporations and their own reinstatement but attacked David as well.

The cry was taken up by the political pamphleteers of the ultra-royalists. Some of their tracts were in the form of biographical dictionaries. The vicious and mendacious J. B. M. Robert, *Vie politique de tous les députés à la Convention nationale* (1814); and the *ci-devant* royal censor A. J. Raup de Baptestein de Moulières, *Petit* [*sic*] *biographie conventionnelle; ou Tableau moral et raisoné* [*sic*] *des . . . députés . . .* (1815), castigated David for his conduct during the Revolution in phrases cribbed from the *Biographie Moderne*. That well known "Manual of the proscribers" by L. G. Michaud and others, *Biographie des hommes vivants,* 5 vols. (1816–19), was only slightly less virulent.

Others wrote so-called "histories" which are today forgotten because of their almost complete lack of historical value but which at the time contributed to the growth of a damaging "Davidian legend." These included the novelist H. Lemaire, *Histoire de la révolution française depuis l'année 1787 jusqu'en 1816,* 3 vols. (1816); the writer R. J. Durdent, *Histoire de la Convention,* 2 vols. (1817–18); the ultra-royalist Vicomte Conny de la Fay, *La France sous le règne de la Convention* (1820); and the ex-Girondin turned royalist, Charles de Lacretelle, whose *Histoire de la révolution française,* 8 vols. (1821–26), was once regarded as a classic. On the other hand, while J. A. Dulaure, *Esquisses historiques des principaux événemens de la révolution française,* 5 vols. (1823–25) did not mention the artist by name, he did reproduce David's *Jeu de Paume,* and praised his festivals.

Some writers of more "liberal" political views such as A. V. Arnault and his collaborators treated David more sympathetically in the *Biographie nouvelle des contemporaines,* 20 vols. (1820–25). Their article

(1822), while not especially well informed on the facts of the artist's life and which regretted his attachment to Marat and Robespierre, recognized the idealistic and patriotic purpose of the "alliance of the painter and the politician" and expressed their desire for the return of the distinguished exile to Paris. Reflecting the neoclassic tastes of the day, they warmly praised the artistic contributions of the "restorer and chief of the French School."

Meanwhile Géricault * had surprised the art world with his *Raft of the Medusa* at the Salon of 1819 and the new spirit was reflected in young Adolphe Thiers' article on the "Salon de 1822" in the liberal *Constitutionnel.* As art critic, the future statesman and historian lauded the romantic style of Delacroix and, while he praised David's *Socrates* as a masterpiece, he pointed out its overemphasis of form at the expense of color. In 1824 Thiers' piece in the *Revue Européenne* on David's *Mars and Venus* praised the master as "the restorer of the arts in France" but concluded that, though his painting was beautifully executed, it was dangerous as a model. David had done his work and should now retire, he concluded. And in fact the appearance of Delacroix' *Massacre de Scios* at the Salon of 1824 has been regarded as marking the advent of Romanticism.†

That same year (1824) appeared the first real biography of David, the anonymous and little known *Notice sur la vie et les ouvrages de M. J.-L. David.* This eighty-page volume attempted to recover David's reputation from the morass of party strife by vindicating his artistic career, distinguishing the artist from the politician, and eliminating the latter from the account. Just after David's death, which occurred on December 29, 1825, this *Notice* was republished, in part textually, in part in expanded form, as *Vie de David, premier peintre de Napoléon par M. A. Th**** (Brussels, 1826) with a Paris edition in larger format and a German translation published at Leipzig (1827). Though written by Antoine Thomé de Gamond, nephew of David's colleague

* Géricault, incidentally, was a great admirer of David and paid a visit of homage to the exile of Brussels in 1820. R. Régamy, *Géricault* (Paris: Rieder, 1926), p. 38; G. Oprescu, *Géricault* (Paris: Renaissance du livre, 1927), p. 106; K. Berger, *Géricault* (New York: Bittner, 1946), p. 19.

† Eugène Delacroix himself had a high regard for David: *Correspondance générale,* ed. A. Joubin, 5 vols. (Paris: Plon, [1935–38]), I, 330, III, 264, V, 61; *Journal,* ed. A. Joubin, 3 vols. (Paris: Plon, [1932]), I, 240, II, 29, 248, III, 53, 261, 270–72, 309–10, 328.

Thibaudeau (*see* p. 177), this apologia is still sometimes attributed to Thibaudeau, to Adolphe Thiers, and even to the art critic Théophile Thoré (*see* p. 152). David the politician is presented as a well-meaning but misguided "dupe" led astray by his classical imagination. David the painter is praised as the greatest of modern masters. Despite its limitations (it seems to be chiefly based on oral tradition and the *Moniteur*) the *Vie de David* still retains a certain value for the study of David.

Grounded in part on the *Notice* and the *Vie de David,* but also drawing on other more original sources, A. Mahul's hitherto neglected article on David (*Annuaire nécrologique,* année 1825 [Paris: Ponthieu, December, 1826], VI, 116–43) made no secret of David's political career and lauded his artistic achievements.

While his own countrymen now tended to take a somewhat more charitable view of the artist's career, David's death did not end the attacks of English writers. Sir Walter Scott, who had recoiled from the artist when he had met him at a dinner in 1815 (J. G. Lockhart, *Memoirs of the Life of Sir Walter Scott,* 10 vols. [Edinburgh: Black, 1902], V, 79), pictured David as a bloodthirsty terrorist and disparaged his artistic genius in his hastily written *Life of Napoleon Buonaparte,* 3 vols. (Philadelphia: Carey, 1827), I, 230n.

That same year, the year of the preface of *Cromwell* and of the Salon of 1827 which marked the appearance of Courbet and the Barbizon School, David's pupils came to his defense. Of a series of apologetic articles on David, the most important was P. A. Coupin, "Notice nécrologique sur Jacques-Louis David," *Revue encyclopédique,* XXXIV (April, 1827), 34–58 which, though warmly sympathetic, was relatively well balanced. Guarded in his references to David's revolutionary role, Coupin says "he pushed love of country and love of liberty too far." He emphasized the artist's human qualities as teacher and family man which had been lost sight of, and his greatness as a painter which "conquered for him an immortality which nothing can ravish from him." More extravagant were other defenders such as J. N. Paillot de Montabert who coined a dictum on David "than whom no one drew the human figure better, without excepting Raphael" (*Traité complet de la peinture,* 9 vols. [Paris: Bossage, 1829–51], VI, 65). All were not so eulogistic. Writing between 1827 and 1830 Alphonse Raabe, "Notice sur Jacques-Louis David," *Biographie universelle et portative des contemporains,* 5 vols. (1830), characterized David's political career as a "long aberration of judgment," and, as a partisan of Romanticism, criticized his paintings for their lack of "spontaneity" and "warmth of emotion."

V

The July Monarchy came in on a flood of liberal enthusiasm and the revolutionaries of 1830 generally regarded David with greater favor from the political standpoint. However, they were divided in their opinion of his artistic merit. Those who admired Romanticism, which was then at its height, criticized David's neoclassic style as cold, artificial and uninspired. The radical young revolutionary Barthélemy Hauréau, in his controversial *La Montagne; notices historiques et philosophiques sur les principaux membres de la montagne* (1834) praised David as "a great citizen and a great painter" because he placed his art at the service of the Republic, but the artist's style left him unmoved. Other men of 1830 derided Romanticism and claimed that David's paintings were more appropriate to the revolutionary spirit than those of Delacroix: "Du Romanticism" and "Salon de 1831" (reprinted in A. Fabre, *Histoire de la révolution française [de 1830]* ([Paris: Thoisnier-Desplaces, 1833], II, 254–61, 279–89).

During the 1830's David's friends, pupils and partisans published historical notices which, while not always sympathetic to his political activities, defended his artistic position and pointed out his excellence as a teacher, the catholicity of his tastes, and his kindly and generous personal character. Of these accounts the following contributed new material: E. F. A. M. Miel's notice written in 1834 and published in the *Encyclopédie des gens du monde,* 22 vols. (1833–44), VII, 578–82 (reprinted in 1840 in *Le Plutarque français,* ed. E. Mennechet, 8 vols. [1835–41], XIII, 228–34); Alexandre Lenoir, "David, souvenirs historiques," in Société des études historiques, *Journal de l'institut historique,* III (August, 1835), 1–13 was especially valuable; J. N. Paillot de Montabert and Valentin Parisot, "David" (1837) in *Biographie universelle ancienne et moderne,* ed. Michaud, 85 vols. (1811–62), supl. vol. LXII, 124–57, maintained that the artist David was the equal of Raphael but was duped by the politicians of the Revolution. Another pupil, L. J. N. Lemercier, read an ode *"Hommage à la mémoire du peintre David"* before a public session of the French Academy on May 2, 1838: *Recueil des discours, rapports et pièces diverses lus dans les séances publiques et particulières de l'Académie française 1830–1839* (Paris: Didot, 1841), pp. 909–23. In 1839 Alexandre Péron eulogized David, defended him from the criticisms of the Romanticists, and called attention to the master's admiration of Rubens and Gothic Art before the Société libre des beaux-arts, *Examen du tableau du Serment des Horaces peint par David* (1839).

In France David had numerous champions and emulators during the 1830's but English estimates of the Revolution and its propagandist did not improve. In fact, Thomas Carlyle's dramatic account, *The French Revolution, a History,* 3 vols. (London: Fraser, 1837), fixed in Anglo-Saxon imaginations a lurid picture of the horrors and atrocities of that "smoke and flame conflagration" which for Carlyle constituted the Revolution. Carlyle execrated "gross David with the swoln cheek" who painted and legislated "with genius in a state of convulsions" and his festivals which were "Scenic Phantasmagories unexampled" and so much unadulterated "Mumbo-Jumbo."

By 1840 French art seemed to be on the verge of a classical reaction and David's artistic reputation rose accordingly. The conservative trend of French politics during the ministry of Guizot (1840–48) did not improve David's standing in official circles but his revolutionary role and the ideological content of his paintings endeared him to many "liberals."

According to Théophile Thoré, ("Les Peintres du XIXe siècle, Louis David," *Trésor national,* ser. 2, III [1843] 65–82), one of the leading art critics of the time, David's work was truly "the art of the people." As a partisan of the Romaniticists, Thoré considered David rather a mediocre painter, but as a political "liberal," he glorified him as a prophet of revolution. He "admired the enthusiasm and resolution" of the Jacobin artist's political career, and praised the great services which he rendered to the arts during the Revolution (pp. 75–76).

Charles Blanc, the art historian brother of the socialist leader, also adopted a sympathetic view of David in his *Histoire des peintres français au dix-neuvième siècle* (Cauville frères, 1845), I, 155–203.* Though he did not care for neoclassicism, Blanc said that David, because of the "triumph of his thought," was just as much in the great tradition of French painting as Géricault. He praised David's paintings for giving "a salutary impulsion to public opinion" and for aiming at "universal regeneration" through revolutionary propaganda (pp. 176, 186). "The Revolution . . . seized upon painting as a means of government; the republican David put his palette at the service of the

* The book was dedicated in "A mon frère, Louis Blanc." Charles Blanc later participated in the Revolution of 1848 and served as minister of fine arts under the Second Republic from 1848 to 1850.

revolutionary idea" (p. 32). Finally, Blanc not only emphasized the enormous European prestige of David and his decisive influence on French painting but also recognized that he was a great artist in his own right.

At the Salon of 1846, there was a retrospective exhibition of art since 1789 which included several of David's works. These, particularly the *Marat* which had not been shown in public for fifty years, stimulated discussion of David. At least some of the critics, including Thoré, came to his defense. While Thoré agreed with the criticism that neoclassicism was overly imitative of sculpture, he spoke warmly in defense of David's career as a Jacobin and praised the *Marat* as his best work. (*Le Salon de 1846* . . . [Alliance des Arts, 1846]).

The art critics among the opponents of the July Monarchy seem to have awarded David a high place, but the historians who prepared the Revolution of 1848 were by no means unanimous in their praise. Léonard Gallois' eulogistic *Histoire de la Convention,* 8 vols. (1834–48) lauded David as "one of the most ardent patriots of the Mountain" whose "talents were worthy of Homer"; but another pro-Jacobin, Alphonse Esquiros, *Histoire des Montagnards* (1847), described him as "cowardly" because he survived his hero Robespierre. The ablest defense of the Jacobins at that time was Louis Blanc's *Histoire de la révolution,* 12 vols. (1847–62). This socialistic historian was much warmer toward David whose "heroic *procès-verbal,*" the *Oath of the Tennis Court* was "the glory of our fathers." On the other hand, as an apologist for the Girondins, Alphonse de Lamartine, *Histoire des Girondins,* 8 vols. (1847), was quite hostile to the Jacobin artist.

Jules Michelet, *Histoire de la révolution française,* 7 vols. (1847–53), frequently used David's works as historical sources but he was too much of a Romanticist to admire the painter's style. Like Charles Blanc, Michelet insisted that the artist thwarted his own natural artistic genius by imitating antique marbles and playing the professor. When he let himself go in sketches and portraits, he showed himself "a great master." Moreover, Michelet was the first to find the true spirit and meaning of the Revolution in the festivals. He showed how the spontaneous federations of 1789–90 were adapted by the leaders for political ends. While he did not approve of David's propaganda demonstrations, Michelet's lyrical descriptions immortalized these ceremonies in a matchless literary form in which poetic license occasionally did violence to the facts. In these as in other colorful pages Michelet exerted an immense influence upon later historians.

VI

In the wake of the Revolution of 1848 came the most eulogistic of all the biographies of David, apparently by an ardent pro-Jacobin, Miette de Villars, *Mémoires de David, peintre et député à la Convention* (1850). The author of this mosaic of earlier biographical notices and speeches from the *Moniteur* claimed that he checked these accounts with the personal testimony of David's pupil Dupavillon and others. Miette de Villars' work was a conscious attempt to rehabilitate all aspects of David's reputation.

With the appearance of "realism" around 1848 and the revival of interest in rococo art, the battle over David's artistic style tended to take a new direction. The aristocratic Goncourt brothers who loved rococo art derided David and neoclassicism in their *Histoire de la société française pendant la révolution* (1854) and later works. On the other hand, E. J. Delécluze's *Louis David; son école et son temps, souvenirs* (1855), (*see* p. 176) was influential in presenting David in a more favorable light. As Vicomte Henri Delaborde said in his review of the Delécluze volume "the passions of the partisans of the rival school [Romanticism] had now calmed down" ("David et son influence sur l'école française," *Revue des deux mondes,* n. s., XXVI [May 15, 1855], 749). Next year, however, Comte Léon de Laborde in the famous report on the London Exposition of 1851, *De l'union des arts et de l'industrie,* 2 vols. (1856), condemned David as a "soulless" and "despotic" reformer who destroyed the true French tradition (naturalism) in order to impose upon art a servile imitation of Roman statuary. He also accused him of vandalism, "political fanaticism, ambition without conviction [and] feeble character." This sweeping denunciation was answered by one of his pupils, L. C. A. Couder, "Protestation en faveur de l'école de David," *Revue universelle des arts,* VI (February, 1858), 419–26.

During the sixties the tide seemed to have turned in favor of David. In the fall of 1860 the publication of an article by Cantaloube, "Les dessins de Louis David," *Gazette des beaux-arts,* ser. 1, VII (September 1, 1860); and the exhibition of paintings by David in the retrospective Exposition Boulevard Italien in Paris confirmed the growing appreciation of the master's drawings and portraits. Thoré for example, writing under his pseudonym "W. Burger," praised the David portraits shown at this exhibition in his article in *Gazette des beaux-arts,* ser. 1, VIII (November 15, 1860), 228–40. Even Ernest Chesneau who in most respects did not consider David a "great genius," praised his portraits and drawings and credited him with initiating nineteenth-century art: "Le Mouvement Moderne en peinture, Louis David," *Revue Européenne,* XV (May 1, 1861), 76–105 (reprinted in his *La Peinture française au XIX*ᵉ *siècle. Les Chefs d'école,* 3rd ed. [1883]). J. Renouvier, *Histoire de l'art pendant la révolution* (1863), who found in his work "the expression of [the Revolution's] greatest energy"; Charles Blanc, *Histoire des peintres de tous les écoles,* 14 vols. (1861–76): *Ecole française,* t. II (1865); and others reflected the new respect with which David was treated. In 1867 a real contribution to the study of David on the basis of new documents was made by Auguste Jal in his *Dictionnaire critique de biographie et d'histoire,* 2nd ed. (1872), which revealed him as "greater, stronger, more admired than before." Despois' epoch-making *Le Vandalisme révolutionnaire; fondations littéraires, scientifiques et artistiques de la Convention* (1868) demonstrated once and for all that David and his colleagues had not encouraged vandalism but rather had fought it with all the weapons at their disposal.

VII

The conservative reaction which followed the French disasters of 1870–71 was reflected in the works of the art historians and regular historians. Louis Courajod, *L'Ecole royale des élèves protégés* (1874), even though he recognized that David saved art during the Revolution, castigated the "ignoble" artists who destroyed the subject of the author's study and imposed a "rigid dictatorship" upon the arts. The antidemocratic bias of H. A. Taine, *La Révolution française,* 3 vols. (1878–85), produced a vigorous indictment of David and his fellow Jacobins as "crazy doctrinaires, thirsting for blood and revelling in destruction." Not only did Taine revive the old legend of David as one of the "instigators, conductors and accomplices" of the September massacres, but he derided the revolutionary festivals as "a sort of opera played in the streets." Other conservatives continued to view David's political activities with distaste and their view was expressed by the phrase "David, the great painter, the afflictive (*triste*) politician": H. Wallon, *Histoire du tribunal révolutionnaire de Paris,* 6 vols. (1880–82), IV, 263–64.

The year 1880 was a landmark in the historiography of David for it was distinguished by the appearance of the monumental official life of the artist by his grandson Jules David, *Le Peintre Louis David,*

1748–1825, 2 vols. (1880–82). The first volume of text was sub-titled: *Souvenirs et documents inédits;* the second of plates consisted of the author's rather bad etchings after the master's works. Jules David was able to use the painter's private papers and family recollections as well as archival materials. The work was the most exhaustive treatment of David and subsequent biographers were usually content to condense and popularize its contents. Unfortunately all the facts and conclusions of the book cannot be accepted without reservation. The author, who wanted above all to express his filial piety by rehabilitating his ancestor's reputation, presented his subject in the best possible light and suppressed unfavorable evidence. His political conservatism made him apologize for and minimize David's role as a Jacobin propagandist, but on the other hand, his admiration for his artistry and personal character knew no bounds. Jules David's uncritical methods resulted in an absence of citations of sources, numerous minor errors in the text, and a total lack of completeness, precision and accuracy in the bibliography. Though weakened by these defects and outmoded in part by later research, the work is still valuable.

In the meantime, the Third French Republic had survived its first stormy decade and its supporters turned once more to the men of the Revolution of 1789 for inspiration. The synthetic work of the republican Spire Blondel, *L'Art pendant la révolution; beaux-arts, arts décoratifs* (1887), for example, was proud of David's part in the artistic and political revolutions. In 1889, the Centennial Exhibition of the Revolution featured the work of David and stimulated a renewed interest in the founder of modern French painting. It might even be said that for many this exhibition marked the "re-discovery" of David by his countrymen and foreign visitors. Certainly such varied productions as a lecture in the Zurich town hall by K. Brun, on *Jacques Louis David und die französische Revolution* (Zürich, 1890), an essay on David in A. Houssaye's *La Révolution* (1891) and Aulard's study of "L'Art et la politique en l'an II" in his *Etudes et leçons sur la révolution française,* ser. 1 (1893) were indicative of considerable academic interest in the artist.

During the three decades preceding the World War of 1914, French historians of the Revolution produced numerous scholarly studies and documentary collections which provided an ever-increasing body of evidence for a new study of David and his propaganda activities. The chief of the republican school, Aulard, who appeared to have no special bias against David, contributed *La Société des Jacobins* (*see* p. 168) and *Recueil des actes du Comité de salut public* (*see* p. 168) mentioned below; articles and documents in the review *La Révolution française* which he directed from 1887 to 1928; monographs such as *Le Cult de la Raison et le culte de l'Etre suprême, 1793–94* (1892); and his masterly synthesis, the *Histoire politique de la révolution française* (1901) which revealed that David had served as Associate Commissioner for Navy and Colonies.

Studies by Aulard's pupils and associates also contributed directly and indirectly to the knowledge of the subject. A. Brette, *Le Serment du Jeu de Paume* (1893), for example, revised the traditional view of the accuracy of David's painting of that event. Henry Morse Stephens, *The French Revolution,* 2 vols. (London: Rivingtons, 1886–91), who introduced English readers to the newer materials unearthed by the school of Aulard, was aware of the significance of the revolutionary festivals and of what he called "the curious influence of David and his pupils upon the Reign of Terror."

Scholarly political rivals of Aulard also contributed materials for the revision of the reputation of David. The distinguished socialist Jean Jaurès, *Histoire socialiste,* vols. III–IV: *La Convention* [1905], said that art, inspired by "new forces and a virile genius [David]," destroyed the Academy in order "to establish . . . a direct communication between the young [artistic] geniuses and the Revolution" (III, 214). Shortly after this French socialist acclaimed David's propaganda plans and demonstrations (IV, 1635), a famous Russian Social Democrat, Georgii Plekhanov published a relatively sympathetic Marxian interpretation of David's revolutionary art in *Pravda* in 1905 (*Sochineniia,* ed. D. Riazanov [pseud. of D. B. Goldendach], 24 vols. [Moscow, 1923–27], XIV, 95–119). Economic determinism and class struggle were also emphasized by Prince Piotr Kropotkin, *The Great French Revolution, 1789–1793* (New York: Putnam, 1909). Kropotkin anticipated the later Communist view by branding David and the Jacobins as *petit bourgeois* and criticizing their festivals as empty ceremonies devoid of real support by or meaning for the proletariat.

Of even greater significance were the contributions of the pro-Robespierre historian, Albert Mathiez. His studies in religious history, such as *Les Origines des cultes révolutionnaires, 1789–1792* (1904); his articles in the organ of the Société des études robespierristes, *Annales révolutionnaires* (continued as *Annales historiques de la révolution française* after 1924), which he directed from 1908 until his death in 1932; and his various monographs such as *Le Club des Cordeliers pendant la crise de Varennes et le massacre du Champ de Mars* (1910); all these illuminated the relation of propaganda art to the history of religion and to the events of the Revolution. *La Révolution française,* 3 vols. (1922–27), which summarized Mathiez' conclusions, paid tribute to the propaganda purpose of the festivals and to David's role as a peacemaker between political factions.

Rather different was the more conservative interpretation of Louis Madelin's volume of the same title (*La Révolution* [Paris: Hachette, 1911], vol. V of *L'Histoire de France racontée à tous,* ed. F. Funck-Brentano). Madelin, a Bonapartist sympathizer, characterized David as " a great artist and a shallow politician," a mere "lackey" who served ably as "official decorator of the Republic" and later as glorifier of Napoleon.

During the same period studies of music during the Revolution were made which contributed to the growing mass of information on the festivals. Julien Tiersot, "Les Fêtes de la révolution," *Le Ménestrel,* LIX–XL (November 12, 1893–July 22, 1894) (republished under the title *Les Fêtes et les chants de la révolution* [1908]); and Constant Pierre, *Musique exécuté aux fêtes nationales de la révolution française* [1894], *Musique des fêtes et cérémonies de la révolution française* (1899), and *Les Hymnes et chansons de la révolution* (1904) were outstanding.

Even more important were the publications during this period of the art historians on the fine arts of the Revolution. Unlike the republican Blondel (*see* p. 156) , the well known authority André Michel was rather hostile in his interpretation of David. In his *Chefs-d'oeuvre de l'art français au XIXe siècle, l'école française de David à Delacroix* (Paris: Librarie illustrée, 1891), and his chapter on "L'Art en France de 1789 à 1799" in *La Révolution française* (Paris: Colin, 1896), vol. VIII of E. Lavisse and A. Rambaud, eds., *Histoire générale du IVe siècle à nos jours,* Michel pictures David as a "despot" and the influence of his style as "fatal." More constructive were two studies of neoclassicism which appeared in 1897: the brilliant interpretation of Louis Bertrand, *La Fin du classicisme et le retour à l'antique;* and the scholarly doctoral thesis of François Benoît, *L'Art français sous la révolution et l'empire; les doctrines, les idées, les genres.*

After the turn of the century, interest in David was reflected in a considerable number of periodical articles; two short popular biographies: Charles Saunier, *Louis David, biographie critique* (1903), and Léon Rosenthal, *Louis David* (1905); and an unpretentious but reasonably good synthesis, Maurice Dreyfous, *Les Arts et les artistes pendant la période révolutionnaire (1789–1795), d'après les documents de l'époque* (1906). Among the more important of the articles were those of Saunier, "La 'Mort de Sénèque' par Louis David," *G.B.A.*, ser. 3, XXXIII (March, 1905), 233–36 and " 'Jupiter et Antiope,' oeuvre de jeunesse de Louis David," *G.B.A.*, ser. 4, VI (September, 1911), 254–60, which showed that David's youthful style was very much like Fragonard's. Moreover, Prosper Dorbec, "David portraitiste," *G.B.A.*, ser. 3, XXXVII (April, 1907), 306–30, and "Le Portrait pendant la révolution," *Revue de l'art ancien et moderne*, XXI (January-February, 1907), 4–52, 133–48 and L. Dumont-Wilden, *Le Portrait en France* (Brussels: Van Oest, 1909) popularized a fact that had long been recognized by experts, namely that David was one of the greatest of French portrait painters.

During the next few years a number of first-rate studies of the origins of David's style exerted a definite influence upon the artist's reputation. André Fontaine's fundamental work on the *retour à l'antique*, entitled *Les Doctrines d'art en France: peintres, amateurs, critiques de Poussin à Diderot* (1909) developed the background of the so-called "Davidian revolution." The doctoral thesis of René Schneider, *Quatremère de Quincy et son intervention dans les arts, 1788–1830* (1910), somewhat exaggerated the importance of the pedantic antiquary and underestimated David, but nevertheless modified contemporary opinion of both men. Jean Locquin's authoritative volume on the aesthetic reform, *La Peinture d'histoire en France de 1747 à 1785* (1912), proved conclusively that neoclassicism antedated David. Similarly Louis Hautecoeur in his dissertation on *Rome et la renaissance de l'antiquité* (1912) analyzed the relationship of the School of David to the international artists' colony at Rome.

Then in 1913 an art exhibit provided another landmark in the evolution of the shifting estimates of David. The exposition "David et ses élèves" at the Petit Palais in Paris not only confirmed the earlier opinions of David's essential greatness as a portrait painter but also stimulated an admiration of his other works, particularly his powerful revolutionary canvases such as the *Marat*. If one may base one's judgment on the numerous articles in the art journals and other periodicals of the day, the exhibition greatly stimulated a wider appreciation of David's merits as an artist and a more general interest in David's personal and political career among both critics and the public.

VIII

This interest was not to be fully satisfied, for within slightly more than a year the outbreak of the World War of 1914 suspended most scholarly work until the coming of peace. During the years 1914–1918 two studies on David were published, both dealing with his caricatures: Mme. J. Lortel, "David caricaturiste," *L'Art et les artistes,* XVIII (March, 1914), 273–75 and André Blum, *La Caricature révolutionnaire, 1789 à 1795* (1916). In 1919 the latter writer discussed another aspect of David's propaganda activities in "Les Fêtes républicaines et la tradition révolutionnaire," *R.F.,* LXXII (1919), 193–200. Blum's article credited David with the preponderant role in inspiring and executing the festivals which, said the author, created a revolutionary tradition and a *culte de la patrie.*

That same year the aesthetic problem was revived by the David specialist Charles Saunier. In his "La Peinture héroïque dans l'école de David," *Renaissance de l'art français,* II (1919), 331–39, Saunier showed how the neoclassicism of David gave birth to the Romantic movement in painting. Jean Locquin's "Le Retour à l'antique dans l'école anglaise et dans l'école française avant David," *Renaissance de l'art français,* V (1922), 473–81, demonstrated that David had been anticipated by various English artists. On the other hand Louis Réau, who favored indigenous rococo art against international neoclassicism, argued in his *Histoire de la peinture française au XVIII siècle [1690–1785],* 2 vols. (1925–26), that the *retour à l'antique* was really of French origin but was employed by the Germans in order to undermine the artistic hegemony of *la grande nation.* Nevertheless, at the same time Réau in his "La Peinture française de 1785 à 1848" in vol. VIII, pt. 1 of *Histoire de l'art,* ed. Michel (1925), recognized that the virile art of David responded to the social needs of the democracy which issued from the Revolution. Later in his *L'Europe française au siècle des lumières* (Paris: A. Michel, 1938), Vol. XXL of *L'Evolution de l'Humanité,* ed. H. Berr, Réau claimed that neoclassicism was Italian in origin and vindicated David as the restorer of French artistic hegemony in his generation.

The centennial of David's death in 1925 was the occasion for the appearance of a great many articles on the artist and his activities. Of these a series of considerable interest and varying worth by R. Régamey, R. Rey, C. Saunier, A. Salmon, J. G. Goulinat, J. Vallery-Radot, and G. Grappe designed to revise popular notions about David appeared in the periodical *L'Art vivant,* I (December 15, 1925), 1–32. The pieces on his doctrines, style, drawings and technique were valuable; those on the artist's revolutionary career, his role as *ordonnateur* of fêtes and his psychology were rather superficial. These and other articles published then and in following years, together with the commemorative exhibitions in Paris and Brussels, helped to reawaken interest in David's work including the perennial mystery of the fate of the *Le Peletier* painting (*see* p. 102) and the technical qualities of the *Oath of the Tennis Court.*

While the works of René Schneider, *L'Art français: XVIIIe siècle, 1690–1789* (1926) and Henri Focillon, *La Peinture au XIXe siècle* (1927), were not especially favorable toward David, others re-examined his role to his advantage. Robert Rey's analysis of classic elements in the Post-Impressionists, *La Renaissance du sentiment classique dans la peinture française à la fin du XIXe siècle* (1929), concluded that French art had once more returned to the principles exemplified by David. Waldemar George, *Le Dessin français de David à Cézanne et l'esprit de la tradition baroque* (1929), interpreted David as a naïve and dynamic "primitive" with a "new vision" who broke with the past and impelled the nineteenth century toward a questioning and recasting of artistic values.

Interest in and writing about David was of course not confined to France. In America, W. R. Valentiner's thoughtful study on *Jacques Louis David and the French Revolution* (New York, 1929) was based upon the author's David sketchbooks and other hitherto unpublished materials. The German specialist W. F. Friedlaender, *Hauptströmungen der französischen Malerei, I: Von David bis Delacroix* (Leipzig, 1930), contributed an interesting interpretation of David's art. A more pretentious work, highly critical of the painter's character and style, was Richard Cantinelli's *Jacques Louis David, 1748–1825* (1930). Though its handsome reproductions were valuable, the book's *catalogue raisonée* left much to be desired in completeness and accuracy, and the brief introductory text did not provide a satisfactory account of David's career. The Danish scholar, Ernst Goldschmidt, *David og hans skole* (Copenhagen, 1934), vol. V of his *Frankrigs malerkunst,* challenged Cantinelli's alleged "discovery" in the Bibliothèque Nationale of a document damaging to David's reputation.

During the past dozen years some interesting interpretations of David have been contributed by Marxist writers. While Agnes Humbert's *Louis David, peintre et conventionnel; essai de critique marxiste*

(1936) was uncritical and exaggerated, it clearly emphasized David's use of his art as propaganda for the Revolution. Mlle. Humbert warmly applauded the artist's intervention in the world of politics in favor of the masses. Similarly an American, Milton W. Brown, *The Painting of the French Revolution* (New York, 1938), presented David and neoclassicism as expressions of the ideals, morality and philosophy of the bourgeosie in their struggle for power. Brown's work, although somewhat hastily done, was based upon a study of at least some of the published documents available. In 1939 the Communist art expert, Joseph Billiet, interpreted David's work in dialectic terms in "The French Revolution and the Fine Arts" (T. A. Jackson, ed., *Essays on the French Revolution,* tr. fr. *Cahiers du Communisme* [London: Lawrence & Wishart, 1945]) and paid tribute to "the indefatigable organizer of great revolutionary celebrations." The most recent and systematic study of the Revolution from the Marxist point of view is Daniel Guérin's, *La Lutte de classes sous la Première République: bourgeois et "bras nus" (1793–1794),* 2 vols. (Paris: Gallimard, 1946). Guérin harshly rejects the more sympathetic interpretations of his predecessors and, adhering rigidly to the doctrine of class struggle, he condemns David and other bourgeois revolutionaries as cynical betrayers of the *bras nus* who had brought them to power. He returns in effect to a hostile interpretation of David similar to that of the writers of the extreme Right.

Other recent studies of David have been primarily devoted to reinterpreting his life and style in sociological and psychological terms. Klaus Holma's, *David: son évolution et son style* (1940), admittedly not a work of historical research, was a critique of David's psychology and style which emphasized his bourgeois background. An excellent study of artistic influences, its illustrations include some useful reproductions of some of David's less known works. The prominent French critic, Raymond Escholier, also made a contribution to an understanding of David in his *La Peinture française XIXe siècle: de David à Géricault* (1941). An Argentinian biography designed for popular consumption, Jorge Romero-Brest, *Jacques Louis David* (Buenos Aires, 1943), attempted a facile but by no means original explanation of David's psychology and career in terms of a "dual personality."

Among periodical articles dealing with David and his art published during the last dozen years the following should be mentioned: Jacques Combe, "Mystère du silence dans l'art classique," *L'Amour de l'art,* XVI (March, 1935), 79–85 and "Le Dessin français et la tentation du baroque," *ibid.,* XVIII (January, 1937), 5–12; Friedrich Antal, "Reflections on classicism and romanticism: David's classicism . . .," *Burlington Magazine,* LXVI (April, 1935), 159–68; M. Heine, "The Blood of the Martyr: documents," *Verve,* I (December, 1937), 28–31—on the paintings of Le Peletier and Marat; E. Bonnordet, "Comment un oratorien vint en aide à un grand peintre," *G.B.A.,* ser. 6, XIX (May, 1938), 311–15—an anecdote connected with the *Horatii*; C. Picard, "David et l'antique," *Revue archéologique,* ser. 6, XII (July, 1938), 112—a correction of the preceding article; H. Dupre, "Some French Revolutionary Propaganda Techniques," *The Historian,* II (Spring, 1940), 156–64—documents on caricatures and costumes by David; E. Scheyer, "French Drawings of the Great Revolution and the Napoleonic Era," *Art Quarterly,* IV (Summer, 1941), 187–204—included unpublished David drawings; Edgar Wind, "The Sources of David's *Horaces,*" Warburg and Courtauld Institutes, *Journal,* IV (April–July, 1940–41), 124–38—attempted to show that the inspiration for David's painting was an operatic pantomime rather than Corneille's drama; E. Wind, "A Lost Article on David by Reynolds," *ibid.,* VI (1943), 223–24—suggested that Sir Joshua's mysterious eulogy of the *Socrates* was suppressed by his literary executor; G. de Batz, "History, Truth and Art," *Art Quarterly,* VIII (Autumn, 1945), 249–60—discussed the problem of truth in historical pictures from the point of view of David's *Marat;* K. Berger, "Courbet in his century," *G.B.A.,* ser. 6, XXIV (July, 1943), 19–40—a re-interpretation of David as a precursor of Courbet which emphasizes his new plastic and tactile "vision" and the moral content of his neoclassic art; K. Berger, "Beginnings of modern art, David and the development of Géricault's art," *ibid.,* XXX (July, 1946), 41–62—showed how the younger artist was influenced by David's "new vision," his spirit of inquiry and criticism and his study of the old masters.

IX

Thus, for more than a century and a half the reputation of David and his art has fluctuated upward and downward according to the pressure of personal, social and political predilections, revolutionary sentiment and artistic taste. At the present time, although opinion is still not unanimous, David is generally recognized as one of the great masters of French painting. There is as yet no similar agreement regarding David's actual role as a member of the government during the Terror.

While this study has not been concerned with David's political career except as incidental to his propaganda activities, the reasons for this dissension may be of interest here. As a political figure of lesser stature than Danton or Robespierre, David has been ignored by professional historians; the persistence of political passions dating from the Revolution has done nothing to revise partisan views; and most serious of all, the lack of published sources on the Committee of General Security and the Commission of Navy and Colonies has left his special activities obscure. The acts, proceedings and other documents of the Committee of General Security which would answer the controversial questions regarding the real nature and intensity of David's police activities have never been published. Even the excellent monograph of Belloni, *Le Comité de sûreté générale de la Convention nationale* (1924) provided little or nothing of a specific nature. Likewise the records of the Commission for Navy and Colonies (David was Assistant Commissioner) remain unpublished. This writer hopes to shed some light upon the problem of David's part in the government by investigating these archival materials.

Whatever the outcome of such an investigation and whatever future fluctuations in personal, political and artistic opinion may take place, it is certain that David will continue to enjoy recognition as one of the significant figures of his time. His achievements as a propagandist will claim for him an increasingly important place in the study of the French Revolution. His true genius as an artist will assure him eternal recognition as a master in the history of painting.

ESSAY ON SOURCES

The problem of selecting individual items for inclusion in an essay on sources for a study of this type is not an easy one. Materials are so diverse in nature and their amount so considerable that it is impossible to include all the works actually used in the space available. Only the more important materials for this particular piece of research are included here. Works of a general nature have been for the most part omitted and the student of the subject is referred to the bibliographical guides mentioned below and, for more specific references, to the footnotes of this study.

This essay then does not pretend to exhaust the possibilities but merely to give an indication of the kinds of materials found useful. Since the research was completed for the most part before travel to France was again possible, the use of archival materials was not available except insofar as these have been published and are to be found in American libraries.

All works referred to were published in Paris unless otherwise indicated.

I. BIBLIOGRAPHICAL AND OTHER AIDS

In addition to the general bibliographical tools such as the *International Bibliography of Historical Sciences,* ed. by the International Committee of Historical Sciences, 13 vols. to date (Zürich, New York, etc., 1926–), and the various periodical reviews, the standard bibliographies of French history for the period, including E. Saulnier and A. Martin, *Bibliographie des travaux publiés de 1866 à 1897 sur l'histoire de France de 1500 à 1789,* 2 vols. (1932–38); Vicomte Charles du Peloux, *Répertoire générale des ouvrages modernes relatifs au XVIIIe siècle français, 1715–1789,* (1926) with *Supplément* (1927); P. Caron, *Bibliographie des travaux publiés de 1866 à 1897 sur l'histoire de France depuis 1789* (1912); G. Brière and P. Caron, *Répertoire méthodique de l'histoire moderne et contemporaine de la France,* 9 vols. (1899–1924), for works published between 1898 and 1913; P. Caron and H. Stein, *Répertoire bibliographique de l'histoire de France,* 6 vols. (1923–38), for works published between 1920 and 1931, were used. As guides to older publications G. Monod, *Bibliographie de l'histoire de France* (1888) and A. Franklin, *Les Sources de l'histoire de France* (1877) were helpful.

For identification and evaluation of obscure, anonymous or forged works J. C. Brunet, *Manuel du librairie et de l'amateur des livres,* 5 vols., 5th ed. (1860–65), with *Supplément,* 2 vols. (1878–80); A. A. Barbier, *Dictionnaire des ouvrages anonymes,* 4 vols., 3rd ed. enl. (1882); and J. M. Quérard, *La France littéraire,* 12 vols. (1827–64), and *Les Supercheries dévoilés,* 5 vols. (1842–53), were indispensable.

Besides these bibliographical tools the catalogues of various libraries were important. Particularly useful among the printed catalogues were those of the Bibliothèque Nationale, *Catalogue générale des livres imprimés . . . auteurs,* 167 vols. to date (1879–); the British Museum, *Catalogue of Printed Books,* 393 parts (London, 1881–1900), *Supplement,* 44 parts (1900–05) and its new *General Catalogue of the Printed Books,* 39 vols. to date (London, 1931–); the President White Library, Cornell University, *Catalogue . . .* vol. II: *The French Revolution* (Ithaca, 1894); New York Public Library, *French Revolutionary Pamphlets; a check list of the Talleyrand and other collections* (New York, 1945); and John Hall Stewart, *France 1715–1815; a guide to materials in Cleveland* (Cleveland, 1940). Outstanding were the card catalogues at Harvard University and the Library of Congress by reason of their completeness and those of the Frick Collection, New York; the New York Public Library; and the Ryerson Library, Chicago Art Institute, by reason of their specialized and analytical character.

Various specialized bibliographies included G. Lanson, *Manuel bibliographique de la littérature française moderne,* 5 vols. (1909–14); L. E. Hatin, *Bibliographie historique et critique de la presse périodique française* (1866); F. Chèvremont, *Marat: index du bibliophile et de l'amateur de peinture, gravure* [*etc.*], (1876) and such bibliographical articles as R. R. Palmer, "Fifty Years of the Committee of Public Safety," *Journal of Modern History,* XIII (September, 1941), 375–97; G. Bonno, "List chronologique des périodiques de langue française du dix-huitième siècle," *Modern Language Quarterly,* V (March, 1944), 3–55; the "Bulletins Historiques" on the French Revolution of G. Lefebvre in *Revue Historique,* CLXIII (January, 1930), 111–59; CLXIX (January, 1932), 116–59; CLXXXVII (January–June, 1939), 63–112, 184–224, 225–56; CXCVI (April–June, 1946), 158–214 and on the history of art by L. Hautecoeur in *Revue Historique,* CLXXI (March, 1933), 352–84; CLXXVIII (November, 1936), 549–95; CLXXXVII (April, 1939), 146–83; H. E. Bourne, "A Decade of Studies in the French Revolution," *Journal of Modern History,* I (June, 1929),

256–79; and B. Hyslop, "Recent Work on the French Revolution," *American Historical Review,* XLVII (April, 1942), 488–517, were used.

Especially important are the bibliographies of the French Revolution being compiled by A. Martin and G. Walter, *Catalogue de l'histoire de la révolution française,* 4 vols. (I–III, V) to date (1936–) and A. Monglond, *La France révolutionnaire et impériale . . .,* 5 vols. to date (Grenoble, 1930–). Indispensable naturally were M. Tourneux, *Bibliographie de l'histoire de Paris pendant la révolution française,* 5 vols. (1890–1913) and A. Tuetey, *Répertoire général des sources manuscrites de l'histoire de Paris pendant la révolution française,* 11 vols. (1890–1914).

The general collaborative histories were of course an excellent bibliographical source. Of these the appropriate volumes of the older *Cambridge Modern History;* E. Lavisse and A. Rambaud, *Histoire générale;* E. Lavisse, ed., *Histoire de France depuis les origines jusqu' à la révolution;* E. Lavisse, ed., *Histoire de la France contemporaine;* and the more recent W. L. Langer, ed., *The Rise of Modern Europe;* together with the standard manuals, P. Caron, *Manuel pratique pour l'étude de la révolution française,* rev. ed. (1947), and L. Villat, *La Révolution et l'empire,* 2 vols. (1936) were especially helpful.

Of more specialized value were the bibliographies included in the various art histories such as A. Michel, ed., *Histoire de l'art,* 8 vols. (1905–29); in the artists' dictionaries such as E. Bellier de la Chavignerie and L. Auvray, eds., *Dictionnaire générale des artistes de l'école française,* 3 vols. (1882–87); and U. Thieme and F. Becker, eds. *Allgemeines Lexikon der bildenden Künstler,* 34 vols. (Leipzig, 1907–40); and most important of all, those in the various monographs and special studies such as Jules David, *Le Peintre Louis David* (see pp. 155–56). Unfortunately the usefulness of the bibliography in the latter work is diminished by the chaotic arrangement, incompleteness and inaccuracy of the items listed.

Among the biographical dictionaries and encyclopedias which might be mentioned in addition to Bellier de la Chavignerie and Thieme-Becker and the more or less contemporary compilations discussed on pp. 146–51 are Vicomte du Peloux, *Répertoire biographique et bibliographique des artistes du XVIIIe siècle français* (1930); A. Brette, *Les Constituants, list des députés . . . de 1789* (1897); and A. Kuscinski, *Dictionnaire des Conventionnels* (1916–19). H. Mireur, *Dictionnaire des ventes d'art . . . pendant les XVIIIme & XIXme siècles,*

7 vols. (1911–12) is disappointingly incomplete; it even omits the two most important sales of David's works (i.e. those of 1826 and 1835).

Because of the nature of this study the catalogues of art museums, special collections and exhibitions were frequently very useful. Among the former the more significant were those of the Louvre, and the Département des Estampes of the Bibliothèque Nationale, particularly the Réserve and the Collection de Vinck, in Paris; and the Museums of Brussels, Versailles, Dijon, Lille, Nantes and other galleries containing works by David. Among the more important exhibitions of David's works were the following: the David sales of 1826 and 1835 in Brussels and Paris; the "Exposition Boulevard Italien" of 1860, the "Exposition Universelle" of 1889, the "Exposition David et ses élèves" of 1913, in Paris; the David centennial exhibitions in Brussels and Paris in 1925 and 1926; the exhibition "David, Ingres, Géricault, et leur temps" in 1934 in Paris; the "David and Ingres" exhibit shown at the Springfield Museum of Fine Arts (1939) and at M. Knoedler and Company, New York (1940); the exhibition of "Masterpieces of French Art" which toured the United States during the second World War; and the exposition sponsored by the Société d'Histoire de la Révolution Française at Wildenstein and Company, New York in 1943. The published catalogues of and the critical commentaries upon these exhibits which appeared in contemporary periodicals and elsewhere not only throw light upon the works shown but also upon the fluctuations of David's reputation discussed in the Bibliographical Essay.

II. CONTEMPORARY MATERIALS

1. COLLECTIONS

Of the older printed collections of documents P. J. B. Buchez and P. C. Roux, eds., *Histoire parlementaire de la révolution française,* 40 vols. (1834–38) reprints contemporary speeches, newspapers, pamphlets and memoirs not otherwise conveniently available. J. Guillaume, ed., *Procès-verbaux du Comité d'instruction publique de la Convention nationale,* 6 vols. (1891–1907) is broader in scope than its title indicates for its annexes include all types of archival documents relative to the propaganda committee. It is indispensable for study of the interaction of art and politics during the Revolution. Aulard's famous *Recueil des actes du Comité de salut public,* 27 vols. (1889–1933) and *La Société des Jacobins,* 6 vols. (1889–97) are not complete or without errors and S. Lacroix' monumental *Actes de la Commune de*

Paris, 15 vols. in 2 ser. (1894–1914), ends substantially with November 10, 1791, so they had to be checked and completed by contemporary materials such as newspapers.

An indispensable source was the great collection of documents on the history of French art published by Philippe de Chennevières and his successors of the Société de l'histoire de l'art français. For almost a century the *Archives de l'art français* and the *Nouvelles archives de l'art français* published documents from various archives and private collections. These and their *Bulletin* and other publications provide a rich mine of source materials for revolutionary art and artists. More specialized compilations such as F. Engerand, ed., *Inventaire des tableaux commandés et achetés par la Direction des bâtiments du roi, 1709–1792* (1910) and A. Tuetey and Jean Guiffrey, eds., *La Commission du muséum et la création du Musée du Louvre, 1792–1793, Documents recueillis et annotés . . .* (1910) also included documents pertinent to this study.

Among collections still useful for contemporary materials, some of which were destroyed during the Communard uprising of 1871, are L. M. Ternaux, *Histoire de la Terreur, 1792–94,* 8 vols. (1861–81), A. Dauban's source studies of public opinion *La Démogogie en 1793* (1868) and *Paris en 1794 et en 1795* (1869); and F. E. Robinet's, *Le Mouvement religieux à Paris pendant la révolution,* 2 vols. (1896–98), for the festivals; and his *Le Procès des Dantonistes* (1879), for the role of David at the trial of Danton.

2. ACTS, LAWS AND DECREES

Of the collections of official acts, laws, decrees, decisions and the like J. B. Duvergier's well known *Collection complète des lois, décrets, ordonnances, règlements et avis du Conseil d' Etat . . . de 1788 à 1824,* 24 vols. (1825–28) was the most convenient to use. However, since the contemporary collection compiled by the printer of the National Assembly, F. J. Baudouin, ed., *Collection générale des décrets . . .* [May, 1789–Nivôse, an VIII], 79 vols. (1789–99), was more complete and accurate, it was used in preference to Duvergier in this study. The texts of the various laws in the *Collection Baudouin,* as it is sometimes known, were compared with and corrected by the proceedings of the several revolutionary assemblies, (*see* p. 170), the reports of contemporary newspapers (*see* pp. 179–85), and the official decrees published in pamphlet form by the government (*see* pp. 186–94). The acts of the Committee of Public Instruction were studied in Guillaume (p. 168) and for the decrees of the Committee of Public Safety Aulard's compilation mentioned above was used with circumspection, and as in the case of the *Collection Baudouin* was carefully checked with other contemporary materials.

3. OFFICIAL PROCEEDINGS, DEBATES AND SPEECHES

Because of the well-known deficiencies of J. Mavidal, E. Laurent and others, *Archives parlementaires,* ser. 1, 82 vols. (1867–1913), this work has been used seldom and then with caution. For the most part the debates were followed in the official proceedings published at the time by order of the various revolutionary assemblies: *Procès-verbal de l'Assemblée nationale* [*constituante*], 75 vols. (1789–91), for the period June 17, 1789 to September 30, 1791; *Procès-verbal de l'Assemblée nationale* [*législative*], 16 vols. (1791–92), with a useful index, for the period October 1, 1791 to September 21, 1792; and *Procès-verbal de la Convention nationale,* 72 vols. (1792–95), down to October 5, 1795.

Since the debates are frequently abbreviated or reduced to a mere mention of the subject, the details of the speeches have to be filled in from the contemporary newspapers. For the early period, besides the commonly used *Moniteur (Gazette nationale, ou le Moniteur universel,* ed. Thuau-Grandville, 152 vols. [November 24, 1789–December 31, 1868]) and the *Journal des débats et décrets,* 42 vols. (August 30, 1789–May 17, 1797) parliamentary happenings may be traced in Le Hodey's verbatim reports in the *Journal des Etats généraux* (April 27–July 11, 1789) and its continuation, the *Journal de l'Assemblée nationale,* 26 vols. (July 12, 1789–August 10, 1792) and the folio *Le Logographe,* 475 nos. (April 27, 1791–August 17, 1792). The newspapers of Barère, Mirabeau, Brissot, Robespierre, Desmoulins and others discussed later in this Essay were of special value for the speeches and opinions of their respective editors. Other sheets whose reports of the debates of the Assembly were particularly complete were *L'Auditeur National, Révolutions de Paris, Journal universel, Annales patriotiques, Journal du soir, Chronique de Paris,* later the *Feuille villageoise,* and naturally the old and well established *Gazette de France* (1631–1917), *Mercure de France* (1672–1820), and *Journal de Paris* (1777–1840). For the period of the Convention, in addition to those journals mentioned above which survived, there were the *Journal de France, Bulletin national, Courier de l'égalité,* and *Décade philosophique.* Especially useful were the *Courier universel, Le Républicain français, Premier journal de la Convention* and *Journal de la Montagne.**

Speeches by various individuals who appear in this study have been collected and published. Some of David's are printed in Jules David's work but largely it would appear from the versions in the *Moniteur.* The collected speeches of Robespierre, *Discours et rapports,* ed. C. Vellay (1908); G. J. Danton, *Discours,* ed. A. Fribourg (1910); and Marie-Joseph Chénier, *Oeuvres,* 5 vols. (1824–26), were referred to but wherever possible the official texts of individual speeches by these men as well as Cloots, Collot d'Herbois, Barère, Mathieu, Grégoire, Merlin de Thionville and others, reprinted by the government in pamphlet form, were used and are listed by author in the appropriate section of this bibliography.

The minutes of the meetings of several of the committees of the National Assemblies have been published in the *Collection de documents inédits sur l'histoire de France.* Of these Guillaume's *Procès-verbaux du Comité d'instruction publique de l'Assemblée législative* (1889) as well as his more monumental *Procès-verbaux du Comité d'instruction publique de la Convention nationale* described on p. 168 were indispensable. For the proceedings of the art commissions we have Louis Tuetey's *Procès-verbaux de la Commission des monuments,* 2 vols. (1902–03) and *Procès-verbaux de la Commission temporaire des arts,* 2 vols. (1912–18); and A. Tuetey and J. Guiffrey's *La Commission du Museum,* already mentioned (p. 169). Finally for David's early political role E. Charavay and P. Mautouchet, eds., *Assemblée électorale de Paris . . . Procès-verbaux de l'élection des députés* [etc.], 3 vols. (1890–1905), was indispensable.

At the trial of the Public Prosecutor of the Revolutionary Tribunal, Fouquier-Tinville, testimony was given which involved David in the condemnation of Danton to the guillotine. This evidence was published in the contemporary periodicals, notably the *Bulletin du Tribunal criminel révolutionnaire: Procès de Fouquier-Tinville,* no. 26 [n.d.], pp. 1–2 and was made much of by the Thermidorian pamphlets of L. Lecointre, *Les Crimes des sept membres des anciens Comités* (1794), p. 111; E. B. Courtois, *Rapport fait . . . sur les événements du 9 Thermidor* (1796), p. 36 and was reprinted in the appendix of Robinet, *Procès des Dantonistes* as previously stated. Court records were also

* These and other journals are discussed more fully under section 7 "Newspapers and periodicals." *See* pp. 179–85.

used in connection with David's drawing for his picture of Le Peletier; *Gazette des tribunaux,* XII, no. 3706 (July 26, 1837), p. 943.

The attitude of the Jacobins toward the use of art as propaganda can be studied in the minutes of their meetings. Since several of the more important sessions are not to be found in Aulard's *Société des Jacobins* (*see* p. 168) primary reliance was placed upon the *Procès-verbaux* in the party organs: *Journal des Amis de la constitution, Journal des débats de la Société des amis de la constitution* (known as the *Journal des Jacobins*) and the *Journal de la Montagne* with its little-known predecessor, the *Premier journal de la Convention nationale;* and various other newspapers such as *Le Républicain français, Auditeur national, Courier universel, Journal des hommes libres de tous les pays,* and *Feuille villageoise.* These same journals contain information on festivals and other propaganda activities of the Jacobins in the *départements* and to them can be added local sheets such as the *Journal de la Société des amis de la liberté et de l'égalité établie à Bruxelles* and the official proceedings of local clubs such as that at Tulle published by V. Forot, ed., *Le Club des Jacobins de Tulle. Procès-verbaux de toutes les séances (1790 à 1795)* (Tulle, 1912); that at Artonne published by F. Martin, *Les Jacobins au village; Documents* (Clermont-Ferrand, 1902); and that at Bergerac published by H. Labroue, *La Société populaire de Bergerac pendant la révolution* (1915); as well as the documents quoted by Louis de Cardenal, *La Province pendant la révolution; histoire des clubs jacobins (1789–1795)* (1929).

The verbal proceedings of the Royal Academy of Painting and Sculpture, indispensable for David's early struggles against corporative authority, were published with an index by A. de Montaiglon and others, eds., *Procès-verbaux de l'Académie royale de peinture et de sculpture (1648–1793),* 10 vols. (1875–1909). After the abolition of the Academy the minutes of the quasi-official artists' societies organized and dominated by David are of similar importance for this study. H. Lapauze, ed., *Procès-verbaux de la Commune générale des arts de peinture, sculpture, architecture et gravure (18 juillet 1793-tridi de la Ire décade du 2e mois de l' an II) et de la Société populaire et républicaine des arts (3 nivôse an II-28 floréal an III)* (1903). The texts of individual speeches, reports and decrees which were separately printed during the course of the artistic feuds have been listed with the pamphlets under the names of their respective authors (*see* pp. 186–94).

4. POLICE REPORTS

Of all the various types of sources of the period one of the most valuable for a faithful daily picture of the public reaction to revolutionary propaganda was the police reports. P. Caron, ed., *Paris pendant la terreur,* 3 vols. (1910–43), published the reports of the special agents of the Ministry of the Interior for the period from August 1793 to March 1794. W. A. Schmidt, ed., *Tableau de la révolution française,* 3 vols. (Leipzig, 1867–71), though reproducing fewer documents, extends into the period of the Consulate; Dauban's works cited on p. 169 also include police reports.

5. LETTERS

Some of the most revealing evidence for the subject was found in the collections of published correspondence. Of special importance of course were David's own letters. Jules David, *Le Peintre Louis David* includes a considerable number of letters to and from the artist but inaccuracies which appear in the transcription of other documents open the texts and particularly the dates of the letters to some question. Moreover, many David letters still extant are not included. Others have been published in various periodicals, notably in *Archives de l'art français, Nouvelles archives de l'art français, La Révolution française, La Chronique des arts,* and in miscellaneous publications such as M. F. A. de Lescure, *Les Autographes* (1865); France, Musée des archives nationales, *Documents . . . exposés dans l'Hôtel Soubise* (1872) and in various catalogues such as G. Charavay, ed., *Catalogue d'une importante collection de documents autographes et historiques sur la révolution française* (1862); *Catalogue des autographes et des documents historiques composant la collection de M. Etienne Charavay* (1900–01).

The official correspondence between Count Angiviller, the Superintendent of the King's Buildings, and Jean-Baptiste Pierre and Joseph Vien, the Directors of the Royal Academy, *Correspondance de M. d'Angiviller . . . avec Pierre* [*et Vien*], ed. M. Furcy-Raynaud, 2 vols. (1906–07), and between Angiviller and Pierre and other Directors of the French Academy at Rome, *Correspondance des Directeurs de l'Académie de France à Rome avec les Surintendants des bâtiments, 1666–1804,* A. de C. de Montaiglon and J. J. Guiffrey, eds., 17 vols. (1887–1908), were essential.

Especially useful for eyewitness descriptions and personal reactions were the official dispatches and secret correspondence of foreign envoys and agents in France including those of the British Ambassador, the First Duke of Sutherland, *The Despatches of Earl Gower . . . from June 1790 to August 1792, to which are added the despatches of Mr. Lindsay and Mr. Monro, and the diary of Viscount Palmerston in France during July and August 1791,* ed. O. Browning (Cambridge [Eng.], 1885); the Ambassador of Spain, Count Fernán Nuñez, *Un témoin ignoré de la révolution,* ed. A. Musset (1924); the Parmesan envoy and chargé d'affaires, the Bailli de Virieu-Beauvoir and the Chevalier de Lama in *La Révolution française racontée par un diplomate étranger. Correspondance . . .* ed. Vicomte de Grouchy and A. Guillois (1903); the Venetian Ambassadors, A. Capello and A. Pisani, *I Dispacci degli ambasciatori Veneti alla corte di Francia durante la rivoluzione,* ed. M. M. Kovalevskii (Turin, 1895); and the agent of the Papacy, the Abbé L. S. J. Salomon, *Correspondance secrète . . . avec le Cardinal Zelada (1791–1792),* ed. Vicomte de Richemont (1898). A valuable source for revolutionary festivals in America was the *Correspondence of the French Ministers to the United States, 1791–97,* ed. F. J. Turner (Washington, D. C., 1904).

Foreign visitors to Paris provided relatively independent accounts. The ardent Hellene and Greek scholar, Adamantios Koraēs, *Lettres . . . au protopsalte de Smyrne Dimitrios Lotos sur les événements de la révolution française (1782–92),* tr. and ed. Marquis de Queux de Saint-Hilaire (1880), the anonymous English woman and Henry Swinburne in *La France et Paris sous le Directoire,* ed. A. Babeau (1888); the former revolutionary Henry Redhead Yorke, *France in 1802; Described in a series of contemporary letters,* ed., J. A. C. Sykes (London, 1906); the authoress Helen Maria Williams, *Letters containing a sketch of the politics of France . . . and of the scenes which passed in the prisons of Paris,* 4 vols. (London, 1795–96) and *A Residence in France during the years 1792, 1793, 1794 and 1795 described in a series of letters,* ed., J. Gifford, 1st Amer. ed. (Elizabethtown [New Jersey], 1798); and the antiquarian Stephen Weston, *Letters from Paris during the summer of 1791 (June–October)* (London, 1792) were especially useful in this study. Even more valuable were the letters of the German visitors to revolutionary Paris, G. A. von Halem, *Paris en 1790,* ed. A. Chuquet (1896), tr. fr. *Blicke auf einen Theil Deutschlands, der Schweiz und Frankreichs bei einer Reise vom Jahr 1790,* 2 vols. (Hamburg, 1791) and F. J. L. Meyer, *Fragmente aus Paris im IV ten Jahr der französischen Republik,* 2 vols. (Hamburg: Bohn, 1798), used also in French translation by C. F. D. Dumouriez, *Fragments sur Paris,* 2 vols.

(Hamburg, 1798). C. T. Weinlig's *Briefe über Rom,* 3 vols. (Dresden, 1782–87), used in connection with David's trip to Naples, Herculaneum and Pompeii; T. C. Bruun-Neergaard, *Sur la situation des beaux-arts en France, ou Lettres d'un Danois à son ami* (1801), the reactions of a Danish art amateur to the artistic controversies of the day; the letters of the great chemist A. L. Lavoisier on the suppression of the academies in *Oeuvres,* ed. E. Grimaux, 6 vols. (1862–93) were helpful.

Illuminating were the letters of native Frenchmen, especially those addressed to their families rather than to posterity. F. J. Bouchette, a provincial attorney and member of the Constituent Assembly, *Lettres,* ed. C. Looten (1909); the Marquis de Ferrières-Marsay, a moderate-minded country gentleman elected to the National Assembly, *Correspondance inédite (1789, 1790, 1791),* ed. H. Carré (1932); the spontaneous and sincere letters of the young medical student E. Géraud, *Journal d'un étudiant . . . pendant la révolution (1789–93),* ed. G. Maugras (1890); the correspondence of the wife of the Jacobin deputy, Mme. Rosalie Ducrollay Jullien, *Journal d'une bourgeoise pendant la révolution, 1791–93,* ed., E. Lockroy, 2nd ed. (1881); and of the wife of the Girondin minister, Mme. Marie Jeanne Phlipon Roland, *Lettres,* ed., C. Perroud, 2 vols. (1900–02); and the hostile views of the royalists and their sympathizers published by P. de Vaissière, *Lettres d' "aristocrates." La Révolution racontée par des correspondances privées, 1789–94* (1907)—all these were drawn upon. In a different category are the open letters to the press of Charles Marquis de Villette, *Lettres choisies . . . sur les principaux événements de la révolution* (1792), of the poet André Chénier, *Oeuvres en prose,* ed. L. Becq de Fouquieres, new ed., (1881), and others which were published to express their writers' views and to influence public opinion.

6. MEMOIRS, JOURNALS AND DIARIES

Although the memoirs of the period provide a wealth of material for a study of this kind, they must be used with considerable caution. In the main apologetic, they are frequently very inaccurate. They have been used here occasionally where they were corroborative or were supported by more reliable evidence; more frequently they have been cited for the opinions expressed by their authors. While not always as satisfactory as some other sources such as private letters, some of the journals and diaries record the contemporary impressions of their authors and are therefore valuable as reflections of public opinion. In some cases the views of an individual are of special value as

Robespierre's "Carnet" ed. crit. A. Mathiez, *A.R.*, X (January, 1918), 1–21.

David himself never wrote his memoirs; the so-called *Mémoires de David* (1850), published by Miette de Villars, are compiled from the recollections of these who knew the artist. The souvenirs of David's pupils, colleagues and friends are essential sources for his life and work. Of these by far the most important are the remarkable recollections of one of his favored pupils, E. J. Delécluze, *Louis David, son école et son temps; souvenirs* (1855). Delécluze's boyhood memories provide vivid and unforgettable pictures of David directing the Festival of the Supreme Being, defending himself in the Convention after Thermidor, and painting and teaching in his studio. As a young art student Delécluze became a close friend of David and heard the master's own account of his revolutionary career. Nevertheless, he did not come into intimate contact with David until 1796 and his recollections were written down fifty years later. While primarily devoted to his own literary career, Delécluze's *Souvenirs de soixante années [1789–1849]* (1860) record the impressions of a boy's life during the Revolution and of a student in David's atelier. Delécluze's "Souvenirs inédits" in the *Revue rétrospective,* though more useful for David's last years, include material on the artist's influence on Talma and the theater.

Comtesse de Genlis, *Mémoires inédites,* 10 vols. (1825) and Mme. Vigée Le Brun, *Souvenirs,* 2 vols. (1869), and, indirectly, Comte d'Angiviller, *Mémoires,* ed. L. Bobé (Copenhagen, 1933) throw considerable light on David's social life before the Revolution and also reveal something of the painter's character and personality. The vividly written memoirs of Charles de Lacretelle, *Dix années d'épreuves pendant la révolution* (1842) not only provide highlights on the Fête of Châteauvieux but also on the salon life in which David moved during the old regime. For this social milieu there are rich memoir materials including those of liberal nobles such as Comte L. P. Ségur, *Mémoires,* 3 vols., 3rd ed. (1824–27) who frequented David's studio in those days and literary figures such as J. F. Marmontel, *Mémoires,* ed. M. Tourneux, 3 vols. (1891).

Of outstanding significance for David's struggles with the Academy is J. G. Wille, *Mémoires et journal,* 2 vols. (1857). The author, an engraver who knew David well, also gives impartial, illuminating and faithful descriptions of daily events, including the revolutionary festivals. For hostile accounts of David's relations with the Academy *see* the Marquis de Paroy, *Mémoires,* ed. E. Charavay (1895), an ardent royalist and associate of the Academy, and the sculptor L. P. Deseine, *Notices historiques sur les anciennes académies royales de peinture, sculpture de Paris* (1814). Angiviller's recently discovered *Mémoires,* (*see* p. 176), together with the new documents there published, throw a more favorable light upon their author's relations with David.

Among the memoirs used for the early festivals which are not mentioned elsewhere in the bibliography are E. Dumont, *Souvenirs sur Mirabeau,* ed. J. L. Duval (1832); A. C. Duquesnoy, *Journal . . . sur l'Assemblée constituante,* ed. R. de Crèvecoeur, 2 vols. (1894), and C. E. Marquis de Ferrières-Marsay, *Mémoires,* ed. Berville and Barrière, 3 vols (1821).

For the period of the Convention the memoirs of David's fellow deputies were essential when used with discretion. B. Barère de Vieuzac, *Mémoires,* ed. L. H. Carnot and P. J. David (d'Anger), 4 vols. (1842–44) written decades later and commonly regarded with distrust, give a sympathetic account of the artist's activities and throw light on their relationship to the public works program of the Committee of Public Safety. The fiery old *Montagnard,* M. A. Baudot, wrote his *Notes historiques sur la Convention nationale, le directoire, l'empire et l'exile des votants* (1893) in exile but they were not published until fifty-six years after his death. As an enthusiastic Dantonist Baudot loathed Robespierre but he shows a high appreciation for David. Another sympathetic evaluation of the artist and his work by one who knew him well was A. C. Thibaudeau, *Mémoires sur la Convention et le Directoire,* ed. Berville and Barrière, 2 vols. (1824). The moderate deputy of "the Plain," P. C. F. Daunou, *Mémoires pour servir à l'histoire de la Convention nationale,* ed. Barrière and Lescure (1848), regarded David as "a man of very distinguished talent." On the other hand, the Jacobin engraver A. F. Sergent-Marceau, *Reminiscences of a regicide,* ed. M. C. M. Simpson (London, 1889) is unfriendly to David but takes credit for his propaganda successes.

Other useful accounts were those of the terrorist J. N. Billaud-Varenne, *Mémoires inédites et correspondance,* ed. A. Begis (1893); the Abbé Henri Grégoire, *Mémoires,* 2 vols. (1837); the "Man of the Plain," P. T. Durand de Maillane, *Histoire de la Convention nationale,* ed. Berville and Barrière (1825); and the Girondins, J. P. Brissot de Warville, *Mémoires* (1754–1793), ed. C. Perroud, 2 vols. (1911), and Mme. M. J. P. Roland [de la Platière], *Mémoires,* ed. C. Perroud, 2 vols. (1905).

Foreign observers also provided materials of some importance.

The Swiss journalist and secret agent of the royalists, J. F. Mallet du Pan, *Mémoires et correspondance,* ed. P. A. Sayous, 2 vols. (1851), was unusually well informed. His recollections were used here for the foreign reaction to the festivals. The contemporary diary of the Scottish physician John Moore, *A Journal during a residence in France from the beginning of August to the middle of December 1792,* 2 vols. (London, 1793), is naturally far more reliable than the later reminiscences of the English surgeon J. G. Millingen, *Recollections of Republican France 1790 to 1801* (London, 1848) of his boyhood in revolutionary Paris. Other British visitors, Viscount Palmerston, "Diary . . . in France. July 6–August 31, 1791" in *Despatches of Earl Gower* (*see* p. 174) and Sir John Carr, *The Stranger in France, or a tour from Devonshire to Paris* (London, 1803), were useful. Both Sir John and the German traveler F. J. L. Meyer, *Fragments sur Paris* (*see* p. 174) describe David's quarters in the Louvre and indicate the libelous legends regarding his revolutionary career which were spread by the royalist artists in the building. The letters of the Swiss J. H. Meister, *Souvenirs de mon dernier voyage à Paris (1795),* ed. P. Usten and E. Ritter (1910) are included here because they were written afterwards. The senile meanderings of Mme. M. G. Tussaud, *Memoirs and reminscences,* ed. F. Herve, 2 vols. (Philadelphia, 1839) include a description of David by one who specialized in faces. Gouverneur Morris' *Diary of the French Revolution,* ed. B. C. Davenport, 2 vols. (Boston, 1939) reveals the cynical comments of the American Minister to France upon the festivals.

For David's role as a member of the Committee of General Security the memoir materials are extremely untrustworthy. The mendacious pamphlets of the recanting terrorist J. Vilate, *Causes secrètes de la révolution du 9 au 10 thermidor* (October 6, 1794), *Continuation des causes secrètes de la révolution du 9 au 10 thermidor* (November 15, 1794), *Les Mystères de la Mère de Dieu dévoilés* (January 27, 1795); and the absurd and calumnious account of another police spy and penitent terrorist, G. J. Senar, *Révélations puissées dans les cartons des comités de salut public et de sûreté générale, ou mémoires (inédits) de Senart* [*sic*], ed. A. Dumesnil (1824), manufactured sensational details on David's police activities which have been repeated ever since. The lurid anecdotes of A. [Garnier]-Audiger, *Souvenirs et anecdotes sur les comités révolutionnaires 1793–1795* (1830) are even less credible.

Miscellaneous data were provided by various royalist memoirs, for example, the governess of the King's children, the Duchesse de Tourzel,

Mémoires, 2 vols. 2nd ed. (1884); the wealthy Marquis de Frénilly, *Souvenirs,* ed. A. Chuquet, new ed. (1909); the conservative statesman, Baron de Barante, *Souvenirs,* ed. C. de Barante, 8 vols. (1890–1901); the celebrated dean of the Paris lawyers, P. N. Berryer, *Souvenirs . . . 1774 à 1838,* 2 vols. (1839); the Bonapartist functionary and Bourbon pensionary P. C. Lecomte, *Mémorial, ou Journal historique, impartiale et anecdotique de la révolution,* 3 vols. (1801–03); the disloyal generals, the Marquis de Bouillé, *Mémoires,* 2 vols. (London, 1797) and C. F. D. Dumouriez, *Mémoires,* ed. J. F. Barrière and M. F. Lescure, 2 vols. (1848); and even the brilliant poet of reactionary Romanticism, the Vicomte de Chateaubriand, *Mémoires d'outre-tombe,* ed. E. Biré, new ed., 6 vols. (1898–1900).

Finally some cautious use was made of the fascinating but highly unreliable literary concoctions of the witty and colorful G. Touchard-Lafosse, *Souvenirs d'un demi-siècle, 1789–1836,* 6 vols. (1836); the lyrical and imaginative Charles Nodier, *Souvenirs de la révolution et l'empire,* 2 vols. new ed. (1857); the posthumous and partly apocryphal [S. E. Monnel], *Mémoires d'un prêtre régicide,* 2 vols. (1829), "edited" by the literary adventurer D. A. Martin; the fantastic and mendacious borrowings of Jacques Labiche called Georges Duval, *Souvenirs de la terreur,* 4 vols. (1841–42); and the apocryphal *Mémoires et souvenirs d'un pair de France et membre du Sénat conservateur,* 4 vols. (1829–30), attributed to that manufacturer of memoirs, Baron de Lamothe-Langon.

7. NEWSPAPERS AND PERIODICALS

The periodical press of the French Revolution is one of the fundamental sources for the study of the history of the period. A number of the revolutionary journals have already been mentioned among the contemporary materials used for legislative debates and speeches and the proceedings of the Jacobin societies (*see* pp. 170–72). Moreover the newspapers of the time were of primary importance here because of the nature of this study. As an analysis of public opinion it deals with the reaction of various individuals and groups to the propaganda techniques of the artist David. Because of the large number of revolutionary journals and the wide variety of their opinions one can find in them expressions of almost every point of view. For this reason the hundred odd examples studied by the writer were of fundamental importance for this study. Some of those used are included here. Needless to say the well-known revolutionary journals such as Mirabeau's *Le Courier de Provence* [sic], 17 vols. (May 2, 1789–September 30, 1791); Barère's *Le Point du jour, ou Résultat de ce qui c'est passé la veille à l'Assemblée nationale,* 26 vols. (June 19, 1789–October 21, 1791); Prudhomme's weekly *Révolutions de Paris,* 17 vols. (July 12, 1789–February 28, 1794); Brissot's *Le Patriote françois* [sic], 1388 nos. (July 28, 1789–June 2, 1793); Camille Desmoulin's *Révolutions de France et de Brabant,* 8 vols. (November 28, 1789–December 12, 1791); Marat's *L'Ami du Peuple ou le Publiciste parisien,* 685 nos. (September 12, 1789–September 21, 1792); Robespierre's *Le Défenseur de la Constitution,* 12 nos. (June 1–August 10, 1792) and *Lettres . . . à ses commettans,* 22 nos. [September 30, 1792–March 15, 1793] and A. J. Gorsas' *Le Courrier des départemens,* 48 vols. (July 5, 1789–May 31, 1793), were studied.

Long-lived and useful were C. F. Perlet's newspaper known as the *Journal de Perlet,* 49 vols. (August 1, 1789–September 4, 1797); L. S. Mercier's weekly *Annales patriotiques et littéraires de la France,* 21 vols. (October 3, 1789–June 30, 1797); Etienne Feuillant's *Journal du soir, de politique et de littérature,* 4813 nos. (October 2, 1791–September 30, 1811), with its morning edition *Journal de France,* 25 vols. (September 21, 1792–September 22, 1798); J. C. Poncelin de la Roche-Tilhac's *Courier français,* 26 vols. (June 30, 1789–October 9, 1793), continued as *Courier républicain,* 19 vols. (October 31, 1793–September 5, 1797); Cussac's *Mercure universel,* 88 vols. (March 1, 1791–June 18, 1798); the *Courrier universel, ou l'écho de Paris, des départemens et de l'étranger,* ed. H. N. de Ladevèze, Husson, and others, 15 vols. (December 21, 1792–January 17, 1800); *L'Auditeur national, journal de législation, de politique et de littérature,* 28 vols. (October 2, 1791–January 18, 1800); *Gazette générale de l'Europe,* 7 ser. (April 26, 1792–May 11, 1798), with its evening edition *Le Messager du soir,* 2 ser. (October 1, 1793–October 8, 1795). These journals owed their longevity to their chameleon-like changes of editorial policy. At first pro-revolutionary, almost all of them tended to support the government in power and ended by becoming conservative and even reactionary during the Directory.

Of comparable duration but more consistently radical were A. F. Lemaire's *Courier de l'égalité,* 1596 nos. (August 16, 1792–January 18, 1797); the folio-sized *Le Républicain français,* ed. M. Gouget-Deslandres, 1856 nos. (November 13, 1792–February 3, 1798); and the Jacobin deputy Charles Duval's *Le Républicain, journal des hommes libres de tous les pays,* 14 vols. (November 2, 1792–September 14, 1800), which evaded persecution by numerous changes of title, notably *Journal des hommes libres de tous les pays.*

While relatively moderate sheets such as the *Correspondance politique de Paris et des départements* [ed. J. F. Lefortier], 3 ser. (June 18, 1792–January 1, 1795), were useful for factual material, it is in the partisan journals that the reactions of various groups to revolutionary propaganda are to be found.

Among the patriotic sheets to be mentioned in this connection were *L'Ami de la révolution, ou Philippiques,* 57 nos. (September 8, 1790–August 5, 1791), attributed to Sylvain Maréchal; Saint Foi's *Correspondance nationale,* 45 nos. (February 15–July 19, 1791); the popular weekly *La Feuille villageoise,* ed. J. P. Rabaut Saint-Etienne, G. Cérutti, P. A. Grouvelle, P. L. Ginguené and others, 10 vols. (September 30, 1790–August 12, 1795), which aimed at spreading revolutionary ideals among the peasants; *L'Instituteur du peuple, ou La Vérité sans voile,* ed. Collignon-Dumont, 5 nos. (undated [1792]); *L'Intérêt du peuple français, ou La Bouche d'or, journal servant à réfuter tous les autres,* ed. J. F. Sobry, 6 nos. (November 22–December 29, 1790); the *Journal de la révolution,* 418 nos. (August 25, 1790–October 3, 1791); M. Labenette's, *Journal du diable,* 83 nos. (March 26–October 18, 1790); Gabriel Feydel's colorful and caustic *L'Observateur,* 2 ser. (August 8, 1789–October 12, 1790); J. A. Dulaure's influential daily, *Le Thermomètre du jour,* 7 vols. (August 11, 1791–August 25, 1793); Tremblay's *Journal du soir sans réflexions et Courier de Paris, des départemens et des frontiers réunies* (1790–April 10, 1794); and P. J. Audouin's *Journal universel, ou Révolutions des royaumes,* 1993 nos. (November 23, 1789–June 2, 1795), one of the most persistent and influential of the pro-revolutionary dailies.

Many contemporary journals spoke for various groups and organizations. The philosophical and masonic Cercle Social had its famous *Bouche de fer,* 2 ser. (January 1, 1790–July, 1791). Founded by the eloquent Abbé Claude Fauchet, under Nicolas de Bonneville it later became one of the most radical political sheets of the day until its editor was proscribed as a result of the Massacre of the Champ de Mars. Other publications of the Cercle Social used were the *Bulletin des Amis de la vérité,* ed. J. Lavallée and others, 121 nos. (December 31, 1792–April 30, 1793); the monthly *Chronique du mois, ou Les Cahiers patriotiques,* ed. E. Clavière, C. Condorcet, L. S. Mercier, N. Bonneville, J. P. Brissot and others, 21 nos. (November, 1791–July, 1793). These as well as Fauchet's satirical *Journal des amis,* 18 nos.

(January 4–June 15, 1793) became organs of the Girondins along with the *Annales patriotiques, Courrier de Gorsas, Thermomètre du jour, Patriote françois,* and the *Chronique de Paris* already mentioned.

Periodicals which expressed Dantonist opinions were also helpful. Pierre Philippeaux's weekly, *Le Défenseur de la vérité, ou l'Ami du genre humain,* 44 nos. (January 5–December 15, 1793), was the personal organ of Danton's friend and fellow deputy who died with him on the guillotine. The well-known *Vieux Cordelier,* 7 nos. (December 5, 1793–February 3, 1794), of Camille Desmoulins was another sheet used for its "indulgent" views.

Marat's *Ami du Peuple* was of course helpful for the positive and sometimes violent reactions of its famous author. Its continuations, the *Journal de la République française,* 143 nos. (September 25, 1792–March 11, 1793) and *Le Publiciste de la République française,* nos. 144–242 (March 14–July 14, 1793) were also used. Similar in style was Stanislaus Fréron's *L'Orateur du peuple, par Martel,* 17 vols. (May 1, 1790–August 12, 1795) which began as a radically revolutionary sheet. After Thermidor it was revived as an ultra-reactionary organ of the *jeunesse dorée. La Tribune des patriotes,* 4 nos. [April 30–July 7, 1792] was a continuation by Fréron and Desmoulins of the latter's *Révolutions de France et de Brabant.*

One of the most significant periodicals for this study was *Lettre*[*s*] *bougrement patriotique*[*s*] *du véritable Père Duchêne,* ed. A. F. Lemaire, 400 nos. (undated [1790–92]) which staunchly defended the Revolution in Billingsgate style. This publication (really a series of radical pamphlets) was continued by the same editor's *La Trompette du Père Duchêne,* 147 nos. (undated [1792–93]). Lemaire's *Père Duchêne* inspired a number of imitations of which J. R. Hébert's *Je suis le véritable Père Duchêne, foutre,* 385 nos. (undated [September, 1790–1794]) was the best-known. Hébert's *Père Duchêne* was even more violent and obscene than the original. Other vitriolic and profane relatives of the redoubtable Duchêne followed including *Lettre*[*s*] *bougrement patriotique*[*s*] *de la Mère Duchêne,* 18 nos. (undated [1791]); *Jean Bart, ou suite de je m'en fouts,* [ed. L. M. Henriquez?], 181 nos. (undated [1790–91]); and *Entretien*[*s*] *entre Jean Bart et le Père Duchêne,* 17+ nos. (undated [1791?]).

The official organs of the various Paris clubs were especially valuable. The Jacobin weekly *Journal des Amis de la Constitution,* ed. M. P. Choderlos, 41 nos. ([November 30, 1790]–September 20, [1791]), and its successors were used. After the split in the Society this sheet merged with the *Journal des débats de la Société des amis de la constitution, séante aux Jacobins à Paris,* [ed. Deflers ?], 6 vols. (June 1, 1791–December 14, 1793), commonly known as the *Journal des Jacobins.* The latter was superseded first by the little known *Premier journal de la Convention nationale, ou le Point du jour,* ed. J. C. Laveaux, 3 vols. (September 21, 1792–June 30, 1793) and then by the celebrated *Journal de la Montagne,* ed. J. C. Laveaux, T. Rousseau and others, 4 vols. (June 1, 1793–November 18, 1794).

While addressing itself to all the various revolutionary societies, the *Journal des clubs, ou sociétés patriotiques,* ed. J. J. Leroux, J. Charon and D. M. Revol, 47 nos. (November 20, 1790–September 11, 1791), was partial to the Jacobins. The official sheet of the famous Society of the Rights of Man and of the Citizen, was the *Journal du Club des Cordeliers,* ed. J. Sentiers [pseud. of A. Etienne] and A. F. Momoro, 10 vols. (June 28–August 10, 1791). The *Journal de la Société de 1789,* ed. Marquis de Condorcet, P. S. du Pont de Nemours, André Chénier and others, 15 nos. (June 5–September 15, 1790) was the organ of the constitutional monarchist Société de 1789.

Other periodicals which expressed the views of constitutional monarchists were the old *Gazette de France* and the *Journal de Paris;* A. M. Cerisier's *Gazette universelle, ou papier-nouvelles de tous les pays et de tous les jours,* 3 vols. (December 1, 1789–August 10, 1792), which was succeeded by *Nouvelles politiques, nationales et étrangères,* ed. P.-L. Monestier, J. B. A. Suard, P. S. du Pont de Nemours, Baron de Barante, C. de Lacretelle, Abbé A. Morellet and others, 5 vols. (November 15, 1792–September 5, 1797), and later by *Le Publiciste,* ed. J. B. A. Suard and others, 32 vols. (September 15, 1797–November 10, 1810); the *Gazette française, papier-nouvelles de tous les jours et de tous les pays,* ed. P. L. Fiévée, 10 vols. (January 1, 1792–December 18, 1797); and the *Bulletin national, ou papier-nouvelles de tous les pays et de tous les jours,* [ed. Dom J. P. Gallais], 3 ser. (November 1, 1792–August 21, 1796). Despite its title the *Courier républicain,* 19 vols. (October 31, 1793–September 5, 1797), the successor of Poncelin's proscribed *Courier français,* was royalist in sympathy as was J. B. Duplain's *Courrier extraordinaire, ou le premier arrivé,* 10 vols. (March 3, 1790–August 11, 1792).

The extremists in the royalist camp had a considerable number of newspapers at their disposal. Of those used the most notorious was the *Journal général de la Cour et de la Ville,* 15 vols. (September 15, 1789–August 10, 1792), founded by Brune, the future Marshal of

Napoleon, and edited by J. L. Gautier de Syonnet from whom it became known as the *Petit-Gautier.* This fashionable aristocratic periodical was the mouthpiece of the ultra-royalists and émigrés. Wittiest and one of the most salacious of the sheets of the period was the satirical *Les Actes des apôtres,* ed J. G. Peltier, and others, 311 nos. (November, 1789–October, 1791). Equally vehement, though somewhat less vulgar and more serious in its polemics, was *L'Ami du Roi, des françois, de l'ordre et sur-tout de la vérité par les continuateurs de Fréron,* 92 nos. (June 1–August 31, 1790). This counter-revolutionary daily was edited by Mme. Fréron, her brother the Abbé Royou, C. F. L. Ventre de la Touloubre, known as Montjoie, and others and published by Crapart. After three months, the editors quarreled with each other and with their printer and three rival issues of *L'Ami du Roi* appeared on September 1, 1790, each continuing the title and numbering of the original. On November 6, Crapart's journal merged with Montjoie's and was edited by the latter until the "day" of August 10, 1792. The Abbé Royou's *Ami du Roi,* the most violent and notorious of the three, flourished until the arrest and death of its editor on May 4, 1792.

Besides these better known royalist journals there were others used such as the rabid and influential *Gazette de Paris,* ed. B. F. du Rozoy, called Durosoi, 6 vols. (October 1, 1789–August 10, 1792), whose career was terminated by the execution of its editor after the fall of the monarchy; *Le Babillard,* 138 nos. (June 5–October 30, 1791), which recorded the gossip of the Palais Royal and the Tuileries; *Le Feuille du jour,* ed. P. G. Parisot, 11 vols. (December 1, 1790–August 10, 1792), the organ of the aristocratic clique of the Opera ballet; *Le Consolateur, ou journal des honnêtes gens,* ed. L. A. Beffroy de Reigny, 63 nos. (January 3–August 7, 1792), reputedly in the pay of the court; *Les Folies d'un mois à deux liards par jour,* [ed. Abbé A. de Bouyon?], 8 "mois" (October 1, 1791–August 10, 1792), whose invective was paid for from the King's privy purse; *La Rocambole des journaux,* 5 vols. (May 1, 1791–August 5, 1792), attributed to David Sabalut; L. C. de Barruel-Beauvert's *Journal royaliste,* 22 nos. (March 16–August 9, 1792); *Le Spectateur national* which absorbed the title and resources of the *Modérateur* to form *Le Spectateur national et le Modérateur,* 7 vols. (April 18, 1790–August 10, 1792); and the two satirical royalist sheets, *Journal politique-national des Etats-généraux et de la Révolution de 1789,* ed. Abbé A. Sabatier de Castres and A. Rivarol and others, 3 vols. (Cambrai [etc.]: 1790); and *Les Sabats Jacobites,* ed. François Marchant, 3 vols. (undated [1791–92]).

Several pre-revolutionary journals supported the royalist cause after 1789. The *Journal général de France,* 10 vols. (January 1, 1785–August 10, 1792) was edited in a counter-revolutionary spirit by L. A. Bonafous, Abbé de Fontenai, until January 1791 when he left to start his own anti-Jacobin newspaper with the same title. The *Journal général,* ed. L. A. B. Fontenai, 3 vols. (February 1, 1791–August 10, 1792) was suppressed along with its original and most other reactionary sheets on August 10, 1792. The venerable *Mercure de France* was divided in allegiance: the literary part was "liberal" but the political articles by the royalist pamphleteer J. F. Mallet du Pan were counter-revolutionary. Mallet's articles were also printed in the *Journal historique et politique de l'Europe,* 81 vols. (Geneva: October 10, 1772–February 28, 1793). The latter periodical was superseded by the *Annales de la République française,* 15 vols. (December 1, 1792–December 21, 1799).

Clerical journals expressed the views of various religious groups. Of these the following were used: the *Annales de la religion et du sentiment,* 3 vols. (1791–92), a little known organ of the non-juring clergy; the *Journal de l'Eglise constitutionnelle de France,* ed. L. P. Couret (1792) claimed to speak for the constitutional clergy; and the clandestine *Nouvelles ecclésiastiques, ou mémoires pour servir à l'histoire de la Constitution Unigenitus,* ed. N. Larrière, M. C. Guénin, J. B. S. Mouton and others (Paris [etc.]: 1728–1803), reflected the opinions of the Jansenists.

Technical journals devoted to literature, the arts and public instruction were especially valuable. *La Décade philosophique, littéraire et politique; par une société des républicains,* ed. P. L. Ginguené, J. B. Say, S. Andrieux, P. J. B. Chaussard, T. C. Brunn-Neergaard, J. Lebreton and others, 54 vols. (April 29, 1794–September 21, 1807); the *Journal de l'instruction publique,* ed. D. Thiébault and J. A. Borelly, 8 vols. (undated [July, 1793–September, 1794]); the *Journal d'instruction publique,* ed. Auguste, A. F. Coupigny, G. F. Fouques-Deshayes, known as Desfontaines, and others, 2 vols. (July 23–December 20, 1794); as well as the older *Journal encyclopédique,* ed. P. Rousseau and others, 304 vols. (Liége [etc.]: 1756–1793) and *L'Esprit des journaux français et étrangers,* ed. Abbé Coster and others, 487 vols. (Liége [etc.]: 1772–1818), were especially useful for legislation and discussions concerning fine arts projects and exhibitions, revolutionary festivals and the political and social utility of the arts.

The continuation of the *Bulletin du Tribunal criminel révolutionnaire* under the title *Procès de Fouquier-Tinville et autre membres du tribunal du 22 prairial,* ed. Donzelot, 48 nos. [March 28–May 6, 1795] was also used.

Except where noted, all the periodicals discussed were published in Paris. At some points foreign periodicals were used, for example: *Courrier français,* 6 vols. (Philadelphia: April 15, 1794–July 3, 1798); *Diario ordinario* (Rome: July 6, 1716–September 19, 1870); *Memorie per le belle arti,* 4 vols. (Rome: 1785–88); and *Journal de la Société des amis de la liberté et de l'égalité établie à Bruxelles,* ed. J. Chateignier, 2 vols. (Brussels: November 18, 1792–March 8, 1793).

8. PAMPHLETS AND BROCHURES

BARÈRE [DE VIEUZAC, BERTRAND]. *Rapport fait à la Convention nationale au nom du Comité de salut public . . . 13 prairial [1 juin 1794], sur l'éducation révolutionnaire, républicaine et militaire; et décret sur la formation de l'Ecole de Mars . . .* ([Paris]: Imp. nat., [1794]). 16 pp.

———. *Rapport fait [à la Convention nationale] au nom du Comité de salut public, sur la suite des événements du siège d'Ypres, et sur les monumens nationaux environnans Paris . . . 13 messidor, l'an II [1 juillet 1794]* ([Paris]: Imp. nat. [1794]). 4 pp.

BARÈRE [DE VIEUZAC, BERTRAND], *et al. Réponse des membres des deux anciens Comités de salut public et de sûreté générale, aux imputations renouvellées contre eux, par Laurent Lecointre de Versailles, et déclarées calomnieuses . . . 13 fructidor dernier; à la Convention nationale* (Paris: Imp. de Charpentier, l'an III [1795]). 112 pp.

BILLAUD-VARENNE, [JACQUES NICOLAS]. *Rapport fait à la Convention nationale au nom du Comité de salut public . . . 1 floréal, l'an II [20 avril 1794] sur la théorie du gouvernement démocratique . . . et sur la nécessité d'inspirer l'amour des vertus civiles par les fêtes publiques et des institutions morales* ([Paris]: Imp. nat., [1794]). 24 pp.

B[OISSIEU], DIDIER. *Réflexions sur la festomanie* ([Paris]: Boulard, [1795?]). 18 pp.

BOISSY D'ANGLAS, [FRANÇOIS ANTOINE, COMTE DE]. *Essai sur les fêtes nationales adressé à la Convention nationale . . . 12 messidor an II [30 juin 1794]* ([Paris]: Imp. Polyglotte, [1794]). 118 pp.

CHAMFORT, [SÉBASTIEN ROCH NICOLAS, *called*]. *Des Académies. Ouvrage que M. Mirabeau devait lire à l'Assemblée nationale sous le nom de Rapport sur les Académies* (Paris: Buisson, 1791). 40 pp.

CHÉNIER, MARIE-JOSEPH-BLAISE. *Discours prononcé à la Convention nationale . . . 15 brumaire, l'an II [5 Novembre 1793] . . . de l'instruction publique . . .* ([Paris]: Imp. nat., [1793]). 15 pp.

———————. *Rapport fait à la Convention nationale au nom des Comités d'instruction publique et des inspecteurs [sur les funérailles de Le Peletier . . . 22 janvier 1793]* ([Paris]: Imp. nat., [1793]). 4 pp.

———————. *Rapport fait à la Convention nationale au nom du Comité d'instruction publique . . . 1 nivôse an III [21 décembre 1794 sur les fêtes décadaires]* (Paris: Imp. nat., [1794]). 9 pp.

[CLOOTS, JEAN BAPTISTE DU VAL DE GRACE, BARON VON] *(known as* ANACHARSIS CLOOTS). *Etrennes de l'orateur du genre humain aux cosmopolites* ([Paris]: au chef-lieu du Globe, 1793). 66 pp.

COLLOT D'HERBOIS, [JEAN MARIE]. *Rapport fait à la Société des . . . Jacobins . . . 26 juin 1791 . . . en réclamation de justice pour quarante-un soldats du régiment de Château-vieux . . .* ([Paris]: Imp. nat., 1791). 31 pp.

———————. *Réponse . . . à des notes barbares envoyées à divers journaux contre les soldats de Château-Vieux, et notamment à celles envoyées par MM. Roucher et André Chénier au "Journal de Paris"; lue à la Société [des Jacobins] le 4 avril [1792]* ([Paris]: Imp. du "Patriote françois", [1792]). 8 pp.

———————. *La Vérité sur les soldats de Château-Vieux [lue à la Société des Jacobins] . . . 30 mars [1792]* ([Paris]: Imp. du "Patriote françois", [1792]). 8 pp.

COUPÉ, [JEAN MARIE LOUIS]. *Des Fêtes en politique et en morale* ([Paris]: Baudouin, [1795?]). 47 pp.

[DAVID, JACQUES-LOUIS]. *Description générale de la première fête républicaine de la réunion . . . célébrée en mémoire de la fameuse journée qui s'est passée aux Tuileries, le 10 août 1792 et à l'occasion de l'acceptation de la Constitution . . .* (Paris: Pithou, [1793]). 32 pp.

———————. *Détail des cérémonies et de l'ordre à observer dans la fête à l'Etre-suprême qui doit être célébrée le 20 prairial d'après le décret de la Convention nationale du 18 floréal [7 mai 1794]* ([Paris]: Imp. nat., [1794]). 12 pp.

[DAVID, JACQUES-LOUIS]. *Détails de toutes les cérémonies qui vont être célébrées dans toute l'étendue de la République française . . . en l'honneur de l'Etre suprême . . . suivi de l'ordre de la marche [etc]* ([Paris]: Prévost, [1794]). 16 pp.

DAVID, JACQUES-LOUIS. *Discours prononcé . . . [à la Convention nationale sur l'érection d'un monument au Peuple français] . . . 17 brumaire, l'an II [7 novembre 1793]* . . . ([Paris]: Imp. nat., [1793]). 3 pp.

————————. *Discours prononcé à la Convention nationale . . . en lui offrant le tableau représentant Marat assassiné . . . 24 brumaire, l'an II [14 novembre 1793]* . . . ([Paris]: Imp. nat., [1793]). 3 pp.

————————. *Discours prononcé à la Convention nationale, le 29 mars 1793 . . . en offrant un tableau de sa composition représentant Michel Lepelletier au lit de mort* . . . ([Paris]: Imp. nat., [1793]). 3 pp.

————————. *Discours [prononcé à la Convention nationale] . . . sur la nécessité de supprimer les Académies . . . 8 août 1793 . . .* ([Paris]: Imp. nat., [1793]). 6 pp.

[DAVID, JACQUES-LOUIS]. *Instruction pour l'ordre à observer le jour de la fête de la réunion, au 10 août, l'an II* . . . ([Paris]: Gerard, [1793]). 4 pp.

DAVID, JACQUES-LOUIS. *Plan de la fête de l'Etre-suprême qui doit être célébrée le 20 prairial, l'an II [8 juin 1794 présentée à la Convention nationale 18 floréal an II (7 mai 1794)]* (Paris: Imp. nat., [1794]).

————————. *Rapport et décret sur la fête de la réunion républicaine au 10 août, présenté au nom du Comité d'instruction publique . . . [11 juillet 1793]* ([Paris]: Imp. nat., [1793]). 10 pp.

————————. *Rapport fait à la Convention national . . . [sur l'érection d'un monument au Peuple français, 27 brumaire, an II (17 novembre 1793)]* . . . ([Paris]: Imp. nat., [1793]). 8 pp.

————————. *Rapport fait [à la Convention nationale] . . . au nom du Comité d'instruction publique, en mémoire des victoires des armées françaises, et notamment à l'occasion de la prise de Toulon [5 nivôse an II (25 décembre 1793)]* ([Paris]: Imp. nat., [1793]). 8 pp.

————————. *Rapport fait [à la Convention nationale] au nom du Comité d'instruction publique . . . pour l'explication de la médaille frappée en commémoration de la réunion civique du 10 août 1793* . . . ([Paris]: Imp. nat., [1793]). 6 pp.

———. *Rapport fait* [*à la Convention nationale*] *au nom du Comité d'instruction publique* . . . *sur la nomination des cinquante membres du jury qui doit juger le concours des prix de peinture, sculpture et architecture* . . . *25 brumaire, l'an II* [*15 novembre 1793*] ([Paris]: Imp. nat., [1793]). 6 pp.

———. *Rapport* [*fait à la Convention nationale*] *sur la fête héroïque pour les honneurs du Panthéon à décerner aux jeunes Bara et Viala* . . . *23 messidor, l'an II* [*11 juillet 1794*] ([Paris]: Imp. nat., [1794]). 14 pp.

———. *Rapport* [*fait à la Convention nationale*] *sur la suppression de la Commission du Muséum* . . . ([Paris]: Imp. nat., [1794]). 8 pp.

———. *Second Rapport* [*à la Convention nationale*] *sur la nécessité de la suppression de la Commission du Muséum, fait au nom des Comités d'instruction publique et des finances* . . . *27 nivôse, l'an II* [*16 janvier 1794*] . . . ([Paris]: Imp. nat., [1794]). 11 pp.

DAVID, JACQUES-LOUIS, *et al.* *Adresse des représentans des beaux-arts, à l'Assemblée nationale* [*constituante*], *dans la séance du 28 juin 1790* ([Paris]: Imp. nat., [1790]). 3 pp.

———. *Mémoire sur l'Académie royale de peinture et de sculpture, par plusieurs membres de cette académie* (Paris: Valade, 1790). 36 pp.

DE BRY, JEAN [ANTOINE JOSEPH, BARON]. *Rapport* [*à l'Assemblée nationale législative*] *sur les honneurs à rendre à la mémoire de J.-G. Simonneau, Maire de' Etampes, fait au nom du Comité d'instruction publique, et décret du 18 mars 1792* . . . (Paris: Imp. nat., [1792]). 8 pp.

Détail et ordre de la marche de la fête en l'honneur de la liberté, donnée par le peuple à l'occasion de l'arrivée des soldats de Château-Vieux, le dimanche, 15 avril 1792 . . . (Paris: Imp. Tremblay, [1792]). 8 pp.

DU PONT [DE NEMOURS, PIERRE SAMUEL]. *Lettre* . . . *à M. Pétion* [*du 13 avril 1792 sur la fête en l'honneur des soldats de Châteauvieux*] ([Paris]: Imp. de l'auteur, [1792]). 16 pp.

———. *Seconde lettre* . . . *à M. Pétion* [*du 27 avril 1792 sur la fête en l'honneur des soldats de Châteauvieux*] ([Paris]: Imp. de l'auteur, [1792]). 19 pp.

Fête civique [*célébrée le 2 mai 1790 au Petit Goave*] (Port-au-Prince: Chez Bourdon, [1790]). 3 pp.

Fête civique, célébrée [*17 avril 1795 à Philadelphia*] *par les patriotes Français, Américains et Hollondais* . . . (Philadelphia: Parent, [1795]). 4 pp.

Fête de l'Etre-Suprême et à la Nature célébrée à Chaumont, chef-lieu du Département de la Haute-Marne, décadi 20 prairial [*8 juin 1794*] ([Chaumont]: no pub., [1794]). 7 pp.

FRANCE. ASSEMBLÉE NATIONALE LÉGISLATIVE. Comité d'Agriculture et de Commerce. *Projet de décret sur les récompenses nationales pour les artistes en exécution de la loi du 22 août 1790 présentée à l'Assemblée nationale . . . 9 Septembre 1791* (Paris: Imp. nat., 1791). 9 pp.

——————. Comité d'Instruction Publique. *Projet de décret . . . sur les réclamations des artistes qui ont exposé au Salon du Louvre* [*en 1791*] . . . ([Paris]: Imp. nat., [1791]). 2 pp.

FRANCE. CONVENTION NATIONALE. *Appel nominal . . . 13 au 14 avril* [*1793*] *. . . sur la question: Y-t-il lieu d'accusation contre Marat? . . .* ([Paris]: Imp. nat., [1793]). 78 pp.

——————. *Appel nominal . . . 16 et 17 janvier 1793 . . . sur cette question: Quelle peine sera infligée à Louis?* ([Paris]: Imp. nat., [1793]). 43 pp.

——————. *Appels nominaux . . . 15 & 19 janvier 1793 . . . sur ces trois questions: 1. Louis Capet est-il coupable de conspiration . . .; 2. Le jugement . . . sera-t-il soumis à la ratification du peuple; 3. Y aura-t-il un sursis, ou non, à l'exécution* ([Paris]: Imp. nat., [1793]). 71 pp.

——————. *Instruction particulière, pour les commissaires chargé des détails de la fête de l'Etre suprême qui doit être célébrée le 20 prairial* ([Paris]: Imp. nat., [1794]). 10 pp.

——————. *Procès-verbal des monumens, de la marche et des discours de la fête consacrée à l'inauguration de la constitution de la République française le 10 août 1793 . . .* ([Paris]: Imp. nat., [1793]). 16 pp.

——————. Comité de Salut Public. *Arrêtés . . .* [*5-28 floréal an II (24 avril-17 mai 1794)*] *relatifs aux monuments publics, aux arts et aux lettres* ([Paris]: Imp. nat., [1794]). 21 pp.

GRÉGOIRE, [HENRI]. *Rapport et projet de décret présentés* [*à la Convention nationale*] *au nom du Comité d'instruction publique . . . 8 août* [*1793, sur la suppression des Académies*] ([Paris]: Imp. nat., [1793]). 14 pp.

JULIEN, MARC-ANTOINE, *et al.* *Adresse lue au nom des Jacobins de Paris par Marc-Antoine Julien . . . à la barre de la Convention nationale . . . 27 floréal [16 mai 1794]; Réponse du président de la Convention; Discours par le citoyen Couthon . . .* ([Paris]: Imp. nat., [1793]). 8 pp.

LANTHENAS, FRANÇOIS XAVIER. *Bases fondamentales de l'instruction publique et de toute constitution libre, ou Moyens de lier l'opinion publique, la morale, l'éducation, l'enseignement, l'instruction, les fêtes, la propagation des lumières et le progrès de toutes les connaissances au gouvernement républicain . . .* (Paris: Imp. du Cercle Social, 1793). 190 pp.

LECOINTRE, LAURENT. *. . . A la Convention nationale, contre Billaud-Varennes, Collot-d'Herbois et Barère, membres du Comité de salut public, Vadier, Voulland, Amar et David, membres du Comité de sûreté générale [11 fructidor an II (28 août 1794)]* ([Paris]: Imp. nat., [1794]). 10 pp.

———————. *Les Crimes des sept membres des anciens Comités de salut public et de sûreté générale, ou Dénonciation formelle à la Convention nationale contre Billaud-Varennes, Barère, Collot-d'Herbois, Vadier, Vouland, Amar et David, suivie des pieces justificatives . . . 20 brumaire an III [10 novembre 1794]* ([Paris]: Imp. nat., [1794]). 244 pp.

MATHIEU-[MIRAMPAL, JEAN BAPTISTE CHARLES]. *Rapport fait à la Convention nationale au nom du Comité d'instruction publique . . . [sur la suppression de la Commission des monuments et son remplacement par la Commission temporaire des arts] 28 frimaire, l'an II [18 décembre 1793] . . .* ([Paris]: Imp. nat., [1793]). 18 pp.

———————. *Projet de fêtes nationales . . . imprimée par ordre de la Convention nationale* ([Paris]: Imp. nat., nivôse an III [1794–95]). 7 pp.

———————. *Projet de fêtes nationales, présenté [à la Convention nationale] au nom du Comité d'instruction publique . . .* (Paris: Imp. nat., l'an II [1793–94]). 10 pp.

MERLIN (DE THIONVILLE), ANTOINE CHRISTOPHE. *Opinion . . . sur les fêtes nationales prononcée à la Convention nationale . . . 9 vendémiaire an III . . . [30 septembre 1794]* ([Paris]: Imp. nat., [1794]). 20 pp.

MIGER, [SIMON-CHARLES]. *Discours lu . . . à l'Académie royale de peinture, dans l'assemblée du 28 novembre 1789, pour servir de supplément à sa lettre addressée à M. Vien, premier peintre, en date du 20 de ce mois* ([Paris]: no pub., [1789]). 5 pp.

——————. *Lettre à M. Vien . . . premier peintre et directeur de l'Académie royale de peinture (20 novembre 1789)* ([Paris]: no pub., [1789]). 15 pp.

[MIRABEAU, HONORÉ GABRIEL RIQUETTI, COMTE DE]. *Adresse des Amis de la constitution à l'Assemblée nationale [constituante 6 novembre 1790]* (Paris: Baudouin, [1790]). 6 pp.

MORELLET, L'ABBÉ ANDRÉ. *De l'Académie française, ou Réponse à l'écrit de M. de Chamfort de l'Académie française, qui a pour titre: "Des Académies"* (Paris: Jansen, 1791). 108 pp.

Ordre de la marche de la fête qui aura lieu décadi prochain 10 nivôse, l'an II [30 décembre 1793] en mémoire des victoires des armées françaises, et notamment à l'occasion de la prise de Toulon ([Paris]: Imp. nat., [1793]). 6 pp.

Ordre de la marche et des cérémonies qui seront observés aux funérailles de Michel le Pelletier . . . ([Paris]: Imp. nat., [1793]). 8 pp.

Ordre et marche de la translation de Voltaire à Paris, le lundi 11 juillet [1791] et sa profession de foi ([Paris]: Imp. du Cercle Social, 1791). 8 pp.

Ordre, marche et détail de la cérémonie décrétée par l'Assemblée nationale [législative], consacrée au respect de la loi, et dans laquelle on honorera la mémoire de Jacques-Guillaume Simonneau . . . laquelle aura lieu le dimanche 3 juin 1792 (Paris: Ballard, 1792). 11 pp.

PAJOU, AUGUSTIN, *et al.* *Adresse et projet de statuts et règlements pour l'Académie centrale de peinture, sculpture, gravure et architecture, présentés à l'Assemblée nationale, par la majorité des membres de l'Académie royale de peinture & sculpture en assemblée délibérante* (Paris: Valade, 1790). 85 pp.

PAROY, [JEAN PHILIPPE GUY LE GENTIL COMTE (later) MARQUIS DE]. *Précis historique de l'origine de l'Académie royale de peinture, sculpture et gravure . . .* (Paris: Gratiot, 1816). 48 pp.

PÉTION [DE VILLENEUVE, JÉROME]. *Réponse . . . à M. Dupont [du 22 avril 1792 sur la fête en l'honneur des soldats de Châteauvieux]* ([Paris]: Imp. Lottin, [1792]). 19 pp.

Pétition individuelle présentée hier soir, samedi 21 avril [1792] au conseil générale de la Commune par un nombre [sic] de citoyens-soldats de la garde nationale parisienne ([Paris]: Imp. L. Potier de Lille, [1792]). 4 pp.

Procès-verbal de célébration de la fête [à Philadelphia] du 23 thermidor [an II] (10 août [1794] v. style) (Philadelphia: Parent, [1794]). 8 pp.

Procès-verbal de la fête qui a eu lieu [à Philadelphia] le 2 pluviôse [an III] (21 janvier [1795] v. st.) (Philadelphia: Parent, [1795]). 7 pp.

Procès-verbal de la première séance du jury des arts [17 pluviôse an II (5 février 1794)] [suivie du] *Procès-verbal de la seconde séance [18 pluviôse (6 février)]* [et] *Opinions motivés des membres du jury sur la peinture* ([Paris]: Imp. nat., [1794]). 90 pp.

Programme arrêté par le directoire du département de Paris, pour la fête décrétée par l'Assemblée nationale [législative] le 18 mars 1792, à la mémoire de Jacques-Guillaume Simoneau . . . ([Paris]: Ballard, 1792). 8 pp.

QUATREMÈRE DE QUINCY, [ANTOINE CHRYSOSTOME]. *Considérations sur les arts du dessin en France, suivies d'un plan d'Académie, ou d'Ecole publique et d'un système d'encouragemens* (Paris: Devaux, 1791). xiv, 168 pp.

————————. *Suite aux considérations sur les arts du dessin en France; ou Réflexions critiques sur le projet de statuts & règlements de la majorité de l'Académie de peinture & sculpture* (Paris: Desenne, 1791). 2, 49 pp.

————————. *Seconde suite aux considérations sur les arts du dessin; ou Projet de règlemens pour l'Ecole publique des arts du dessin; et de l'emplacement convenable à l'Institut nationale des sciences, belles-lettres & arts.* (Paris: Desenne, 1791). 2, 103 pp.

RENOU, [ANTOINE]. *Esprit des statuts et reglements de l'Académie royale de peinture et sculpture, pour servir de réponse aux détracteurs de son régime* ([Paris]: Hérissant, 11 novembre 1790). 18 pp.

RENOU, [ANTOINE], *et al. Adresse à l'Assemblée nationale [constituante] par la presque totalité des officiers de l'Académie royale de peinture et sculpture, auxquels se sont joints plusieurs académiciens* ([Paris]: Hérissant, 30 novembre 1790). 8, 36 pp.

ROBESPIERRE, [MAXIMILIEN MARIE ISADORE DE]. *Rapport fait [à la Convention nationale] au nom du Comité de salut public . . . sur les rapports des idées religieuses et morales avec les principes républicains et sur les fêtes nationales . . . 18 floréal, l'an II [7 mai 1794]* (Paris: Imp. nat., [1794]). 45 pp.

SOCIÉTÉ DE 1789. PARIS. *Règlemens de la Société de 1789 et liste de ses membres* (Paris: Imp. de Lejay, 1790). 57 pp.

SOCIÉTÉ POPULAIRE ET RÉPUBLICAINE DES ARTS. PARIS. *Considérations sur les avantages de changer le costume français* . . . ([Paris]: Imp. Fantelin, [1794]). 4 pp.

TALLEYRAND-[PÉRIGORD, CHARLES MAURICE, PRINCE DE BÉNÉVENTE]. *Rapport sur l'instruction publique, fait au nom du Comité de constitution, à l'Assemblée nationale* [*constituante*], *les 10, 11 et 19 septembre 1791* . . . (Paris: Imp. nat., 1791). 123 pp.

Voeu des artistes ([Paris]: Gueffier, [1789]). 4 pp.

III. DAVID'S SKETCHBOOKS AND DRAWINGS

Among the most valuable of all sources for the study of David's life, art, and ideas are the sketchbooks which he filled with drawings during his long career. "Douze grands livres de croquis," dating from the artist's student days in Italy, figured as no. 66 at the sale of his effects after his death.* Of these, four were used by this writer for the present study. Two were examined at first hand: one owned by Dr. W. R. Valentiner is in its original binding; the second, a part of the Grenville L. Winthrop Bequest (Acq. no. 1943. 1815. 19) at Fogg Museum of Art of Harvard University, has its pages remounted in a large album. The contents of two similar sketchbooks now preserved in the Louvre were studied by means of reproductions (*Inv. dess.*, IV, 83–108). Three other original David sketchbooks devoted to studies for his Napoleonic propaganda paintings, *The Consecration* and *The Distribution of the Eagles,* were also placed at this writer's disposal: two through the generosity of the Fogg Museum of Art (Winthrop Bequest Acq. nos. 1943, 1815. 12 and 1943. 1815. 13), and another through the courtesy of Georges Wildenstein.

These sketchbooks, together with various original drawings for the *Jeu de Paume* (*see* pp. 37–38) and other subjects (e.g., the allegorical drawing referred to on p. 66 and the preliminary study reproduced opposite p. 194), are the basis for the conclusion that David was not only the finest draftsman of his day and one of the greatest artists of modern times, but that his drawings constitute an unexploited historical source of considerable value. Though a number of brief discussions of the technique and artistic value of some of David's sketches have appeared during the past eighty-five years,† a thorough and scholarly study of his drawings as historical sources has yet to be made. This writer has begun to gather materials for such a study, has included some of his conclusions in this study, and hopes to continue the project at a later time.

* *Catalogue des tableaux* [*etc.*] *de M. Louis David . . . dont la vente publique aura lieu . . . 19 avril 1826 . . .*, pp. 16–17.

† A. Cantaloube, "Les Dessins de Louis David," *G. B. A.*, [ser. 1], VII (Septemoer, 1860), 284–303; C. Saunier, "Les Dessins de Louis David," *L'Art vivant,* I (December 15, 1925), 13–18; W. Heil, "Some French Drawings of the Nineteenth Century," Detroit Institute of Arts, *Bulletin,* XII (January, 1931), 37–41; E. Scheyer, "French Drawings of the Great Revolution," *The Art Quarterly,* IV (Summer, 1941), 188–93; M. Sérullaz, *Jacques Louis David . . . quatorze dessins* (Paris: Musées nationaux, 1939), pp. [1–8]; Waldemar George, *Le Dessin français de David à Cézanne et l'esprit de la tradition baroque* (Paris: Ed. Chronique du jour, 1929), pp. v–xli.

INDEX

D

E

F

G

H

I

J

K

L

M

N

O

P

Q

R

S

T

U

V

W